"There's nothing worse than feeling you're l[...] there's nothing better than having a roadma[...] [...] that hurt and toward closeness and health that you *knew* parenting could be like! You'll find a way forward in this new book, and new look at connecting caring *and* correction that can change your and your child's life. I highly recommend this to stressed-out and just-starting-out parents at all ages and stages."

John Trent, PhD, Moody Theological Seminary; author, *The Blessing* and *LifeMapping*

"In the age of helicopter parenting and global anxiety about the future, Jim and Lynne Jackson bring a grace-filled message of hard-won wisdom for weary parents like me. Their four essential messages will connect with your kids and launch them into the world as confident and capable human beings."

Steve Wiens, senior pastor, Genesis Covenant Church, Minneapolis; author, *Beginnings: The First Seven Days of the Rest of Your Life*

"*Discipline That Connects With Your Child's Heart* has been more transformational for our family than any other book. The 'peace process,' in particular, has changed conflict from a wedge that drives us apart into an opportunity to grow together."

Chad and Liz Caswell, changed parents of three

"The DTC material has been a game-changer with my family. Additionally, I have partnered with Connected Families as a pastor and military chaplain and have presented the material to my church and airmen families in base retreats. This is a biblical, practical, and simple approach to parenting."

Capt. Michael Golay, chaplain, USAF

"This book has changed how I parent! Thank you to the Jacksons for sharing these needed actionable parenting strategies in an authentic and even vulnerable voice. I needed it. I used it. It worked. Thank you."

David Horsager, CEO, Trust Edge Leadership Institute; bestselling author, *The Trust Edge*

"This is a 'why' book and a 'how' book. The Jacksons speak into a way of thinking, acting, and being that forms us and changes our collective character, habits, and practices. Parents will be helped. Children will be glad. Homes, schools, and communities will be transformed."

Joel Johnson, senior pastor, Westwood Community Church, Minneapolis

"Good, solid, practical advice and insights for parents—with some surprisingly simple and effective ways to discipline that may never have occurred to you. You'll enjoy this book!"

Cynthia Ulrich Tobias, author, *The Way They Learn* and *You Can't Make Me! (But I Can Be Persuaded)*

"The Jacksons empower parents to reframe 'problem behaviors' to invitations for connection with God, with each other, and with the needs of the world. They trumpet the call for parents to offer messages of safety, love, value, and responsibility while simultaneously examining their own lives. This is a great book!"

Dr. Denise Muir Kjesbo, PhD, Children and Family Ministry chair,
Bethel College

"Typical parenting books offer strategies intended to control your child—what a setup! The Jacksons equip you with insights and practical tools to be the parent God created you to be. As parents lead with grace, kids follow and grow in wisdom and true respect. This book will bring peace and joy to you and your home."

Peter Larson, PhD, and Heather Larson, MA, authors,
10 Great Dates: Connecting Faith, Love & Marriage

"Being the mom to four young boys, I've struggled to balance grace, training, and boundaries (often more like a mix of yelling, threatening, and frustration). Thankfully, God led me to Jim and Lynne Jackson and their straightforward approach in *Discipline That Connects*. Now I can confidently communicate the four messages while driving carpool, sitting around the dinner table, or tackling bedtime chaos."

Heather MacFayden, blogger, God Centered Mom

"As the mom of three young (and full-of-life) kids, I want to prayerfully raise kids who follow God but who also choose love and connection over a bunch of shoulds and should-nots. Because of this, *Discipline That Connects With Your Child's Heart* immediately appealed to me. I was not disappointed— inside the pages I found helpful tips, connection-based ideas, and best of all the encouragement I needed to connect with my kids as I disciple them."

Erin MacPherson, author, *Christian Mama's Guide* and *Free to Parent*

"It's obvious after reading just a few pages of this book that the Jacksons know the true meaning of the word *discipline*: to train. Parents and caregivers alike will find practical help from the many stories and examples in each chapter on how to touch a child's heart by helping them feel safe, loved, called and capable, and responsible. This book even helps a grandparent like me. I will be assigning it in my Family Ministry courses."

Scottie May, PhD, associate professor, Wheaton College; author, *Children Matter: Celebrating Their Place in the Church, Family, and Community*

"A practical, proven, and powerful framework for parenting. Every concept and example in the book illuminates its central message: Love kids with the same grace and insight that we've received through Jesus. I intend to cherish this resource as a parent and will refer to it many times over."

Matt Norman, regional president, Dale Carnegie Training;
former 40 Under 40, *Minneapolis/St. Paul Business Journal*

"In *Discipline That Connects*, we found not only an amazing philosophical parenting resource, but a non-formulaic, practical parenting discipleship tool. Our family is forever changed by applying these biblical principles to our parenting journey. We've gained peace, direction, and vision as we implement the book's messages in our home."

David and Michelle Swanson, transformed parents of five

DISCIPLINE THAT
CONNECTS
WITH YOUR
CHILD'S HEART

DISCIPLINE THAT CONNECTS WITH YOUR CHILD'S HEART

Building Faith, Wisdom, and Character in the **Messes of Daily Life**

JIM AND LYNNE JACKSON

BETHANY HOUSE
a division of Baker Publishing Group
Minneapolis, Minnesota

Published by Bethany House Publishers
11400 Hampshire Avenue South
Bloomington, Minnesota 55438
www.bethanyhouse.com

Bethany House Publishers is a division of
Baker Publishing Group, Grand Rapids, Michigan

Previously published by Connected Families

Printed in the United States of America

Library of Congress Control Number: 2016938458

ISBN 978-0-7642-1847-7

Cover design by Dan Pitts

Cover photography by Getty Images

Authors are represented by WordServe Literary Group

21   22   7   6   5

We dedicate this book to all the parents we've been privileged to journey alongside. Though you may have come to us for guidance, you have been our guides as well, sharing the stories of your lives and learning. Your hunger to grow and your Spirit-led applications of things we teach keep us ever humble, curious, and eager to serve more parents like you.

Contents

Acknowledgments

This book would not exist without the encouragement of many parents who sat under our teaching and kept asking us to put our thoughts in writing. The essence of the content grows out of our combined personal and professional experiences with people who have embodied grace with us—even in our worst moments.

Our parents, though by no means perfect, taught us about faithfulness in marriage and to love no matter what. Our kids—Daniel, Bethany, and Noah—accepted both our stumbling efforts to practice what we preach and our many apologies for blowing it.

We've had many mentors who showed us that discipline can be wise and gentle. Our past colleagues at Courage Center, Oxboro Church, Grace Church, TreeHouse, Rolling Acres, and Capable Kids showed us the importance of grace for all people, and to look beneath the surface of challenges to find the gift in each person. Our beloved pastors—Dave and Donna Heinrich, Joel Johnson, and Kevin Sharpe—persistently pointed us to Jesus and encouraged us to walk in our calling. And since 1990, a team of faithful donors have given sacrificially so that we could share the grace we've grown in with thousands of families.

Once we typed our ideas into a reasonable format and painstakingly agreed on them, Greg Johnson strongly believed this project had something unique to offer in a sea of parenting resources, and introduced us to the wonderful folks at Bethany House Publishers. Our editor, Christopher Soderstrom, persistently and graciously took our stumbling efforts to express ourselves and made the concepts flow.

Finally, to our amazing colleagues on the Connected Families and Safe-Generations teams: You put wind under the wings of our passion to inspire and equip parents to embody God's grace and truth!

Foreword

How do you fill your home with discipline and grace? Is it possible to build character in your child without crushing his or her spirit? Is there a strategy that will help kids to one day become responsible adults who love God? I believe the answers to these questions are found in this incredible book by Jim and Lynne Jackson. *Discipline That Connects With Your Child's Heart* is a strategy of parenting that is healthy, positive, and authentic. Jim and Lynne bring years of successful experience working with families, as well as having raised their own children. They know firsthand that parenting isn't always easy.

The principles in this book work whether you are trying to create a media-safe home, talk with your kids about healthy sexuality, build healthy morals and values, deal with homework, or help a child think through the consequences of unwise choices. I tell people all the time, if you're married, read at least one marriage book a year; likewise, if you're a parent, read at least one parenting book a year. This is *the* parenting book.

I absolutely love the way the Jacksons have laid out a simple (but not easy, because life isn't easy) plan for connecting with your child's heart. Their brilliant Correct, Coach, Connect, and

Foundation graphic gives us words, actions, and a strategy for helping our kids thrive, and helps us stay connected with our kids even as we discipline and give them boundaries. Let's face it: There is pain in life. I like to say, "It's the pain of discipline or the pain of regret." Paul taught his disciple Timothy to "discipline yourself for the purpose of godliness," and in essence, that is a purposeful goal for every parent.

I'm so glad you have chosen to invest your time reading this book. Parenting will be the most meaningful job and most difficult job you will ever have. But you will gain some great wisdom and be more effective as you put these wonderful principles into practice.

Jim Burns, PhD
President, HomeWord

Dear Reader

In 1992 Lynne was shifting her occupational therapy career to serve kids with high sensitivities and behavior challenges, and Jim started leading support groups for parents of high-risk teens. The parents we served were overwhelmed, tired, and discouraged, and they found conventional teaching lacking. Determined to offer God's grace along with practical tools, we developed a simple framework that offered fresh hope and new skills.

Meanwhile, we had three preschool kids and were dealing with ADHD, allergies, and asthma. When we were considering a fourth child, a good friend said, "You are the most stressed family I know. Your three kids are like nine. Why would you want twelve?"

We stopped at three. You'll get to know each of them as you read through this book, as they were at the center of our learning journey.

Like the parents we served, we were overwhelmed. But as we applied what we were learning, we found hope and purpose in our chaos. We paid close attention to ensure we were teaching not just theories but useful tools. We considered:

- Is this transferrable to every family? (Yes!)
- Is God's grace firmly at the center? (Yes!)
- Do parents of all kinds find these ideas helpful? (Yes!)

Spurred on by those we served, we embarked on our calling to inspire and equip parents to embody God's grace and truth in compelling ways.

The book you're holding is the culmination of our twenty years of experience working with parents every day. In its pages you will find an approach to corrective discipline that focuses on a cross section of the larger framework that guides all our efforts (see more at disciplinethatconnects.org).

In brief, effective parents build a strong **Foundation** on God's grace and truth that spills over to their kids. They communicate the message, *"You are **safe** with me."*

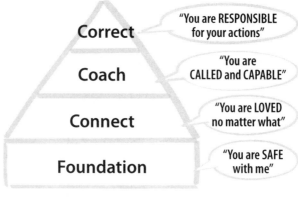

"You are RESPONSIBLE for your actions"

"You are CALLED and CAPABLE"

"You are LOVED no matter what"

"You are SAFE with me"

4 Actions, 4 Messages

As they do this, they **Connect** with their kids by loving, enjoying, and celebrating them. This conveys, *"You are **loved** no matter what!"*

These parents **Coach** their kids to grow into their calling as unique creations of God, thus communicating, *"You are **called** and **capable**!"*

Despite parents' best efforts, kids will misbehave. Thoughtful parents **Correct** their children with wisdom and love, aiming for more than right behavior, as they build sound identities anchored in the message, *"You are **responsible** for your actions."*

Discipline That Connects With Your Child's Heart is an exploration of how to give your best disciplinary effort by breathing life into these four messages.

This way of parenting brings God's love, grace, and truth to life, even in squabbles and challenges with your kids. Like one mom said, "Discipline that Connects isn't a quick fix, it's a lasting fix!" If you're looking for truly long-term impact, this book is for you.

Our kids need this—and our world needs them!

CHAPTER 1

The Lessons Our Kids Truly Need

Karla was fed up.

"My son, Nathan, has been nothing but trouble lately," she told us. "Every day after school, he just drops his backpack in the entry and goes straight to his computer obsession. When I confront him for playing games before doing his homework, he sasses me and storms off. So I've grounded him from the computer and from going outside.

"Sometimes I work hard at setting consequences to make this stop. Other times I feel so tired that I just let him do what he wants. Yesterday he had another huge meltdown about it, but this can't keep happening. He's got to learn!"

Karla was exhausted, irate, overwhelmed, and searching for answers, all at the same time.

"What are you hoping he will learn?" I (Jim) asked.

"I'm hoping he'll learn his lesson," she said.

"I see. Which lesson?"

"That getting away with disrespect in this house just isn't going to happen," she said, growing more angry and determined.

"So far, how well do you think he's learning the lesson?"

"That's the problem—it seems the harder I try, the worse he gets. I've read books and been to seminars. Sometimes I've been pretty tough to let him know who's the boss; that just made him madder. I tried diplomacy, but he just doesn't listen. I've tried time-outs. I take away his iPod or computer. I ground him. Sometimes I ignore him and hope he'll learn on his own. *Nothing* I do connects with him. None of it works."

● ● ●

Karla's experience illustrates two extremes that parents often embody—extremes that illustrate common difficulties regarding how to discipline. Many bounce between a tight, controlling grip and a discouraged, exhausted surrender when they're too tired or preoccupied to keep trying. Whether it's through aggressive dominance or through passive resignation, they're hoping that somehow *something* works to make their kids behave.

But when parents approach discipline this way, their children rarely learn the desired lessons. While parents aim to communicate the importance of respect, responsibility, and, in the big picture, faith, instead they often convey an altogether different set of messages. They end up arguing through a snowballing cycle of frustration, defiance, and disillusionment. This ultimately gives kids the sense that they control their parents' emotions. Worse yet, the attitudes and actions they're seeing in their parents imply to them that parents aren't worthy of their respect.

But parents can get out of this negative spiral as they connect with their child's heart during discipline. You *can* connect with your child's heart through discipline! We've witnessed the Discipline that Connects approach powerfully transform the experience of families whose parents embrace it. It's centered on four biblical principles (see chapter 2). They are simple yet profound concepts that guide parents to think, act, and love in alignment with God's heart for discipline.

Parents who learn and apply these principles often see dramatic improvements in their family relationships. Even if changes in their children's behavior come more slowly than they hope, parents themselves learn to be peaceful and confident in their efforts, driven more by what's best for each child than by the urgency of the moment.

Further, as parents grow, their children will see the difference. As parents become calmer, grounded in peace and purpose, they become far better positioned to influence their children toward wiser responses and decisions.

Connection Makes All the Difference

Let's revisit Karla's situation to see how these principles might guide her.

Karla notices Nathan's unopened backpack in the entry and hears the unmistakable sounds of a computer game coming from his room. Instantly she begins to feel angry about his repeated disregard for her instructions. Recognizing her growing agitation, she realizes that a big power-grabbing reaction won't get her where she wants to go. She also acknowledges that some of her anger has been the result of a stressful day at work.

Taking all this into account, Karla slows her pace, takes a deep breath, and prays, "Lord, you love Nathan, and so do I. I need your wisdom to deal with this situation. Help me to be a *safe* parent."

When Karla walks into Nathan's bedroom, she gently places her hand on his shoulder and sits beside him. In a nonthreatening but firm tone, she asks, "Honey, do you remember what I've asked you to do before playing computer games?"

He shrugs, saying nothing.

"I know you love this game, but I want to make sure you're listening when I explain the consequences for playing it before doing homework." She pauses, hoping he'll stop the game on his own.

When he doesn't, she continues calmly, yet slightly firmer, "You're so persistent. I love that about you. But at the moment, it's not helping you. If you pause the game right now, you can play again after homework. If you don't, then I'll decide how long before you can play again."

Nathan hits the pause button, looks grudgingly at his mother, and mutters, "What's the big deal?"

Karla softens. "I appreciate your attention. The 'deal' is that you're still disobeying by playing before finishing your assignments."

He takes a quick breath, which tells her a complaint is coming. So she adds, "I've seen that you're really good at this game—maybe that's part of what tempts you to ignore responsibilities?"

She pauses again, this time wanting her statement to sink in while she determines how exactly to empathize with her son. Once she's sure of herself, she goes on: "Sometimes I struggle with things this way too. We could talk about that, or we could talk about how you can manage homework and still get to enjoy the game. What do you prefer?"

(Note that so far, in their brief exchange, Karla has skillfully offered Nathan choices and put the decision in his hands. She's managed this not only without compromising her parental role, but also, as she had intended, with a touch of empathy.)

"Whatever," Nathan says. He's off balance. Usually by now he is fighting back; this time his mom's kindness has dropped his usual defensiveness. While he hasn't really listened to the choices she offered, he also isn't feeling trapped.

Ordinarily Karla's anger and combativeness frustrate Nathan and center his focus on her. Now that she's in control of herself, he is feeling the weight of his own choices.

His response surprises her. "I just hate my math teacher. And the homework is stupid. It's so confusing, and I'm never going to use this stuff in real life!"

"Ah, I get it," she says, gently. She feels a surge of both satisfaction and hope at realizing she's learned the root of his homework avoidance—without having had to lecture or badger him. She empathetically rephrases his words.

"Things a little tough at school right now?" she asks.

"Yeah. No kidding." Nathan looks at the floor.

"Sounds like you're pretty frustrated and discouraged. How about this: Why don't I help you get started on your math? Over dinner, let's figure out what could help you feel better about math and follow the rules about homework."

Nathan isn't enthused, but at least he is opening up to her.

Karla's discipline is *connecting*.

She set the stage for a constructive process of coming alongside her son as a guide. She didn't allow herself to be drawn into Nathan's drama. She created a safe place for him to share his real feelings. Building on this foundation, she now was *with* him, no longer seen as an opponent or a controlling authority figure.

Karla lovingly kept her position of authority, put responsibility into Nathan's hands, and gained respect. This scenario illustrates one way Discipline that Connects principles have helped hundreds of parents strengthen their influence and bond with their children through the kinds of situations that often drive families apart.

Typical Discipline vs. Connective Discipline

Parents generally respond to their children's misbehavior in one of two ways. The first is *domineering*—charging into the situation and controlling outcomes through demands for immediate obedience and either threats or use of strong consequences. The main aim of this approach is, "That behavior must stop—now!" The parent's own strong feelings of anxiety, anger, embarrassment, and confusion are oftentimes hidden beneath this primary goal. These intense emotions can cause parents to get as loud and demanding as needed in an effort to "win."

In a real sense, then, that approach is about kids being defeated. If "winning" equates to gaining instant control, then these tactics might be effective for a time. However, no one really wins when this is a parent's standard approach to discipline, because kids either comply to stay out of trouble or eventually rebel against the control. Either way, they never learn how to be self-guided, and once they're free from the controlling parent, they tend to lose control of themselves—and their lives.

The other typical parental response is *passivity*—giving in or giving up. Sometimes parents allow the kids to get away with various choices and actions because they believe certain situations and confrontations are just too difficult, especially as the kids move from being toddlers to teenagers. Even if there is little or no peace, parents in this mode are trying to "keep the peace" anyway. They turn their backs on battles, clean up the messes, and hope they aren't offending and alienating their kids.

They tend to feel weak and wounded. They regularly say (for example) that they feel like doormats, or that their kids don't appreciate them. Their kids are likely to grow up feeling entitled and accustomed to getting what they want.

Virtually every parent is capable of getting stuck in one or both of these extremes. But none of us wants to live there! Parents who commit to Discipline that Connects with their children's hearts can little by little find their way into a new normal. If you want to learn a way of disciplining that will profoundly influence your children's behavior, their development, their future, and their faith, keep reading.

Our hope and prayer is that as you grow in your understanding of the following principles, you will set goals for discipline that go far beyond merely controlling or avoiding your child's misbehavior. We pray that your goals will encompass modeling God's grace, truth, and love in all situations, no matter how difficult. To any extent that up to now you may have "missed the mark," be sure of this: Living this new way will have a lasting impact on your children as they see faith come alive in your home.

Discipline puts to the test what we most deeply believe. Is Christ's love longer, wider, higher, and deeper than our children's (and our) misbehavior? Is God's mercy present in our ugly conflicts, ultimately drawing our hearts back together— and to Him? Does God's Word truly bring valuable protective wisdom that gets us back on track after we sin? Is the Holy Spirit's power more than sufficient to keep us growing in faith and character even when we struggle?

Simply stated, *corrective discipline is a wonderful opportunity either to reinforce or to tear down our efforts to train kids to know, love, and follow Jesus.* If we ourselves are Jesus-followers and want to pass on our faith, but we err foundationally in how we discipline them, they will likely conclude that the elemental spiritual principles of our faith don't meaningfully reach into real life.

Discipline that's effective in *discipleship* will flow from a parent's heart of humility, forgiveness, wisdom, love, and vision for a child's life. It must make sense to the child to win his or her respect. We can know that discipline has connected with our child's heart when he or she is developing a desire to know and love Jesus and to walk in the grace of obedience.

MY RESPONSE

- What stands out to me about the heart-connection approach to discipline?

- In what way(s) have I exhibited one or more of the elements of Karla's thoughtful, connective approach when I've disciplined a child?

- What aspect(s) of my current disciplinary methods would I say could use the most adjustment or change? What are the adjustments or changes?

"You Are SAFE With Me."

Kids learn the best when they feel safe.

Correct	"You are RESPONSIBLE for your actions"
Coach	"You are CALLED and CAPABLE"
Connect	"You are LOVED no matter what"
Foundation	"You are SAFE with me"

CHAPTER 2

Four Essential Messages

This chapter is an overview of the four basic messages of the Discipline that Connects approach to parenting. We hope that by the end of the book these will be deeply imprinted on your heart and that you'll have learned numerous practical ways to communicate—and demonstrate—them to your children.

(1) "You are SAFE with me."

To learn life's most important values, a child must feel emotionally and physically safe. Parents often take for granted that because their kids are complying with demands, they're learning the values parents desire for them. This is not the case. *If parents engage with a misbehavior focused only on the need for control, they seem either subtly or overtly unsafe to their child.* The child might actually be learning to be intimidated by anger.

So if I want my discipline to connect, I have business to take care of before I engage. As I calm down, I can be thoughtful, even prayerful, about my goals. This equips me so that when my child is defiant, whining, or lying, I'm guided by more than what I feel.

In the heat of the moment, preparing might be as simple as taking a deep breath. It could be a prayer or taking a step back instead of charging in thoughtlessly. The point is to replace any goal of making the problem go away immediately with a goal of modeling God's grace and truth. Then I can enter the situation focused on what my child really needs and communicate a powerful message: *"You are safe with me!"*

Becoming safe begins by doing some difficult work to understand what's going on inside us.

Think back to Karla from chapter 1:

- She was aware of her volatile emotions, what was causing them, and what would happen if she allowed anger and anxiety to drive her interaction with Nathan.
- She took a deep breath and waited to engage her son until she was calm enough to focus on her love for him.
- She prayed for wisdom and asked for a heart of forgiveness.

All this was fixed on her own state—*before* she approached Nathan. By taking responsibility for her attitude and actions, Karla became a safer parent.

When we understand and own what's going on inside us, we send the message, "You are *safe* with me." This message anchors the Discipline that Connects approach and sets the stage for us to communicate the other three:

"You are *loved*, no matter what."
"You are *called and capable*."
"You are *responsible* for your actions."

(2) "You are LOVED, no matter what."

"Sure," some parents say, "I show my kids love when they misbehave—it's tough love, the kind that hurts me more than it hurts them." There is merit, occasionally, in "tough" measures as one element of loving discipline. However, if that's primarily what children receive when they act up, then they're missing out on the fullness of God's heart for sinners—for misbehaving people. We know from experience that it's easy to justify punitive discipline from an angry heart. We also know from experience that very rarely is tough discipline delivered with forgiveness and grace.

Conversely, some parents show "love" by letting their kids off the hook. At times there may be good reasons to show leniency. But if we habitually ignore misbehavior and don't hold them accountable, they won't be drawn into the reality that "God is not mocked, for you reap whatever you sow" (Galatians 6:7 NRSV). When leniency happens, kids don't learn responsibility for their actions. The key is to demonstrate love in ways that hold them accountable for learning, without exasperating them. (See Ephesians 6:4.)

John, Jesus' disciple, describes God's love as *lavished*! (See 1 John 3:1.) Through thick and thin, good and bad, belief and unbelief, His love never diminishes. If we'll open our hearts to receive it, He'll pour love over us till it's all-consuming. And not because we've got our act together:

> God demonstrates his own love for us in this: While we were still sinners [filled with disobedience, defiance, disbelief, and all manner of darkness], Christ died for us. (Romans 5:8)

How might it look if our driving purpose in discipline was to respond as a three-dimensional demonstration of Christ's love? In the illustration we saw, it looked like this:

- Karla sat down next to Nathan and softly placed her hand on his shoulder.
- She spoke gently, keeping their connection lighthearted.
- She responded with empathy when he expressed frustration.
- She was authentic and vulnerable and admitted that fun activities sometimes tempt her away from responsibilities too.

When love like this shows up during discipline, rigid defiance tends to melt like ice on sun-warmed pavement. It doesn't let kids off the hook, but it communicates a powerful message: "You are *loved*, no matter what."

(3) "You are CALLED and CAPABLE."

Paul's proclamation of our design and purpose casts a vision for us all:

> We are God's handiwork, created in Christ Jesus to do good works, which God prepared in advance for us to do. (Ephesians 2:10)

God has already planned good works for each one of us—every parent and every child. This is our calling! And with that in mind, He created us with unique gifts and capabilities to equip us. When kids misbehave, those gifts and capabilities don't disappear, they just show up in selfish and unhelpful ways—most misbehavior involves *some* sort of skill. Parents can either try to suppress the gift to stop the behavior, or redirect it for honoring purposes. Todd, the father of a spicy eight-year-old, learned to respond to Lily from the simple thought, *God made you.* This helped him to reframe her challenging behavior as something to be guided, not squashed.

Daniel, our oldest, always had a quick wit. Early on, he frequently used that skill to disrespectfully slice and dice us, his siblings, other children, and even his teachers when he was upset. We knew that this trait was a raw skill in need of shaping, so we held him accountable for his disrespect and encouraged him to use his words in honoring ways. As Daniel grew in wisdom and kindness, he learned to put that verbal prowess to much better use. He has a knack for teaching others with clever analogies, and he has spoken very persuasively (publicly and privately) about God's love.

When kids misbehave, we typically dwell on the wrong or sinful part of what they've done. As a result, what we commonly communicate during discipline—verbally and/or nonverbally—is, "*You* are the problem."

When my child misbehaves for what seems like the umpteenth time in a day, it can be a stretch to believe she's capable of anything but making me crazy. Yet with a little encouragement and guidance she can learn wise uses of her gifts that may even point her toward her calling. This inspires me to seek out the skill beneath the sin and acknowledge it as one way of encouraging her.

After affirming a trait of Nathan's, Karla offered reasonable choices to help him respond rationally:

- "Your persistence is something God can use someday; did you know that? It just isn't helpful at the moment," and "I've seen that you're really good at this game."
- "If you pause the game right now, you can play again after homework. If you don't, then I'll decide how long before you can play again."

By focusing on his potential rather than on his failure, Karla set Nathan up to succeed—and in a way that still kept him accountable for his behavior.

These types of responses, respectfully delivered, open up whole new realms of possibilities for guiding our children through behavior challenges. We can learn to anchor our discipline in these principles: I stay safe and communicate to my child, "You are loved no matter what, and you are fully capable of wise choices." This connects with my child's heart and often intercepts or redirects the misbehavior.

(4) "You are RESPONSIBLE."

Despite our best efforts to follow these principles, our children will still sometimes misbehave, and disciplinary measures will be needed. Our ultimate model is God, who "disciplines us for our good, in order that we may share in his holiness" (Hebrews 12:10).

That's what this book is all about: discipline that leads our children into a deeper connection with God's holiness and love. So we administer consequences not with the belief that enough pain will lead to change, but knowing that learning to follow in the Father's ways can sometimes be painful. (See Hebrews 12:11.)

When our consequences are rooted in love—not frustration, impatience, fear, or anger—they can effectively communicate, "You are fully capable of wise choices; you are responsible both for your actions and for making amends when you've done wrong."

Well-administered consequences don't just force kids to "serve their time"; rather, they show how to value restitution that leads to reconciliation. Wise consequences help them to feel remorse for what they've done and to experience a sincere desire to make things right. Instead of being punitive, consequences become constructive, leading to internally motivated kids. Until I achieve this goal, there's no telling how they will act when out from under my authority.

A few examples of constructive consequences:

- A child who disobediently watches TV before completing homework is required to install a filter or timer on the TV and teach his parents how to use it.
- A child who disrespectfully yells at a sibling can rest and calm down until she is ready to sincerely share four encouraging and loving things to the sibling.
- A child who refuses to finish clearly communicated chores gets his privileges back when the chores are done and he compensates any inconvenience caused to others with an extra chore.
- A child who has lied helps create a workable plan to restore trust in her affected relationships.

There are so many possibilities. (See specific topics in the appendix for details.) But keep in mind that even a constructive consequence imposed in a controlling or angry manner will not ultimately lead a child toward real heart change.

*   *   *

If you're unfamiliar with this approach, these principles and suggestions might seem unrealistic. That's what Dave thought when he came to a seminar, but he was desperate enough to attend because his nine-year-old son was spiraling out of control. His wife, Karen, called us several days later and said, "I can't believe the difference in Dave and how he deals with our son! Where can I get more of your materials? We need to steep ourselves in these ideas."

We often see the following cycle in families: Parents worn out by struggles become more angry and controlling with their discipline, causing the children to become progressively more resentful and less and less likely to respond well. Over time this sets the tone relationally as home life becomes branded with frustration and disconnection.

We can reverse this cycle as we learn to approach our kids in grace-filled ways and give truly constructive consequences. When children learn to expect grace and encouragement rather than demonstrations of power and control, their hearts become more open, not only to their parents but ultimately to the gospel's redemptive power. This is because instead of just hearing about the gospel of grace, they're experiencing it in tangible ways:

- God loves you *always*. Sin cannot—hasn't, doesn't, won't *ever*—separate you from His love.
- You are God's unique creation, capable of fulfilling the calling for which He created you.
- It's not my job to control you—you are responsible to God for your life and your actions, and to make right whatever your behavior has wronged.

When kids experience such support and assurance in the context of discipline, they begin to believe the messages of grace and truth that stand behind it. They learn to do the right things for the right reasons. They become people who understand and grow in God's love, which they then naturally come to share with others.

MY RESPONSE

- Which of the four "messages" in this chapter feels most familiar to me, and why?
- Which feels least familiar, and why?
- Thinking back to when I was disciplined as a child, what sort of messages did I receive? What effects do I remember these messages having?

CHAPTER 3

Forward Progress Begins With a Backward Step

Kids learn best when they know they're safe; this is the foundation necessary to best teach any value, skill, or lesson. Building an emotionally safe and secure relationship with kids keeps their trust in us high, and wins us the true respect and authority needed to guide them into a strong relationship with God and healthy relationships with others. The key question we answer in the next four chapters is, "How can I become a safer parent?" Once our kids perceive us to be safe, they're receptive to our love and guidance and are drawn into a relationship with a loving God. And, ironically, this best prepares them to go into a world full of danger as messengers of God's grace and truth.

* * *

One day I (Jim) arrived home from work deeply stressed. The whole drive I had been mulling over a contentious issue, mentally playing and replaying an intense dialogue. I exited the car irritable, tired, and hungry. I wanted a straight and un-cluttered path to a quick snack before landing in my recliner.

Instead I walked into the midst of a loud dispute between all three children, who were gathered around the table and argu-ing about a magazine. I dove right in, grabbing the magazine and bellowing, "Would you kids be *quiet*? You're being rude and disrespectful. It's been a hard day—the last thing I need to come home to is your bickering!"

They looked up at me in shock, as if to ask, "Who's being rude here?" Instead of railing back, my eldest wisely asked, "Hey, Dad, where's the love?"

Ouch.

I closed my eyes and drew a deep breath. "I'm sorry," I said, and meant it. "Can I have a do-over?"

* * *

The Discipline that Connects principles have helped us on two fronts. First, the four messages have succinctly described for us the goal of our discipline. Sharing them with our kids helps us be better accountable to the kids *and* the messages. Second, our accountability helps us know when we've blown it. If we don't recognize this, our kids usually do! Walking this path means that even when we mess up, there's a clear guide for getting back on track.

When I asked for my do-over, the kids nodded. I retreated outside and closed the door. I knew I hadn't been safe; I had not been in touch with my love for them. They knew it too. So I readied for re-entry by praying in a whisper: "Lord, forgive me. Help me to let go of my stuff from today. Give me peace and wisdom. Help me to do better this time."

I felt myself calming, my attitude changing. As I reappeared, my sons and daughter were waiting expectantly. They had settled as well, just knowing the direction we were taking together.

"Hey, kids," I said with a smile. "It's great to see you." I ambled over and sat with them. "I see you're having a disagreement about that magazine. Do you want my help with it, or do you think you can respectfully work it out on your own?"

"We've got it covered," Bethany offered. They were all smiling too. "Good do-over."

"Thanks to you," I replied. "One other thing: If you do need more time to resolve your issue, please take it either downstairs or outside. I've had a stressful afternoon and need a little quiet time to recuperate."

As they headed out together, I could tell they'd already resolved the matter.

Results of Charging Into Discipline

Since that day it's become clear to Lynne and me that almost all forward progress with our children begins by taking a step back: to breathe, to pray, to prepare our hearts and minds for the challenges ahead. This activates safety.

In this sense, parenting is similar to a quarterback executing plays for the offense. Usually, after taking the snap, the QB immediately moves backward, either to hand off or to survey the field before his next decision. Without those regressive steps, he gets no separation from the two lines crashing in front of him; he can easily and quickly be buried. Every once in a while it works to just plow forward, but if that became the norm it would be highly ineffective. The backward steps create the opportunity for forward progress.

When I marched into the house that afternoon—when I took the snap of my kids' conflict—I charged right into the fray. I just lunged ahead, wielding the weight of my stress and the force of my agenda. I didn't take a step back (let alone several) and didn't survey the field to consider, to understand,

and to wisely decide. Not only did I make no progress, I lost yardage.

In those brief moments outside, I realized that it needed to be just God and me before I engaged with my family. That short time to prepare helped me relate to my children not as a demanding bully but as a gentle guide.

Many parents describe transitioning into their child's teenage years something like this: "We had a few bumps here and there when she was younger, but things were pretty normal. Lately, though, it's like the lid has blown off. What has happened?! We don't even know this kid!"

While hormones and shifts in brain development surely contribute to some craziness, we've found that there's usually more to it. The following account, which illustrates "the blowing of lids," is an example of parents using consequences just to gain immediate control. It's also a lesson about what kids learn when this happens.

● ● ●

"You're so old-fashioned!" screamed twelve-year-old Natalie. "This makes no sense!"

Joe had just grounded her for failing to clean the kitchen before using the computer. "How dare you talk that way to me?" he shot back, rising to his full height. "Go to your room! And if you expect to wear that silver jacket ever again, you will apologize—*now*."

Joe's frustration was boiling over. He couldn't figure out what had come over his daughter in recent weeks. To him, she'd seemed increasingly irrational and emotional. Well, *enough*. This would end—today.

Natalie felt trapped. She was exasperated with her dad's tactics and confused about what her new jacket had to do with any of this. She wasn't the least bit sorry, but she didn't want to lose the special birthday present from her parents. Not able to put her feelings into words, and knowing better than to erupt again for fear of his reaction, she gave in.

"I'm sorry." She forced out the words, then walked down the hallway to her room and shut the door.

Joe huffed, then uncrossed his arms. He thought Natalie might be learning her lesson, yet he still worried about how difficult her behavior had become. *I'm just doing what I've always done, and she's getting worse.*

He prayed that God would convict his daughter regarding her attitude and that somehow she'd get over this apparent season of rebellion. Beneath his prayer, Joe himself had emotions he neither understood nor had words to express. He had a deep fear about where this was heading, but he managed to avoid looking too deeply at his own heart and at his responses to Natalie's misdeeds; he kept his focus on his daughter.

Meanwhile, in the relative safety of her room, Natalie's fury gave way to sobs. Any potential for remorse was trampled by confusion, hurt, and a sense of helplessness. She blamed her dad for how she felt. As thoughts and feelings boiled, she grew determined not to give in so easily next time.

As a budding adolescent, she sometimes felt more able to take on her parents. *He better not try this again,* she thought, *or he'll be sorry. I won't back down next time. I don't care if he freaks out. They can't keep pushing me around like they have all my life.* Taking some comfort in newfound resolve and the beginnings of a plan, she slowly drifted into sleep.

● ● ●

So many parents, and many adolescents, have shared stories like this one. Pent-up emotions from feeling squashed by misguided discipline tend to reveal themselves in ugly ways if parents don't seek more than just instant control of misbehavior. In Joe's case, his actions and threats had "worked" only if that meant Natalie muttering the words *I'm sorry*. But clearly a storm was brewing.

When our kids are young, we can get away with being harsh and unloading on them. To a great extent they'll do what we say—not because they have learned to respect us or truly desire to do what's right, but because they're still sufficiently afraid and they want to get on with life. Most of them know they'll get shot down if they challenge us. They generally won't go toe-to-toe *until* they realize how strong they can be.

This begs for our application of the apostle Paul's teaching to parents:

> Do not exasperate your children; instead, bring them up in the training and instruction of the Lord. (Ephesians 6:4)

Mirroring: Learning by Imitation

Once, when interviewing some teens, I (Jim) asked, "Do you think when you misbehave that your parents ever misbehave too in the way they react to you?" Without hesitation one answered, "They sure do!" while adding, "But there's no one to hold them accountable for it." Another jumped in: "Since there's no one to hold them accountable, I have to get even with them."

Her strategy: When her parents were punitive, she was vengeful. And this doesn't happen exclusively "later" either—many strong-willed younger children will square off with Mom or Dad as well. We were with a dear friend when the following explosion happened with her toddler.

> Kirsten firmly announced to her two-year-old son, Owen, that it was time to stop playing and leave. As she reached for his hand, he yelled, "NO!" then dodged her hand and took a swing to hit her.

Kirsten felt caught between her child's disobedience, her own emotions, and a desire for immediate control. And she reacted loudly: "You will not say no to me or hit me!" She picked up her son roughly and plopped him onto a small chair for a time-out.

Owen stomped his feet, flailed his arms, and went on screaming, "No! No! No!"

Kirsten continued yelling also, her face just inches from his: "You stay in that chair, and don't move till the timer goes off! Do you understand me?"

"NO!" he screamed, and stood up out of the chair.

It was plain he did not understand. In truth, she wasn't understanding herself. Embarrassed and angry, she was doing what she'd learned from her own mother—fight to seize the reins. When parents get irate and yell to gain control, kids are inclined to simply follow suit or to shut down altogether.

Kids learn less from what we say than from how we act. And they in turn demonstrate what they've learned by imitating or mirroring us.

Kirsten was clearly out of tactics. Feeling overwhelmed and desperate, she burst into tears and stormed off, saying, "I don't need this right now."

Owen imitated her again in the transition from anger to anguish. Where only moments earlier he'd matched her anger with defiance and screaming, he now sat back down in his chair, deflated. Huge tears rolled down his cheeks as he sobbed, "Mommy! . . . Mommy!"

The persistent, creative, selfish misbehavior of children can trigger impulsive, irrational responses in usually rational adults. When parents become unpredictable and intimidating, kids feel threatened.

Just like adults, kids who are frightened tend either to fight back or be intimidated into compliance. Either way, they're not at all thinking about how to learn from their mistakes—they're just protecting themselves, so their learning has nothing to do with respect or obedience or wisdom.

Again, parents might continue doing this as long as it "works," that is, as long as it seemingly gives them a sense of control. Yet over time, as the child's mistrust or resentment builds, he grows more and more able and determined to fight back. When the angry approach no longer results in a "fix," parents either resentfully ramp up their efforts and escalate conflicts—fueled by *their* resentment of their kids—or become more passive, even avoiding conflicts altogether and increasingly letting the kids run the show. Many end up flipping between the two responses as the day and mood dictate.

Either way, there are subtle yet significant messages communicated by both harsh and passive discipline. Jesus said, "Out of the abundance of the heart the mouth speaks" (Matthew 12:34 NKJV). When a parent's overflow is muddied by anger, anxiety, or insistence on control, the messages children perceive might be:

- "I'm out to get you."
- "You are a problem."
- "You make me angry" (i.e., you are in control of my emotions).
- "When you act this way, I don't love you."
- "You aren't worth the stress of trying to set boundaries."
- "I'm afraid of you."

These messages are diametrically opposed to what we truly want to convey. They also work against goals we may have for our kids—for instance, taking responsibility, respecting others, completing what's started, getting to bed on time, and so on. If your child resists your goals, examine whether he feels entirely safe with you and what messages he may be receiving.

Remember: Kids complying through intimidation are rarely learning wisdom and developing character.

The early years in the Jackson household were characterized by irritable, impulsive kids and stressed-out, reactive parents. Daniel, our strongest-willed and oldest, used to say to Lynne, "Mom, you just bursted all over us." He and Jim had word wars for the ages.

Our children were learning what we were teaching, all right, and it wasn't what we wanted. We realized we had to find a new road, take it, and stay on it. We couldn't do this without learning to become safer parents.

MY RESPONSE

Consider a typical behavior challenge you have with one of your children. In that situation:

- What goals/desires do I have for my child?

- What messages might he/she be receiving from my words, posture, tone, body language, etc?

- How do these messages seem to affect my child's response?

- What messages do I want to share with my child?

CHAPTER 4

Keeping My Kids Safe From My Baggage

One parent, while learning for the first time about the importance of becoming safe for her kids, said to us, "Oh, I get it—that's how to protect them from my baggage!" We love this analogy to illustrate the importance of entering discipline situations with peace and insight.

It's a fact: Whether ours fits into the overhead compartments or takes up half the plane's cargo hold, we *all* have baggage.

● ● ●

Linda was parenting as a single mom. She'd been raised by demanding and domineering parents and, since that was familiar, had married a man who shared those traits. But when her then-husband began physically abusing, she feared for her life. Church-led attempts to support and counsel the couple failed, and after receiving a restraining order to protect their sons, she ended the marriage.

Still, Linda refused to let baggage define her.

As she began her healing process, which included counseling, prayer, and efforts to rebuild relationships, she could see how her wounds frequently spilled over into her parenting. She was resentful about her parents' heavy-handed control. She feared that her kids could turn out like their father. These and other issues would surface when the boys were disobedient or defiant.

Realizing how unhelpful it was to allow baggage to compel her discipline, Linda set her sights on calming down before dealing with the boys' misbehavior. No matter how much they acted up or made wrong choices, she wanted to be safe for her children.

One exhausting day, they battled intensely over a broken Lego creation.

"You wrecked it!" one boy cried out.

"I did not!" came the second's embattled reply.

The third chimed in, "I saw you step on it!"

They were getting physical, and Linda headed toward them, determined to take charge and mete out "justice." Yet this time, when she felt a familiar rise of rage, the kind that had led to so many ugly outcomes, she caught herself and screeched to a halt. Then, not knowing what else to do, she counted loudly to ten.

As her kids stared with "what's-wrong-with-Mom?" shock, a still-angry Linda counted to ten again, slowing down and relaxing a bit. She needed a third ten-count to feel completely relaxed. After this final repetition she was able to smile. The boys began to giggle, and then they all burst into laughter.

With the tension dissipated, Linda was able to guide them through a constructive resolution. More important, she'd modeled how to make a wise choice and calm down when upset. Like most kids, her boys were watching.

The next day she overheard her middle son coaching his younger brother, who was revving up for a tantrum. "Wait— don't get mad. Count to ten," he said. Linda was reaping what she'd been sowing. She liked it.

• • •

We all carry difficult memories and unresolved emotions—from our earliest years with parents and siblings, to more recent hurt from someone's unkindness or dishonesty, to trauma from unexpected loss, or just our current stressors. When our baggage fuels our discipline, we lay a heavy burden on our kids—requiring that they behave primarily for our benefit.

When instead I take the backward step to consider what's going on under my own surface, and how I can calm myself, I protect my kids from things that have nothing to do with their misbehavior. I represent safety.

And then my child is likely to perceive altogether different messages, the ones I truly want to send:

- "You are safe with me."
- "I love you, no matter what."
- "You are called to be a blessing and are capable of learning wisdom."
- "You are responsible, and whatever comes from this, I will be here to support you."

These reflect *God's* messages to *us*. Again, when we discipline in ways that preserve safety and show love and confidence, our children will open their hearts to our influence and to the message of the gospel.

The Positive Power of Example

When kids (like anyone else) feel attacked or unsafe, they'll be defensive—even if the "attacker" is Mom or Dad. People on the defensive don't think about what they've done wrong; they're focused on their foe's actions and posture. Do I want my kids thinking about *my* response, or *their behavior*? For example, if Mom raises her voice with Aidan for picking on his little sister, Sandra, Aidan's brain can't give attention to his misbehavior until he feels safe. Rather than feeling remorse for his own actions, he's likely to think "Mom's mean" or "Mom always takes Sandra's side." Then, instead of pondering how he could have been more respectful, he's more likely to think about how he can either get away or fight back.

Conversely, children are far more likely to take responsibility for words and actions if their parents set the example for this. When parents calm down and seek wisdom, they can shift their focus from battling the child's behavior to helping him consider what a wiser response could be in the future. When a child senses that his parent truly has his best interests in mind, he's much more likely to *desire* to make that wiser choice.

God created our brains with cells called "mirror neurons," which, among other aspects, cause us to experience what we see happening to other people. They might prod us to stand on our tiptoes when we watch a high jumper, or nod when the person speaking with us nods first. They can spark empathy when we listen to someone share something deeply emotional. They also are the cells that cause children to learn so much from observing their parents (for instance, think back to Owen on the time-out chair in chapter 3).

Parents who seek to become calm and safe before discipline help their kids mirror and practice an essential life skill: how to cool off and think clearly when upset. This becomes possible when we act on our trust that Jesus is always present and merciful, whatever our circumstance. Imagine how my child's future marriage, ministry, and work experience can be strengthened if she learns to calm down and seek wisdom before engaging in challenging interactions. Even when I have no clue how to respond to a given behavior, if I take some time to consider it first, I've modeled something significant.

MY RESPONSE

- When have I seen the mirror principle at work in discipline situations (both unhelpful and helpful emotion-mirroring examples between my child and me)?
- What could I do before engaging with my child that would help us to resolve conflicts?
- How can I begin doing this when a situation next arises? What will be my first step?

Thinking Aloud: Authenticity and Influence

Children can learn even more effectively from our example if we talk out loud about our process: describing our feelings and sharing the strategy we use to calm down.

When Daniel was a teen, he and I (Lynne) butted heads with some intensity. I remember once, when he launched a sarcastic blast, I pointed my finger at him and said, with as much "authority" as I could muster, "You can't talk that way!" However, in his mind, when I blustered out statements like these, I had no real authority. Of course, he *could* talk to me that way. He just had, and likely he'd do so again.

We began coming to better and quicker resolutions when, beginning to get wound up, I learned to say things like, "Daniel, I'm feeling really angry right now, and I'm afraid I am going to be disrespectful to you—so I want to take a break. Let's finish this conversation when we're both calmer."

The goal of keeping my own head cool and explaining my thinking helped tremendously. Not long after this, Daniel began to follow my lead. The change in him took place over a period of years. Now, as a young adult, he almost always remains calm during conflict.

We've seen this approach benefit kids as young as two. Zoe, an intuitive child who quickly detects under-the-surface anxiety, starts acting up when she experiences subtle changes in her mom's responses to her. Fortunately for them both, Melissa has learned that when she is calm, so is her daughter.

Recently, when nervous and fretting about an event that night, mother and daughter were mirroring each other's anxiety and demonstrating the initial signs of a power struggle. Melissa realized what was happening, picked up Zoe, and gently said, "Mommy is really stressed. I know this stresses you too. Let's calm down together." After those soothing words, they snuggled briefly and then spent the evening joyful and connected.

These examples demonstrate how parents can learn to think aloud with their kids about their emotions, their efforts, and even their guiding principles for parenting. This yields two accomplishments.

First, it becomes an example for our kids. When they hear how we think about things, they can learn valuable insights. If we keep our thoughts to ourselves and don't share, they won't learn as much from our responses.

Second, putting our thoughts and feelings into words holds us as parents accountable. We've asked many to name concrete thoughts that come to mind during discipline situations with their kids. Often they'll say, "I'm just trying to get him to do the right thing" or "I wanted to teach her some respect." But as to what specifically was stirring inside at the time, many can't answer.

In my early attempts to squelch whining, I (Lynne) often barked, "Your whining is not okay, so stop it!" No insight into my emotions, my issues, or why I had chosen that particular response. The intensity of my attention and energy actually rewarded (and therefore fertilized) the whining.

But when I began to think through and then share aloud my internal rationale, I also learned to stay calmer (and even smile sometimes) in response. One of my statements was, "If I give you what you want when you whine, that would teach you that whining is a good way to get what you want. And that's not true."

The following are some practical examples of thinking out loud that often help keep the interaction calmer and more constructive:

- "I'm feeling angry. Maybe you're angry also. What could we do to calm down?"
- "I've had a tough day, and it seems you're having a tough time too."
- "I don't want to disrespect you."
- "I want to be sure you feel loved, even though I'm going to talk with you about what you did."
- "I want to affirm the good part of what you did before we deal with your misbehavior."

MY RESPONSE

- What expressions or assurances are helpful in a typical conflict around my home? (From the list above, from my own thoughts, or from the ideas of others.)
- Where could I post a list as a reminder when I need them most?

Using Scripture Wisely

God's Word provides tremendous, timeless principles for discipline, but all too often we see and hear parents using the Bible to scold their kids, leaving a stain on children's spirits. The words and actions of their parents, who are to be reflections of God's character to them, are likely projecting God not as a loving Father but rather a Cosmic Police Officer whose primary disposition toward them is displeasure or even disdain.

When a child misbehaves, a parent might growl, "Even if *I* didn't see it, the *Lord* was watching!" Or fire off something like, "The Bible tells us to be generous—*that* was selfish." Our daughter-in-law remembers the vivid shame she felt when a teacher frowned at her and said, "That made Jesus very sad."

Pronouncements like these clearly do not communicate truth with grace. And this shows plainly why we must discipline with discernment and humility. Kids who hear Scripture used primarily to correct their misbehavior are almost certain to develop distaste for it.

If I want my kids to value God's Word, the starting place is my example. Do I value the gospel's grace-filled truth? Am I encouraged and guided through my own struggle with sin? If so, do I speak with my kids about the wisdom and joy of obedience? Conversations like this help kids see that conviction from God's Word is helpful, not shameful.

In addition to discernment and humility, we also need a calm spirit to use Scripture well in discipline situations. If I don't have one, then it's best to wait. I need to stop and consider whether my use of Scripture will woo or wound my child at this moment.

In the midst of a conflict, Scripture can come to life when God's Spirit gives insight from His Word. It might be a prompting to stay peaceful or to ask forgiveness, or something that indicates what my child most needs to hear. It might be a truth that shaped me, which we then discuss. When we model how to apply what we want our kids to learn, *then* we'll have credibility to proactively teach and encourage them.

One day, Daniel and I (Lynne) spent much of the morning strongly at odds. He finally said, "Mom, I think we should go play some tennis. We've had a rough morning." On the court, though,

I was still sour, and when I smashed yet another shot into the net, my son quizzically asked, "Mom, are you still mad at me?"

A verse I had memorized to help me with my frequently critical attitude flashed in my mind: "Whatever is true, whatever is noble, whatever is right, whatever is pure, whatever is lovely, whatever is admirable . . . anything [that] is excellent or praiseworthy—think about such things" (Philippians 4:8). I walked forward and said, "Daniel, I've still been focusing on what you did wrong earlier. But just now the Lord convicted me about not noticing something you did that was really cool: You invited me to play tennis because you wanted to reconnect by having fun together after we were mad."

I shared the entire verse with him, and his face lit up. "I love that verse!" he exclaimed.

God's work in me spilled over to my son; since then, he has been drawn to that verse many times during difficult interactions with others.

Another means to wooing our children this way is proactively sharing with them a positive (a "do") that counteracts a negative (a "don't"). For example, our family had been having issues with name-calling. So when all was peaceful, we talked about the benefits of "speaking the truth in love" (Ephesians 4:15). Then we looked for chances to affirm our kids for doing so with each other.

After that foundation had been laid, we could occasionally gently encourage them in conflict to "speak the truth in love." If they did, we might point out how much better that felt.

MY RESPONSE

- How might I humbly model and quote a favorite verse or two during peaceful times?

- What verse(s) might proactively inspire and strengthen my child to avoid a particular misbehavior? (For additional ideas and inspiration, some like to Google "Bible verse" and the character quality they're considering.)

- What was a time I witnessed my child living out a particular "do"? How could I casually remind my child and affirm his or her action or attitude?

• • •

Once again: We've all got baggage. None of us has been perfectly graced and loved. Almost everyone has leftover emotional challenges as a result of being raised and surrounded by imperfect people throughout their lives. Understanding this reality and growing in my ability to receive grace from God and from others prepares me to better demonstrate grace with my kids.

It's essential to our parental calling that we believe and walk in this truth: My value is based not on what my kids do but on what Christ did for me on the cross, in the ultimate act of love.

The most important work I can do as a parent is "to grasp how wide and long and high and deep is the love of Christ" for me (Ephesians 3:18). The more I believe, the more I receive His peace, love, and grace. The more I receive, the more I pass on to my children as well as to others. This is at the core of preparing my heart for discipline so I can provide safety for my kids to learn and grow.

MY RESPONSE

What strengthens me in God's love for me (e.g., something to read or listen to, a favorite way to spend time, a person with whom to spend time, a place to be . . .)? How could I incorporate more of that into my life?

CHAPTER 5

Becoming a Calmer Parent

At the outdoor gathering his family was hosting, Ethan accidentally threw a Nerf football into a group of visitors, drilling one in the forehead. His mom, Ellen, immediately shot out of the crowd, scolded her eight-year-old for his carelessness and disrespect of their guests, then ordered him inside.

It's reasonable to want kids to learn how to be careful. It's right to correct them when they're reckless. However, the way we do this can either shore up or erode the child. We can encourage, or we can discourage.

Ellen discouraged Ethan. Had she briefly taken stock of what primarily was driving her reaction—embarrassment—she could have learned exactly what had happened. Ethan hadn't aimed anywhere near the guests, but the ball his friend had was shaped differently than his own and flew out of his hand in a direction he hadn't anticipated. When he saw the ball sailing off its intended line, Ethan called out a warning and walked slowly toward the group. He was clearly upset and obviously regretted what had happened.

Ellen didn't seek any details, ask how Ethan felt, or consider how he might deal with the accident. In short, his punishment stemmed from his mom's humiliation—she was worried about how what had happened would reflect on her. By not taking the time to ask or learn, she missed an opening to address his error in judgment so as to build up rather than tear down.

● ● ●

Most misbehavior requires no instant intervention. Still, we parents often feel an instant need to do *something*. Many of us have a default inclination to dive in with urgency—seeking control—and then to justify our actions "because of my child's misbehavior." That's rarely helpful; discipline interactions flow from a multifaceted combination of what's happening with the child and what's going on inside the parent. Becoming safe begins with acknowledging and understanding these dynamics.

Safety also requires our use of practical tools for avoiding what makes kids feel *un*safe. Their brains have a self-protect mode that gears for either a defensive or aggressive reaction to anything *fast*, *large*, and *loud*. In a small percentage of situations (when danger is imminent), children might need our startling intervention. But usually our intimidation provokes the defensive/aggressive reactions that cause us all to climb "Crazy Mountain" together.

At seminars when we've discussed escalation of intense emotions, many parents have had an *aha!* moment, realizing that the situation isn't primarily about their children but really about themselves. If we want to help our kids feel safe enough to calm down and solve the problem with us, instead of fast, large, and loud we should aim for *slow*, *low*, and *listen*.

"Slow, Low, and Listen"

Slow

When you first find yourself eager to enter a conflict, stop (if no one's physical safety is at risk) and take stock of what's physically happening to you. Your ears may be burning, or maybe there's a knot in your stomach, or your jaw is clenched, or your vocal tone has changed, or your muscles have become taut—one or more of these can give you an intimidating, conflict-escalating presence. These physical symptoms are being fueled by your thoughts and feelings.

Once, when I (Jim) saw my kids starting to quarrel, with unkind words flying every which way, I tensed to leap in. But as I inhaled to unleash my reaction, I felt my ears getting hot—the first obvious sign that I'm getting upset. Recognizing the impulse, I stopped and remained silent. There was no need to hurry. No one was in danger. I waited to see what would unfold.

Maybe it took a little longer than I'd have preferred, but within minutes the kids had worked it out, apologized, and were happily interacting again. Instead of hearing from me how disagreeable and unsatisfactory they were—and being hammered with unhelpful consequences for their errors—they'd landed on a far more preferable outcome. They learned about resolving conflicts on their own and saw the effects of apologizing and making things right.

The key to "Slow" is to buy time to de-escalate the intensity. Here are some ideas to help yourself slow down:

- Physically take a step back (instead of forward).
- Walk slowly (instead of rapidly) toward the situation.
- Go to a different room for a few minutes, after letting your child know you're going to cool down before trying again to resolve.
- Simply speak slowly instead of firing a barrage of words.

Low

Once I've stopped the charge, I can physically calm myself and consciously choose a nonthreatening posture. The body can help the brain function better and access the skills needed to handle a given challenge, because "motion changes emotion."

Jake, a tall and imposing dad, told us his strategy to calm and connect in discipline is to "take a breath and get small." After he started practicing this, his wife, Hannah, began to notice significantly better interactions between him and their sons.

At its heart, "Low" is really about keeping my energy low and calm and my posture non-intimidating. Some ideas that have proven practical and effective:

- Sit down, lean back, and put your feet up. (It's hard to yell at anyone from this position.)
- Instead of towering over your child, sit beside him. One mom said, "I couldn't believe what a difference it made when I began to just sit down next to my son and gently put a hand on his shoulder to address an issue."
- Set your small child up on a counter or chair, and sit below her level before engaging.
- Put your hands behind your back or in your pockets; unfold your arms; unclench your hands, or even turn your hands palm up to short-circuit an angry or defensive response.
- Breathe deeply and slowly (releases endorphins, calms your brain). Kids often will start to breathe in sync with you, without even realizing it.
- Develop a specific calming routine and let your kids know to expect it. For example, one mom shared, "I keep a small bottle of hand lotion in my pocket. I take the [misbehaving] child aside, but I don't say a word until I've put lotion on my hands and finished rubbing it in. By then, I've usually calmed down and have come up with a helpful plan."

MY RESPONSE

- What's my first physical clue that I'm escalating to anxiety or anger when my kids misbehave?
- At times when I've stayed calm, how have I accomplished it?
- What new "going slow" and "getting low" idea(s) would I like to try?

Listen

"You are not listening! You need to listen to me!" Sound familiar?

James, the brother of Jesus, reminds us, "Everyone should be quick to listen, slow to speak and slow to become angry" (James 1:19). *Everyone.*

As parents, we get to go first and model "Listen." How can we do this?

- Listen to your child. Give kids space to be first to talk. Ask gentle quesitons to help them open up, like, "What's happening here? And what can we do to solve it?"
- Listen to your heart for your child. To keep from blowing an incident out of proportion, keep ready a fond memory or something you love about your child: When has she been respectful? tenderhearted? kind? obedient? and so on. One wise dad simply reminds himself, *Ah, I love this kid.*
- Consciously walk in your child's shoes. Ask yourself, *What is he feeling? When have I had similar emotions? What does he need right now?*
- Listen to God's Word. One mom's favorite verse for parenting stress is, "Whatever you did for one of the least of

these . . . you did for me" (Matthew 25:40). When really upset, she'd recite it out loud, which also seemed to calm her child.

• Say a quick prayer asking God for guidance, and expect an answer! (See James 1:5–6.) Jim's favorite was, "God, give me wisdom. And give me your heart for my child." Lynne found that asking "Lord, what's the opportunity here? How can I connect, or encourage, or build life skills through this?" was very helpful.

Listening for God's wisdom in the heat of the moment led to an important *aha!* experience for me (Lynne) one day. I was locked in nose-to-nose conflict with Daniel. We were stuck in our classic roles: He was upset about something, and I was determined to stop his tirade and get compliance. I felt the weight of my discouragement becoming oppressive as we escalated, but as I slowed to seek a different perspective, I became aware of God's loving presence in the midst of our mess. I felt His compassion for the difficulties of our intense personalities and for our efforts to get along together.

I looked my son in the eye and said softly, "You know what I'm thinking right now?" He appeared puzzled, but I went on, "God has so much mercy on us in our struggle."

This simple acknowledgment settled us both. Calmly, we worked things through with respect. And this again strengthened our relationship. Even though it happened years ago, the memory is still vivid for me, and I've returned to the truth of God's mercy and presence during numerous other untidy family-life moments.

If these ideas are new to you, pick just one that seems doable and try it. The more you practice them, the more natural they become!

MY RESPONSE

- What question, truth, prayer, verse, or other thought could help me keep a grace-filled heart toward my child during stressful times?

- How can I remind myself when things get tough?

Success of Any Kind Is Progress!

When your child misbehaves and you find you're on that mental speedway with all the well-practiced angry responses, don't just mumble an apology and vow to do better next time. Take the exit labeled "Do-Over"—it's the best way to make the road less traveled (a calm response) a superhighway of its own. Practicing the responses you want to give, even after a rough start, strengthens helpful neural connections. Those wiser, calmer responses will become part of your wiring, and your kids just may follow your example.

●　●　●

Lana's eleven-year-old son, Mike, was frustrated by learning challenges. He hated being behind most of his peers in school. More and more often he was having volcanic outbursts; plus, the two of them seemed to be at odds frequently, especially over homework and other responsibilities. Then Lana heard the Discipline that Connects principles and began to work on self-calming and regrouping—with a do-over if she felt she wasn't demonstrating self-control.

One day, Mike started to escalate during conflict over a math assignment but then suddenly stopped and said, "Mom, can I have a do-over?" She realized the value of the self-awareness and humility she'd modeled. Over time, staying calm during conflicts became easier for them both. Years later Lana sent us a thankful note, describing Mike as a high school senior and an amazing young man.

Another helpful way to foster "staying cool in conflict" is to focus on what's gone well in your efforts to stay calmer in response to misbehavior. Even if the success was small, name it. For example, "I didn't yell as loudly or for as long this time," or, "I did my best to listen before raising my voice."

Focusing on satisfaction with *whatever* has gone a little better will grow more success. When you manage to discipline a bit more peacefully, make a mental note, share the good news with someone else, or simply thank God. No matter what, rest in His grace and assurance. Remember, this incremental process brings lots of ups and downs but can have big payoffs in the long run!

● ● ●

Jeri and I (Lynne) had several coaching sessions where part of our focus was on Jeri staying calm when her intense and sensitive daughter would have a meltdown. Jeri was particularly discouraged at her own angry responses when, for example, Kayla would start screaming about the texture of the towel on her car seat. On the verge of tears, Jeri said, "I feel so guilty for yelling at her like that." I asked whether there was anything good or praiseworthy (remember Philippians 4:8!) in her response. She thought and answered, "Well, it wasn't pretty, but I guess I didn't lose it completely."

I challenged Jeri to place her focus on whatever it took to "not lose it completely." She said, "I try to go slow and keep my voice down; it works for a bit and seems to keep me from big blowouts." I encouraged her to keep building on what she'd already done.

This wasn't easy. Her daughter was consistently struggling with huge tantrums; for instance, the sensation of getting her nails clipped could send her into frantic, angry howls. However, Jeri was learning to stay calm during chaos. After a few months she emailed a review of her progress that said, "I'm amazingly calm most of the time."

Bottom line: When things don't go well, keep a faith-filled perspective. God *is* at work for His good purpose. Jim and I struggled greatly in learning how to remain peaceful in discipline. He often had quick-tempered reactions, and I battled perfectionism, which made me critical of the kids and myself. The entire family had to be happy and respectful before I could feel good . . . and so I rarely felt good. Anger often rose slowly in me throughout the day, along with discouragement.

I have painful memories from those days. On two separate occasions, I slapped a child across the face in exasperation. Many times I lamented how I was getting nowhere toward becoming a more peaceful, loving parent.

At one especially low point I felt hopelessly stuck in rigid perfectionism and figured I might as well give up on seeking change. But the Lord granted the insight I needed, essentially this: I will always struggle. So will my kids. Do I want to model despair and defeat, or am I willing to persevere in a step-by-step process? Of course my answer was *Be an example of faith through struggle*. This gave me the courage to keep pursuing God's peace and love amidst the chaos—with gradual but significant changes over time. Though our kids are grown and gone now, Jim and I are both still growing in these ways.

MY RESPONSE

- How might I equip my child and myself for more do-overs? (For example, choose a secret or silly code word that means "pause and do-over.")

- When was a time I stayed fairly cool in conflict? How did I do that, and how might I repeat it more often?
- What do I most want to work on from this chapter? How could I share that with my child, as a statement of my desire for a safe, loving home?

CHAPTER 6

Renewing My Mind for Parenting

Most parents at some point get locked into unhealthy habits and patterns when they focus on changing surface behavior without changing the thinking that drives it. When conflict persists, despite firm resolve and best efforts, it may be time to look beneath.

God's Word exhorts, "Do not conform to the pattern of this world, but be transformed by the renewing of your mind" (Romans 12:2). Part of the world's way is ignoring or denying what's real and focusing instead on appearance. Well-intended parents can slip into this. To an angry child they may command, "Don't you dare say that!" To a sad child they may say, "Don't cry, it will be fine." The "pattern of this world" gets repeated when we sweep our unresolved frustration, sadness, tension, or other real issues under the rug without resolving them.

Though they can't reason through it all and articulate the nuts and bolts of the matter when they're little, our children sense that something's wrong with this. If we live the world's way, we attend to surface-level appearances and others' perceptions. We tend to disregard—and possibly not even notice—deeper dynamics.

"The pattern of this world" is further reinforced when parents blame kids for a problem without looking at their own motives or actions. We ultimately lose our kids' respect when we say, "This is for *your* benefit," without awareness of our own selfish striving for control.

Being "transformed" is about real, substantial, inside-out change. The renewing of our minds is about allowing God's Spirit to fuel new thoughts and develop new attitudes in us. We invite the Lord to search our hearts, shining His light on everything He chooses, and "take captive every thought to make it obedient to Christ" (2 Corinthians 10:5). In *The Message*, we fit "every loose thought and emotion and impulse into the structure of life shaped by Christ."

This isn't a restrictive or discouraging burden! A "life shaped by Christ" is filled with grace and hope. God sees all of our "yuck" much more accurately than we do—and He loves us intensely. He has plans to free us from it as we let Him show us, encourage us, and guide us toward the truth about us and our kids that will get us unstuck and growing together.

To truly grow as a parent, I examine *my* thoughts, feelings, and motives, and I surrender them to God's grace and truth. The strong emotions, actions, and statements revealed when I discipline are a strong indicator of what's happening under the surface. They provide me a mirror to see what's really in my heart. In a unique way, these insights can become the subject matter for my time with God. Once I acknowledge these things, His Spirit can begin transforming work in my heart.

Here are a few of the common beliefs that parents have identified and allowed God to transform.

"You should obey because I'm the parent."

I (Jim) grew up in a home where arguing with my dad was absolutely not allowed. As a result, I developed some deep-seated beliefs, a set of unwritten rules: "It is not okay to argue with Dad. He's right because he says he is."

I would come to realize I needed my mind renewed regarding a recurring scenario with our firstborn. When Daniel began arguing with me, I was unaware of operating by my own father's rules. I simply got irritated with the challenge and judged that my son should know better. From my vantage, he was causing needless problems; I frequently found myself saying (and believing) he should stop arguing "because I am your dad, and I said so!"

However, Daniel was less fearful of me than I was of my father. So even when I said no, he persisted. He didn't necessarily want to defy me, he just desired to hear the rationale for my decisions. My answer, "Because Dad says so," didn't satisfy his need to have concepts make sense. So he kept at it.

I tried to find new strategies and new consequences that would make him stop. Yet as long as I had the unexamined "Because I said so" commandments locked into my heart's unsearched corridors, and Daniel had a need-to-know mindset, nothing I tried was effective. Finally, when he was a young teen, we had our defining moment in relation to this dynamic. Another quarrel had my mind spinning and my defenses high. Feeling challenged and disrespected again, I flat-out said, "This is one of those times when the answer is *no* because I'm the dad! You need to stop this *now*—I'm getting really frustrated by your intensity!"

Fascinating how, when we say aloud the thoughts and feelings that drive us, they can suddenly sound outrageous. I'd basically just revealed my unwritten rules and admitted that my frustration was the reason I was saying no. It had nothing at all to do with what was best for Daniel.

What he said next is forever etched in my mind. "Okay. You win." His statement rang hollow—I didn't feel like a winner. He continued, "I'll do what you ask. But if you want me to respect you the way I *want* to respect you, you'll help me understand this better."

His words bored through all my layers and barriers. He wanted to respect me! And at last I was compelled to look inward and ask a few questions:

- Why am I being so demanding right now?
- Why do I so need to make him stop when he wants so sincerely to understand?
- What does my frustration have to do with anything?
- What makes me think "Because I'm the dad" is a sound rationale?

I also wondered if his statement was the heart's cry of many children who appear contentious or disrespectful. At the core, kids *want* to respect their parents, but often we aren't aware of *our* disrespectful attitudes and words.

I realized, even after years of working on being a God-honoring dad, that I was addressing my son by the same dad-centric rules implanted in me as a youngster. And this was a hard pill to swallow. I confessed my selfishness and said, "I'm sorry for being so harsh. I still have some old rules about Dad always being right and respected. I want to do better. I do have a few reasons, and I'm happy to let you in on them. Will you forgive me first?" He did, and I went on to give him the rationale. He still didn't agree, but he did feel respected, and he accepted my answer.

This typifies how God transforms us by renewing our minds. When we're confronted with imperfections and sinfulness,

God speaks truth to our minds and hearts through His Word. In my outward statements, an inner struggle was revealed. I could ignore it or I could face it, inviting God to help me grow through it. I chose the latter, praying for wisdom to develop new convictions.

These are a few of the renewed thoughts God shaped in me:

- When Daniel misbehaves, I expect him to own up to it and take responsibility for his part. I will win his respect by taking responsibility for my part.
- For my *no* to be respected, I need a sound rationale behind it.
- Sometimes I'm wrong. I'd best take care about thoughtlessly demanding that my children comply.
- Daniel is miraculously created; part of his God-given disposition is to question and solve. I can force him to conform, and likely build resentment in him, or I can find ways to draw out that miracle.
- There are times I will require immediate obedience without explanation, because I am convinced it is best. At those times, heartfelt obedience will result if I've proved respectful and trustworthy the rest of the time.

This does *not* mean that anytime a parent speaks, children should get to argue until satisfied with the rationale. Even so, parental accountability to give a reasonable explanation for decisions helps kids understand and also become more reasonable themselves. Like adults, children follow (even more so!) when they understand.

This turned out to be a helpful process for Daniel. And as we helped him comprehend reasons, he grew increasingly obedient. He really did want to understand and cooperate, and this was his way of wrestling with our values.

MY RESPONSE

- To what extent do I believe I should always be obeyed without question or explanation?
- How does this belief influence how I respond to my child?

"My child is a real problem—
I fear where this will lead her."

Seeing children struggle with behavioral issues can cause high anxiety in parents, especially when parents project the problems into the future. The anxiety often surfaces as anger; parents may view the struggle as a character flaw, wonder if they're to blame, and worry about what will happen to their child.

I (Lynne) battled a thought pattern like this. My early parenting experience was filled with stressful conflicts and dark thoughts, sometimes playing like a recording that looped again and again in my mind. My interactions with Daniel left me feeling like a failure as a mom, and I also felt guilty about how much I resented him.

The belief I remember most clearly was *I'm an angry mom, raising an angry child; when he gets to be a teenager, it's going to be horrible.* This anxiety fueled my discouragement and angry words. It also made me bent on quick control, hoping to prevent the future "terrible teen" scenario I feared.

The Holy Spirit began to confront me about how I wasn't speaking the truth in love to myself. I realized I needed to develop a "truth phrase" to substitute for that unhelpful belief whenever it came up. After some prayer and reflection, I finally landed on, "I'm an intense mom raising an intense child, and we butt heads—but we love each other!" I consciously practiced those words in quiet moments. Then, when Daniel and I started into a conflict, recalling them would calm me down so I could respond wisely.

Over time, as I learned to look at the big picture of our relationship through the lenses of faith and hope, I developed a new belief that raising Daniel was a hilarious adventure. He grew to be a teen with strong character and a passion for Christ; he was witty, intense, and occasionally exasperating but very endearing. By God's grace he was nothing like what I'd dreaded.

*   *   *

Ryan was shaken after hearing this story in a workshop. He raised his hand and confessed before many peers, "God has so convicted me about this. When my daughter has one of her big meltdowns, I think to myself, *This kid is just a train wreck!* I don't say it to her, but I know she feels that from me."

A few days later we received an email describing his "renewed mind."

> *I quickly came to see that beneath the surface of her intensity, Anna is a stunningly creative, passionate, and gifted person who loves God and other people with all of her heart. For her, life is an opportunity to put the pedal to the metal and just go for it. And when she goes for it, the results are beautiful. She's not a train wreck; she's a masterpiece. I am so thankful that I've begun to see her as God sees her.*

Years later he described the transformation that followed as he lived out this belief:

> *I began to look for opportunities to understand and come alongside, instead of react with a power encounter. I realized Anna wasn't being naughty; she was very physically*

and emotionally sensitive, which caused her to have legitimate needs. I also realized that my own sensitivities had fed my reaction to her. For example, when she enters the room now I simply work to dial down our noisiness or TV volume and connect with her for a bit to ease the transition for her.

As a result of understanding myself and my daughter, I have learned from God how to be a better grace-giver to Anna and to others. I no longer see Anna as a problem but as someone who needs to experience the grace, comfort, and growth that can only be found in the body of Christ.

Like Lynne and Ryan, many parents say things about their children that reveal concerns about the future. Untended, the concern grows into fear and can become defining. So listen to the words you speak about your kids. Are they words of truth, spoken in love? If not, you're not alone, and you can begin today to take these matters of the heart to the Lord. Confess the fears and the judgments. Remember, "Perfect love drives out fear" (1 John 4:18). Ask God to place words of love and truth in your heart, for yourself and for your kids.

"My kid is my report card."

Stated so bluntly, that statement obviously isn't true. But it's still a powerful and subtle belief for nearly all parents. Who doesn't fight the temptation to get our value from our child's behavior or performance? From glowing Facebook posts to "Proud parent of an honor student" bumper stickers, we have a tendency to believe, *If my child behaves well or succeeds, I'm a good parent. If my child really blows it, I'm a bad parent.* Unfortunately this puts tremendous pressure on us to control our kids, and on them to get it right. That can lead to an emotional roller coaster as we overreact to normal behavioral ups and downs.

* * *

Our son Noah was a lively, bright little guy—both inquisitive and impulsive. The day he was caught lighting matches in the church provided a real-life test of my (Jim's) ability not to allow his behavior to determine my value. Apparently, he and some friends had gathered under a stairway between services, and their experiment was quickly spreading the distinct odor of sulfur around the church. I was quite embarrassed when I heard of it from, of all people, our pastor's wife. To make matters worse, one of the younger boys who'd followed our young Pied Piper into this delinquency was her son.

Lynne and I are our church's endorsed parent educators. My credibility was at stake! *How could he do this, and in front of so many people?!* My first impulse was to hunt him down and punish him so everyone would know I had things under control. You know, to save face. But I'd learned long ago that my first impulse is rarely a helpful response. So I took a deep breath and slowed my inner inclination to jump into action.

In this space I could think more clearly and less selfishly. I could see that Noah's behavior was not about me; it was mostly childish lack of judgment. I actually said aloud, "Even parent-educators' kids misbehave." I could then focus on how to help my son learn from this, not on how to reduce my embarrassment. After I found him, we walked to a quiet place. It was evident instantly that he felt bad and was ready to discuss a plan to resolve the issue.

Letting go of managing our own reputation when dealing with misbehavior frees kids to feel the weight of responsibility for their actions. To get started, we can remind ourselves, "This child is not my report card!" Then, because we don't need to control the situation, we can guide kids to face the problem they've created.

"I deserve peace, quiet, and obedience!"

Another hidden belief that triggers overreaction is some variation on "I have a right to peace and quiet, a compliant child, a supportive co-parent," and so on. It's even more common for parents who are going through tests and trials.

One young mom, Karra, impatiently scolded her fussy toddler: "Waking up at five-thirty does *not* give you the right to have a tantrum!" Her frustration with his lack of cooperation was evidence of her core conviction that she deserved a good night's sleep, a well-behaved kid, and a low-stress life. When Lynne asked, "If he could, what do you think your son would have said to you right then?" Karra chuckled and admitted that she'd been having a tantrum too.

Rob's belief was similar. He told me (Jim) that his goal when he came home before dinner was to see "a clean house after a long day at the office. I think that's pretty reasonable, and I've made it clear to Paxton that just because Mom isn't well these days is no excuse for him sloughing off. So it's disappointing when I come home to regular messes and chaos. He should know better. That's why I get upset, but it's not working."

"You can't control how clean the house is," I said. "But you can control how you enter the house. What kind of parent do you want to be when you walk through the door?"

His stern face softened, and he replied, "I guess I want to be the kind that would love Paxton and support Lyla." When Rob changed his objective—merely from focusing on something he couldn't control to something he could—he fairly quickly became less resentful and more grace-filled at home.

"Why can't my kid just do what she's supposed to do?"

One of the most complex parent-child pairings is a "get it right/ get it done" personality type raising an intensely wired, highly emotional child who struggles in life.

Britt, a take-charge person, was furious that she couldn't get a handle on her daughter's disobedient and disrespectful behavior. During one of her early phone-coaching sessions with me (Lynne), she started with a few choice labels for Katie. Growing louder, she ranted, "*Why* can't she just do what I *ask*? Seriously—it's simple stuff, like 'brush your teeth' or 'leave your sister alone.' Or, 'be *quiet* while I'm *on a call*!'"

Then her voice became muffled as she yelled, "For heaven's *sake*, Katie! *STOP* it! I told you I'd be on the phone! Can't you *just be QUIET?!*"

I asked how tough it was to be patient when her daughter was acting up. She sighed. "I've had it. Honestly. My fuse is so short these days."

I summarized: "So she's frequently misbehaving, and you're frequently angry. Sounds as if you're both stuck." I realized that overhearing their real-life conflict was providing an opportunity, so I said to Britt, "As your coach trying to help you with this, I'm gonna take a real risk." I paused to shift gears, then harshly commanded, "Britt, you need to just *stop* it! Can't you just be *patient* with Katie?!" During a brief silence, I wondered if I'd lost a client.

"Oh, I get it," she said more softly. "Thanks for doing that." She got it. She saw right away that get-it-right demands don't inspire a person toward growth. We dove into understanding the stress and discouragement driving her conflicts with Katie. Their relationship (and Katie's behavior) gradually transformed as Britt's compassion for Katie guided gentler, more empathetic responses.

"I do not deserve to be treated this way."

We hear plenty of stories about kids who lash out with, "I hate you!" or "I wish I had different parents!" Moms and dads hearing words like these report how hurt they feel and how tempted they are to retaliate. Many ask, plaintively, "What did I ever do to deserve this?"

What usually helps most is when parents learn not to take such words or actions personally—to let them slide. Doing this requires knowing that the behavior is far less about the parent and far more about the child's stress. It could be revealing discouragement, anxiety, even the erratic behavior of a developing brain. This doesn't mean not addressing the behavior; it means addressing it with grace and compassion instead of anger and resentment.

●　●　●

Dan was livid with his daughter. "It's terrible," he said. "She treats us like dogs." He and his wife, Carla, were suffering real abuse from Tina, whom they had adopted as a young teen. She would mock them, tell them they were terrible parents, and generally taunt them about anything that might provoke a reaction. On rare occasions she'd explode in vicious physical attacks.

Carla and Dan were emotionally drained and felt deeply hurt by the seeming rejection. Yet they realized the intensity of their reactions fueled the cycle, so they decided to focus on discovering what Tina really needed from them. They would come to see her outbursts as signs of shame and pain.

During one highly volatile episode, Dan endured Tina's rage for thirty minutes, all the while remaining present to protect her and Carla, and to model the never-leave-or-forsake love of Jesus. Previously he would have responded with fury, fueling another escalation. Now, though, he was filled with compassion, which compelled him to begin to pray for Tina. As he prayed, she softened. Her tense posture relaxed. And then she began to sob in remorse.

Love broke through.

Over time, the damaging behavior and abuse became less frequent as Tina grew more confident of Dan and Carla's love for her. One day she came home from school stressed. Where once it had been common for her to blow up first thing upon arrival, this time she burst in anxiously and announced, "I need a love sandwich." Her parents enveloped her in a bear hug as she poured out her heart about her difficult day.

What a breakthrough—growth rooted in tenacious grace.

When Anger Is More Than Anger

Many parents say they feel angry with their children especially during discipline. However, another emotion frequently lurks beneath. For most people, anger feels more powerful and less vulnerable, and thus is more "comfortable" than shame, hurt, inadequacy, fear, sadness, disappointment, grief, despair, or confusion. Parents who are brave enough to look deeper than the surface may discover that anger is a protective casing around other more fragile feelings.

Getting to the root of these other emotions is crucial to renewing our minds with the truth of Christ.

MY RESPONSE

- Is anger a common emotion for me?

- What would I feel if I couldn't feel angry?

- Do I sense other emotions that, however concealed or buried, may be the real issue? What stands out to me?

This will likely require some reflection and/or journaling, but the answers can be revealing and will help you think more effectively about managing those feelings. If you sense you have stumbled upon a deep well of difficult emotions, you may consider receiving professional help through your church or a counseling agency. We both have undertaken such soul searching at different points, with rich results. You and your family are absolutely worth it.

Learning to Be Okay When My Kids Aren't

As wonderful as worship services and Bible studies are, home is the test of what's real in life. If we depend on our kids to love unconditionally or act in ways that make us look or feel good, their shortcomings and errors will really push our buttons. Our overreactions likely reveal that in some way we feel anxious, inadequate, or rejected, which means we're depending on our kids to help us feel peaceful, sufficient, and loved. This tells them, "I'm not here for your needs; you're here for mine." That's a setup for disappointment and worse.

In contrast, when we believe God's love is enough, we can be okay even when our kids are unkind, exasperating, or insolent. Modeling this attitude over time can establish this reality in our homes: "My value doesn't depend on how others treat me. God's love is more than sufficient."

Only because of God's love and forgiveness through Jesus am I full, complete, and *not* dependent on my kids to feel okay. The more I remind myself of these truths, even in tense situations, the more my parenting transforms from the ground up.

Here are some "grace and truth" beliefs that have helped hundreds of parents—including us—become safer:

- My child is not my report card. I get my value from Christ's love.

- It is not my responsibility to make everyone happy.
- This behavior is just a moment in time; it doesn't define me, my child, or our future.
- Jesus is always with us, full of mercy in our struggles.
- My child and I are gifts to each other, given by God for His perfect purposes.
- There is a significant opportunity in every challenge.

You might also embrace these verses:

> You desire truth in the innermost being,
> And in the hidden part You will make me know wisdom.
> (Psalm 51:6 NASB)

> By wisdom a house is built,
> and through understanding it is established. (Proverbs 24:3)

In her book *She's Gonna Blow!* Julie Barnhill shares that God doesn't give us our kids to fix them or whip them into shape; God gives us our kids to make us more like Jesus. Becoming a safe parent means becoming more like Jesus. I'm off to a great start if I identify the beliefs beneath the hurt that get triggered when my child acts up, and then replace those beliefs with God's truth. Clinging to the truth is faith in action, in my own home, for my whole family to watch and learn.

MY RESPONSE

- What most stands out to me in this section about becoming content in God's love and His purposes for me, even when my child is hurtful or aggravating?

- What truth or verse do I want to embed in my heart to help prepare me for becoming a safer parent?

KID CONNECTION: My Home's Safety Team

Talk with your children about the importance of safety. Walk around the house, inside and out, examining and discussing things that help keep your family physically safe. You can even share and show things that help keep the family financially safe (bank accounts, insurance policies, etc.).

Paraphrase for your kids:

- "It's good to do what we can to be safe; physical safety keeps us from being hurt. But there are also other ways we can be hurt in our own home. Sometimes our words can hurt each other's hearts."
- Read Proverbs 12:18 (explain as needed):
    "The words of the reckless pierce like swords,
    but the tongue of the wise brings healing."
- "I want to work at helping you feel safe by better managing my feelings and words." (Explain why this doesn't mean they won't receive consequences for misbehavior.) Then you might provide an example of when you've been selfish and angry, and ask forgiveness if you haven't done so already. Let them know they can respectfully tell you if they don't feel safe.
- "What are ways we could work together to keep everyone's hearts safe?"

Brainstorm ideas for how each person or the entire family could protect others from their anger and stay calm when they're upset: e.g., develop a sign or a signal to take a break; list activities to do or a place to go for calming down when someone's upset; practice deep breathing; etc.

As you carry out these ideas, keep the initial focus on "What's going better? Who did something special to calm down when upset?" Invite sharing and questions, and be sure to lead by example.

"You Are LOVED, No Matter What."

Misbehavior is the golden opportunity for unconditional love.

Pyramid Level	Message
Correct	"You are RESPONSIBLE for your actions"
Coach	"You are CALLED and CAPABLE"
Connect	"You are LOVED no matter what"
Foundation	"You are SAFE with me"

CHAPTER 7

Misbehavior: The Golden Opportunity for Unconditional Love

Chuck was almost sure his preteen daughter knew he loved her no matter what. Wanting his "almost" to be an "absolutely," he asked her, "Honey, do you know that you are loved, even when you misbehave?"

Sasha replied quickly, "No." She didn't explain her answer.

Chuck was shocked. He was a caring dad who, in his mind, had clearly communicated his love. Yet his daughter was swift and decisive to say she believes she's not loved when she misbehaves.

This is a common disconnect. Parents believe that their kids understand their love, when in fact their kids do not. How does this happen?

* * *

There's an art to communicating love to your kids—not so they can get it, but so they *can't miss it*! A key aspect of conveying unmistakable love is timing. Most parents realize the importance of expressing love, but many of us miss opportunities when our love is most needed.

Simply stated, if we mostly convey love only when we like how our children are acting, we're showing them conditional love. Conversely, if we habitually express love when they're doing nothing in particular, we show them they're loved for who they are, not for what they do.

Imagine a "bank account" of emotional security in your child's heart: Each confirmation from you is a deposit of "I'm loved and valuable" currency. In most relationships, small deposits happen when parents express love as their kids do well, or for no particular reason. But the biggest deposits occur when kids *mis*behave. This means their misbehavior is an irreplaceable golden opportunity! It's the only time we can convince our kids that they're so prized and cherished that we will continue loving them *despite* anything they do.

At a deeper level, this is what grace is all about. Theologians define grace as "unmerited favor." It's the love God showed even when we were still filled with sin (see Romans 5:8), and it's the same love we can make real to our kids while they're "still sinning." When kids experience grace like this, they go into the world prepared to deflect arrows of "ungrace" and to offer grace to others.

Keeping the Message of Love Alive in Our Discipline

Imagine if every time we disciplined our children we kept these powerful teachings at the forefront:

- "I pray that you, being rooted and established in love, may have power, together with all the Lord's holy people, to grasp how wide and long and high and deep is the love of Christ" (Ephesians 3:17–18).

- "The goal of our instruction is love" (1 Timothy 1:5 NASB).
- "God demonstrates his own love for us in this: While we were still sinners, Christ died for us" (Romans 5:8).
- "God is love. Whoever lives in love lives in God, and God in them" (1 John 4:16).

Since God's very essence is love, it only makes sense that we practice His love as we discipline our children.

Most of us parents say we deliver even our firmest consequences out of love for our children. We desire to teach right from wrong and to protect them from even harsher real-life results in the future. Yet while parents believe their discipline sends the message "You are loved," hundreds of the kids we've asked about this perceive an entirely different set of messages:

- "I'm a problem."
- "I'm a pain in the butt."
- "I'm a bad kid."
- "I'm not important."

And so on. This is the great disconnect. What parents *want* their kids to hear and believe, and what kids *are* hearing and believing, are often polar opposites. To explore whether there's some disconnect going on with your kids, we invite you to consider a few questions:

- If a camera were recording me when I discipline, and I gave the video footage to an unknown Sunday school class of kids my kids' age and turned down the volume, what would those kids say it's like to be the child receiving the discipline?

- Judging by my facial expressions and body language, what would my child say are the messages I'm delivering? (Begin with the words, "Child, you are _____!")
- How would my kids say my love for them changes when they misbehave?
- When was a time my child would say he felt loved by me during discipline? What did I do to make that happen?

MY RESPONSE

- How might I talk about my unconditional love with my kids? When there's opportunity for relaxed, open conversation, I can ask my child, "Do you feel like I love you when you misbehave?" However he/she responds, also ask, "Would you share with me anything I do that causes you to feel that way?"
- I can share Romans 5:8 and express my honest desires to better share my love with my kids when they misbehave, just like God does with us.

Love Without Conditions

Even well-disciplined children can have behavioral tailspins. After all, they're free to choose how to act and how to respond to correction. They can get discouraged despite our best efforts. They can forget they are loved.

We can't control this; we *can* control our own attitude and actions. We can remain intentional about expressing our love in all circumstances. We can follow the example of our loving and gracious Savior, who attracted marginalized people in droves because He showed them they were loved as-is, right where they were. Demonstrating this kind of love in the messes of family life brings the gospel to life in our homes!

• • •

Mitch *hated* math.

Mitch's dad, Andy, a mortgage banker, said the subject had always given his son struggles. Now, though, in the sixth grade, Mitch was having real troubles keeping up with his class. Andy was concerned and made a firm rule that Mitch couldn't play with friends until his homework was done. This was reasonable but had an unintended result: Mitch was spending less and less time with his friends while becoming more and more discouraged.

Sometime during the school year, Mitch started to lie about completing his homework so he could go out and play. He got away with the ruse until his teacher called. Andy was a great dad and loved his son, but he hit the roof when he found out how little of the math was being turned in.

"No son of mine is going to behave this way," he said to Mitch. "You're grounded on weekdays till you're back on track. And from now on, I'm looking at every assignment before you leave the house."

Considering the circumstances, Andy's decisions seemed sensible. But Mitch grew increasingly frustrated and disheartened as the studies became more and more difficult. Andy would arrive home each day around five o'clock and ask to see the progress. Mitch's other subjects were fine, but the math was never done. He made excuses, whined, and protested that math was dumb.

Most nights ended in exasperation, and sometimes Mitch sobbed as Andy sat trying to help his son understand the math. It got to where Andy was essentially completing the problems so Mitch could turn in the work. Mitch felt increasingly ashamed at seeing his father's deep disappointment, and Andy knew

Mitch wasn't really learning. The entire situation grated on every aspect of their relationship.

When I (Jim) suggested to Andy that he make sure Mitch felt loved in the midst of all this, he was almost in disbelief. "Are you kidding?" he said. "He knows I love him. Are you telling me Mitch should feel more loved when he's failing math? That'll just make him think it's okay—and it's not."

I asked Andy if he had any other ideas about how to help Mitch feel more encouraged. After conceding that he'd tried everything else, he reluctantly agreed to somehow express his love to Mitch.

"Just be certain," I cautioned, "that when you let him know you love him, you do it in a sincere way, not expecting or demanding a change in his behavior, or he will just feel manipulated."

Andy nodded.

God loves us in the midst of any sin we commit or could commit; this draws us toward, not away from, His righteousness. So it's untrue that showing our children unconditional love somehow reinforces negative behavior. We've repeatedly found that children's attitudes soften if parents emphasize their love when kids misbehave.

When I saw Andy the following week, his eyes were bright. "You wouldn't believe it," he said. "The day we last talked I prayed that God would help me to be more in tune with my love for Mitch during this whole math thing. That day after work, Mitch was in fine form. He threw every excuse in the book at me. I was getting frustrated, but then I caught myself. Instead of launching into him the way I normally do, I just waited and let him go on awhile. I felt a new sense of compassion for him. Then it dawned on me: I really do love this little guy! He's my beloved son. I felt calm, which I hadn't felt in the middle of this before. Mitch could sense it too.

"I relaxed and sat down on the stairs where he'd met me so that we were on the same level. I looked him in the eyes and said, 'Mitch, doing well in math is important. But do you know what's far more important?' I was kind of solemn. He shook his head, not knowing what to expect. 'What's far more important is that you know how much I love you, and whether or not you're good at math can't change that.'

"Mitch's eyes filled with tears. He jumped into my arms and began to sob. 'I'm really sorry, Dad! I'm just not very good at it.'

"'It's okay, son,' I said. I hugged him for a while and then asked if he wanted my help to get it done. He said he did, and while it was still hard for him, the resistant attitude was gone. He asked questions and worked harder than ever, and I was less frustrated and became a much better teacher.

"As the week went on, I did less of the math and Mitch did more. Last night he completed the assignment on his own, and when he finished he was proud to show it to me. I was gentler when I noticed some errors, and he was patient when I worked with him to correct those problems. He's a different kid. And I have to admit, I'm a different dad."

Whether or not Mitch had changed his attitude or improved his math efforts, Andy could sincerely say he was more satisfied with his approach to his child, having prepared his own heart to express genuine love. The change in approach made all the difference. Andy's heart was deeply sincere, and he communicated love in a way Mitch couldn't miss it!

God's Spirit: Our Powerful Resource for Loving Discipline

In Galatians 5:19–21 Paul lists "misbehaviors" (sins) to exceed any parent's worst nightmares, including immorality, witchcraft, hatred, rage, drunkenness, and more. Then, in complete contrast: "But the fruit of the Spirit is love, joy, peace, patience, kindness, goodness, faithfulness, gentleness, self-control" (vv. 22–23 NASB). One list is about sins, the other about the antidote to sin—walking with the Spirit.

The two lists inform Paul's instruction in Galatians 6:1: "If someone is caught in a sin [as in 5:19–21], you who live by the Spirit should restore that person gently [as in 5:22–23]." If that's how to correct adults snared by sin, doesn't it make sense for us parents to patiently correct our children with the same Spirit-filled gentleness?

This means when we're upset at our misbehaving child, we can pray confidently for two things:

- "Holy Spirit, I need your love (or patience or gentleness or kindness or ____) for my child."
- "I know you want to restore and build wisdom here, so show me how to do it." (Then take a few moments to listen.)

MY RESPONSE

- What are the misbehaviors that most commonly upset me (the ones to which it's hardest for me to respond in love)?
- What practical strategy, statement, calming thought, verse, or prayer will best fit each one and allow me to express love to my child? For example:
  » Sibling conflict—statement: "You two often have a lot of fun together. Arguments can be fun-stealers, can't they? What help do you need to solve this?"
  » Messy room—prayer: "Lord, show me how to help this be more fun, less overwhelming."

» Back talk—verse: "The mouth speaks what the heart is full of" (Matthew 12:34). How can I access my child's heart instead of fixating on the misbehavior?"

Insight Into the Need That's Driving the Misbehavior

The Holy Spirit is a powerful resource, both for the peace and patience to discipline gently and for the insight to know what's going on in our child's heart. The following story from Susan about getting to the root of her son's constant whining illustrates the benefit of looking beneath the surface to identify needs.

• • •

A few weeks ago my husband, Don, read that fear often is the primary feeling behind anger. He and I talked a lot about how addressing underlying fear can put the anger into perspective and make it easier to handle. We also talked about how this applied to our kids. I remembered Lynne saying Bryan seemed anxious, and that his whining could be a way of coping with anxiety. This stuck with me because I was frustrated and ready for some fresh angles on dealing with this issue.

Even as a little guy, Bryan had perfected the art of whining, relentless and annoyingly high-pitched. We read all the books about managing it—and we tried them all:

"Talk to me in a normal voice."
"Go to time-out until you can use a regular voice."
"You will lose your favorite stuffed animal if you choose to whine."

We were usually calm as we'd make these statements and then follow through on the consequences we'd set. Yet by the end of the day there'd be a big pile of confiscated animals, and he'd still be whining. In moments of exasperation I'd push my hand forward and say, "*Stop*, Bryan. Stop that whining voice."

I knew intense energy from me actually rewarded his whining, but I didn't know what else to do. Nothing worked—until we focused on something else.

The day after Don and I had the discussion about fear, Bryan was using the high-pitched voice when he couldn't find a DVD. Don tried the "stop" command; the whining got worse. Then I tried a whole new way. "Bryan, are you scared that we won't ever find the DVD?"

He visibly softened. "Yes."

I said I would come down and look with him, but I got distracted on the way. When he tired of waiting, Bryan came to me and asked, with a super calm voice, "Mom, can you help me find the DVD, please?"

I about fell over. We went together and quickly found it. What a difference!

Since that eye-opening night, we've continued to address his underlying anxiety instead of his tone. We calmly say things like, "I can see you're really upset about that. It's hard being upset, isn't it?" He doesn't always stop right away, and we don't force it. But usually within a few minutes he calms down and accepts simple encouragement or problem-solving about the situation.

This seems simple now, but we'd been off base for five years. I've become more empathetic and affirming (rather than controlling), and Bryan is whining less. He has entire days when he doesn't whine at all! We talk in the evening about how much better life goes when he uses his regular voice. Regarding what makes him anxious or afraid, we keep reminding him how God can bring peace to us when we acknowledge our fears and give them to Him.

Instead of trying to stop the whining—which wasn't working anyway—now we're building faith, insight, and skills that will last our son a lifetime.

Love Casts Out Fear . . . Shame . . . Anxiety . . . Discouragement . . .

Susan and Don learned to address not what was disruptively breaking the surface but what was still submerged. Their main change wasn't another strategy but another sightline; not a tactic but a perspective. And they grasped a valuable opportunity to help Bryan feel understood and accepted. From there they could help him recognize and navigate his difficult feelings and learn to calm himself. His behavior then improved dramatically.

In our work with children and youth who are posing extraordinary challenges to their parents, we nearly always find that either anxiety or discouragement or both are at the root of chronic misbehavior. We've seen children passionately and tenaciously stick to a lie because they feared what their parents would do to them or what telling the truth might reveal about them personally. Some scream out criticism and blame a parent because they're ashamed or feel inadequate. Or they act apathetic, as though they don't care, because they're deeply discouraged and have little hope of success.

If kids think they can't measure up to expectations, they'll seek attention in other ways. It's as if they subconsciously think: *A negative behavior is predictable—safe. I know I can control a lot of people's attention and emotions in the process. Setting out to feel like I belong or have significance through positive behavior is risky: I can easily fail; that's lonely, discouraging, and painful.*

In a child's eyes, getting a big reaction to misbehavior is better than being ignored. Over time, this can build an unspoken but powerful identity as "I'm the kid who misbehaves to get attention."

* * *

Liz, a conscientious daycare provider, was determined to protect two-year-old Tony from the aggression of her own three-year-old daughter, Ava. She'd already tried everything she knew to curb the behavior but still felt stuck, so she called us.

As Liz spoke about her approach to Ava's behavior, it seemed evident that Ava felt threatened by Tony. We wondered if Ava's belief was, *I'm not as important to Mommy anymore* or even *Mommy loves Tony more than she loves me.* If these thoughts were driving her actions, then Liz's frustrated responses were forming yet another layer of negative beliefs: *I am a problem. I get attention by hurting Tony. My feelings don't matter.*

It can be very difficult to know what a three-year-old really believes, but this idea seemed sensible to Liz. She decided to make sure that she remembered her love for Ava and then warmly communicated it.

That afternoon, Liz clearly and emphatically conveyed, "Mommy loves you most because you're my little girl!" Ava's aggression immediately turned to concern for Tony's feelings, evident when Liz helped her problem-solve a conflict between the two of them. And, unexpectedly, Ava's persistent thumb-sucking also improved dramatically. Liz realized it had been her way of coping with the anxiety of feeling unloved by her mother.

Liz had spent weeks fruitlessly trying a variety of methods to answer the question, "What should I do?" regarding Ava's mistreatment of Tony. By asking the deeper question, "What's truly going on with Ava?" she found an entirely new approach to Ava's actions. The discovery motivated her to make sure her daughter knew, beyond any doubt, that *Mommy loves you.* Once Ava did know, the change in her was profound.

MY RESPONSE

- What's a persistent behavioral challenge for one of my children? How can I prayerfully consider what might be underneath the surface of that behavior?

- What might my child feel or believe about himself/ herself?

- What messages might my child have received from me on this issue? What messages do I want to give him/her?

- What does my child most need from me?

Now, kindness is no magic bullet to halt all misbehavior. Some parents still have their hearts broken because, despite their best efforts to show and give love, their children have chosen the path of rebellion. This can happen; it happened in the Garden with Adam and Eve. But God never ceased to love them. And Jesus makes it vividly clear, with His sacrificial love, that God never stops pursuing, welcoming, and offering mercy to messed-up sinners.

So we can bask in that love for us, and when kids rebel we can keep on loving as well. No matter what. Instead of getting jaded or resentful, we can confront poor choices and wrong actions with hearts of love and forgiveness. Our humility and vulnerability just might be what reaches their hearts and draws them back.

CHAPTER 8

Putting Love-No-Matter-What Into Action

We have emphasized the need for giving unconditional love to our children entirely outside of what they do, positively or negatively. Now let's look at some practical ways to convey "I love you, no matter what" in misbehavior situations. Before we do, a quick warning.

After one seminar, a mom angrily told us, "I've tried saying 'I love you' when my daughter has misbehaved, and it doesn't work!" Our guess is that the daughter saw this for what it was—not actually love, "just Mom's latest attempt to control me."

We implore you, expressing love is no guarantee that kids will change their behavior. If that's the reason we show love, it's really nothing more than a form of manipulation, not something we want to teach our kids to yield to.

So do the spiritual work of finding your heart of love for your child. Then, when you express that love, guard your heart against any inclination to get what you want because of it. Stay safe. If kids feel safe with you, turning the tide of negative discipline encounters can sometimes take mere seconds through simple approaches like these:

- Put "I love you" into words.
- Give gentle touch if your child is open to it.
- Demonstrate empathy. ("Sometimes I feel sad too" or "You're upset, aren't you?")
- Truly listen. Repeat back what you hear them say. ("So you're angry with me?" or "I'm hearing that you're deeply frustrated.")
- Let your face show your love.

Verbalizing "I Love You"

If you express your love frequently, at times when kids aren't misbehaving, they will trust that love is this relationship's main ingredient.

One woman said, "My folks once went to a parenting class. After they came back, every time we were in trouble, we heard, 'Now, you know I love you, but . . .' That phrase, which we didn't hear a lot at other times, just has negative memories for me. I don't want to do that with my kids."

Well, you don't have to! Make sure love surrounds your interaction both before and after. Express it with a sincere energy that your kids can't interpret as rote or manipulative. Be creative. Be surprising. Be persistent. Lavish love on them like our heavenly Father lavishes love on us.

My (Lynne's) mother was diligent to do just that, despite my being "the liveliest and messiest" of her five kids. She communicated her love and enjoyment of me in convincing ways every day, so that when she spoke of her love when I misbehaved, I totally believed her. My strongest childhood memory (I got in trouble a lot) was her saying with an amazingly lighthearted tone, "Lynnie Marie Williams, I love you, but . . ." She would always stop, smile at me, and let that sink in. It simply reminded me (and her too) of all the love she'd previously expressed. She'd then deal gently with what I had done. To this day I have never doubted Mom's love for me in all circumstances.

Offering Affectionate Touch

Safe, affectionate touch is a powerful communicator of love. Saying "We're both pretty upset" and asking "Would you like a hug?" can be comforting and reassuring, opening the door for parent and child to reconnect and think more clearly. Lightly placing a hand on a child's shoulder can convey that I'm joining her as a coach or mentor rather than as an adversary or critic.

If parents have no hidden or coercive agenda, affectionate touch is usually quite effective—but not always. If either of us put a hand on Daniel's shoulder during an argument and he sensed a hint of control, he would react angrily. We had to work to learn when and when not to offer a gentle touch.

Claire, who had three young children, was struggling with her oldest. Tyler, an intense five-year-old, had been unraveling over seemingly minor issues or changes in his schedule. At Lynne's recommendation, Claire began giving affectionate touch much more frequently during the day—when all was well. This helped Tyler become more receptive to touch during stress.

A few weeks later Claire reported that she was avoiding many blowups with her sensitive son by gently rubbing his shoulders when he began winding up. "I can't believe what a difference this has made," she said. Tyler responded well because the touch had positive connotations; his mom was consistently showing love to him in this way when his world was peaceful.

Showing Empathy

When she was in fifth grade, Bethany and I (Lynne) locked in a forty-five-minute battle over a jungle-in-a-shoebox assignment. She was bent on going to a certain craft store where a high-achieving classmate had bought elaborate supplies. I was resisting because I knew we had a good selection of creative options at home.

I didn't want to feed into what I judged to be motivation based in insecurity and competition, but it didn't feel right to say, "No! Just deal with it!" So we were stuck, and the conflict began to escalate.

At one point I stopped for perspective and asked myself, "What's it like to be my daughter right now?" I realized I was making Bethany feel opposed, not joined—like I was against her, not for her. I took my best shot at putting words to what I figured she was feeling. "I'll bet it's frustrating to be you right now. You really want to do a good job on your school project, and your mom is making it hard. Is that how you feel?"

"Yes!" she exclaimed.

I continued, empathetically matching her energy. "I'm glad you work hard on your assignments!" She started relaxing, so I followed her lead and spoke more gently. "How about we get started with what we have, and if you don't feel good about the results, we'll go to the store tomorrow?"

With a little understanding and affirmation, I went from being her opponent to her teammate. She eagerly dug in with the supplies we had and went on to be thrilled with what she created.

This principle of empathy—identifying with and validating feelings—is a helpful way to connect with struggling children, from toddlers to teens. Take your best guess at what your child might be feeling and make an observation, or simply ask. If she doesn't have words or says "I don't know," suggest some ideas.

When a toddler starts to pitch a fit and pound his high chair before a meal, emphatically say, in basic kid language, "You're hungry. You want food. Mommy's getting it." We can say from experience in our home, it will almost always calm a child down. Great influence comes through joining struggles with understanding rather than fighting them with demands.

One mom reported that right after one of our workshops, with these thoughts fresh in her mind, she tried this with her tantrum-throwing child. "I just said, 'You're really mad right now. You wanted to stay and play.' I was shocked by how well this worked and by how it's worked ever since."

And whether or not empathy and validation will calm our kids, they still communicate important messages: "You are understood. What's important to you is important because *you* are important."

The empathizing approach can feel counterintuitive. But identifying with my kids' feelings and letting them know I understand helps them calm down, and then together we can work to solve the problem. This process also is a reflection of how Jesus responds to us. He *gets* us. And *because* He gets us, He can *help* us! (See Hebrews 2:18 and 4:15).

Truly Listening

When my child feels he's being heard, he feels respected. When he feels respected, he's likely to be far less inclined to continue down defiant paths. Rephrasing what I hear him say requires me to pay attention and take real interest in his perspective. Often his response switches from explosive to evaluative as he realizes I truly want to understand what he's trying to say.

Sometimes our kids just need us to be silent for a little while. One day Daniel was loudly voicing some intense frustration over a situation for which I (Lynne) was partly responsible. I was sitting at the top of our basement stairs while he vented emphatically from the landing below. He was bordering on disrespect, and normally I'd have stopped him to firmly present my viewpoint, but this time I hadn't a clue what to say or how to help. I almost felt like God had His gentle hand across my mouth, protecting my son from what might become a condescending lecture.

So I sat and said nothing—only listened, with a soft expression that I hoped would convey my understanding. The more I listened, the more rational Daniel became. Then he finished and stared back for a few seconds. I still had nothing to say, but apparently he felt satisfied—he went and constructively solved his problem.

During that whole interaction I hadn't spoken a word, but I felt like Daniel and I had connected well. It taught me the power of non-verbals that communicate true empathy.

Welcoming Expressions and Gestures

Social scientists tell us that the majority of communication is non-verbal. Yet many parents have no idea what their non-verbals convey to their kids, who are ever watching, learning, and interpreting. If the facial expression a child sees when his parent corrects him is the same the parent made when scowling at another driver, or complaining about a politician, he will attach to himself a meaning similar to what his parent expressed about the driver or politician.

If we eke out a few kind words but are scowling, a child will interpret the scowl more than the words. The goal is to have our bodily expressions of love match the words. And sometimes no words are needed! Maria gained insight into non-verbals by recording a common conflict, and her report was telling:

> Bedtime stories are always challenging. The kids compete to get the center of my lap and fight over the page-turning. It almost always ends with yelling. Wanting to get an objective view of it all, I set up my phone on a dresser to record and then see if I could learn anything from it.
>
> The video painfully revealed all the non-verbal cues I didn't realize I was giving off, probably the very cues my kids were feeding off—frustration, fatigue, a rush to "get through it," rolling my eyes multiple times, sighing, and the list goes on.
>
> It was a wake-up call, to say the least! After seeing myself, I thought, *I wouldn't want to respect me either*. I now have a concrete image in my brain that comes up when I feel the same emotions resurface. It enables me to catch myself early and correct the old habits.

Another mom reported the blessing of gentle facial expressions. A few weeks after Micki fully committed to expressing love during correction, her son asked, "Mom, why do you smile when you discipline us?"

"Because I'm remembering how much I love you!" she said. The tone in her home was changing rapidly as even corrective situations became peaceful.

In addition to facial expressions, our body language also communicates powerful messages. When Dustin's passionate, defiant son stormed off across the yard in anger, Dustin didn't chase him or command that Nate "get right back here!" He just stood and looked at his son with a gentle smile, waiting in true "Kid Whisperer" fashion. After some moments of looking at each other, he held out his arms. Nate ran to him in tears and they resolved their issue.

MY RESPONSE

Which ideas from this chapter do I want to work on?

- **Putting "I love you" into words:** I'll clearly let my children know I love them, even and especially while addressing conflicts or misbehavior, e.g., "You two (siblings) are angry right now, but I love you, and I believe you can solve this."

- **Touching affectionately:** I'll offer a hug, provide a shoulder rub, or invite a younger child onto my lap.

- **Showing empathy:** I can help my child put words to his or her emotions by filling in the blanks for this sentence: "I'll bet you feel really _____ because _____," or for a younger child, "You're really _____ [emotion]. You want _____." (It's important to fully understand and connect with how my child is feeling before I fill in the blanks.)

- **Really, truly listening:** I'll ask my child what he or she is upset about, and ask clarifying questions that don't start with "Why" (which can sound like an accusation), e.g., "How are you feeling about _____?" Then I'll ask myself, *What do I feel in a similar situation? What would I be concerned about?* I can express my agreement on one point that my child makes without quickly defending my position on points where we disagree. (We'll address that in later chapters.)

- **Using loving facial expressions:** Practice this. In front of a mirror, with my eyes closed, I'll start talking as though I'm addressing my child about a misbehavior. Then I'll open my eyes and look at my expression. Now I'll practice saying it with the expression I want to use.

CHAPTER 9

Eternal Impact: When Love Begins to Rule

Perhaps the most significant benefit of communicating love-no-matter-what to our kids is paving the way for them to truly understand God's love for them:

> I am *convinced* that neither death nor life, neither angels nor demons, neither the present nor the future, nor any powers, neither height nor depth, nor anything else in all creation, will be able to separate us from the love of God that is in Christ Jesus our Lord. (Romans 8:38–39, emphasis added)

This is so wonderful, yet lofty for children to grasp. Imagine if they truly believed and experienced it this way:

> I am *convinced* that neither failure nor lying, neither tantrums nor defiance, neither whining nor complaining, nor any disrespect, neither forgetfulness nor messes, nor any other

misbehavior, will ever change my parents' love and God's infinite love through Christ Jesus my Lord.

As parents, we hope our children will walk in love and truth, so we would do well to consider how we want our children to view God when they mess up.

A young dad named Ted sent this story of an opportunity to share grace with his misbehaving daughter, along with a lifelong lesson about our heavenly Father's character.

> I was working hard to encourage Liddy, my seven-year-old, in her piano practice. She was having a rough day and it spiraled into a huge meltdown. As she was shouting and screaming, I subtly began to record her outburst on my phone. I wanted it to build insight in a grace-filled way, so I waited until we connected that night at bedtime. I showed Liddy the video and asked if she liked feeling that way. She was discouraged and ashamed. "Daddy, I don't like seeing that," she answered.

This is where we can tend to say things like, "If you don't like how you acted, you can choose a different response next time." Ted went another route.

> The Lord helped me to see Liddy's struggle with eyes of compassion. I saw a great opportunity to shape her heart with a valuable truth. I explained that because of what Jesus has done for us, when we ask for forgiveness, God forgets our sins and doesn't look back. "It's like He erases the tape," I explained. Then I asked if Liddy wanted to say anything. She looked up and said, "I want your forgiveness and God's forgiveness. And I want to erase the tape."
>
> She watched me hit the delete button and smiled in relief as the vivid reminder of her failure disappeared. As we said bedtime prayers, she thanked God for His forgiveness.

Liddy is learning to harness her intensity, and she still struggles, but less all the time. As her parents persist with grace, she's learning about a God who loves her at her worst and will forgive in all circumstances. In these moments, parents can have a unique and intimate influence on their children's hearts. After all, there is no one better positioned to influence a child's heart than her parent.

Consistently expressed this way in families, love begins to define household life. Squabbles and trials will still emerge, but they'll lose their defining power as kids and parents alike learn to regain love-no-matter-what when they struggle. Parents will model forgiveness by seeking it. True reconciliation will occur. Then, as parents become more thoughtful about how to demonstrate and talk about God's love in the midst of difficult behavior, children will be powerfully discipled. They'll grow to truly believe, "I am loved, no matter what!"

MY RESPONSE

- How might I use our struggles to share about God's love, grace, and forgiveness with my children?

Kids Aren't the Only Ones Who Change

Early in our ministry, Melanie came to a weekly parenting class with "Angry Mom" etched in scowl lines across her face. She'd grown up in a home where yelling and punishment were the reaction to all errors—childish or intentional. She'd rarely felt that she pleased her parents or that they enjoyed her.

Melanie came to faith as an adult. And now she was finding that this pattern of interaction was largely repeating itself in her own family. When we talked after a class session, she quickly focused on all the difficulties she had with her daughter, Anna. She continued to be skeptical about our teaching to let misbehaving children know they're loved no matter what.

The next week she shared the story of what became a major life event for her. Anna had played with a soccer ball in the living room, near her mom's most beloved possession: the lamp from Melanie's grandma, the only person who'd seemed to love Melanie without strings. Before long, the ball ricocheted off a chair and smashed into the precious, fragile antique, which exploded into shards all over the floor.

Melanie's instinctive response to the disobedience was to do the same—explode all over her daughter. But as she escalated into all-too-familiar rage, she noticed something for the first time. She saw Anna's fear. Her daughter was cowering, awaiting certain wrath, "because that's what she'd seen before."

Melanie felt a pang of tenderness and reflected on what she'd heard in our class: "Love her now, because this is when it matters." She stopped and prayed. Then she dropped to her knees, gathered her terrified daughter into her arms, and, from her newfound heart of compassion, said, "That lamp was really special to me, but I love you so much more than that lamp!"

Relief poured out in Anna's deep sobs as Melanie held and rocked her. Dealing with the mess could wait until later. Love was the immediate need.

Not long after, Melanie and Anna volunteered to do a dramatic presentation of what had happened. This was so well received that they ended up "touring" moms' groups around their community, reenacting and then sharing about the importance of *Love no matter what.*

Saturation in this truth about God's love and grace began to heal the wounds from Melanie's childhood. She gradually forgave her parents for their rage and rejection, joyfully expressed unconditional love to them, and eventually helped lead her terminally ill mother to faith in Jesus. This cascade of God's love and power, which broke the pattern of generations, all started with a simple decision: "I will let go of the anger ('You are *safe* with me') and communicate, 'You are *loved*, no matter what' to my struggling child."

We connected again with Melanie seven years later. She was vibrant and joyful. "That class was absolutely a turning point in my life," she said. "I realized I didn't have to be the parent my parents were."

∎ ∎ ∎

Many others likewise tell of the marvelous interplay between giving unconditional love to their kids and growing in their own understanding and embrace of God's passionate love and mercy for them when they struggle. You can tell the story too!

KID CONNECTION: Celebrating Unconditional Love

Plan a special time with your family—whatever would collectively bring joy. Your plans might include an overnight stay at a hotel, an all-together basement sleepover with popcorn and movies, a bonfire with marshmallows and s'mores, a special meal everyone has a part in preparing . . . be creative, and make it memorable! (Tell the kids the date and time but don't give details.)

As you gather, read Romans 8:38–39 and talk briefly about ways you're growing in understanding God's unconditional love. Then, as a family, rewrite the verses to fit your family's challenges. (See the example at the beginning of this chapter.) Ask each person to contribute (parents first) at least one thing that sometimes causes him/her to feel unloved.

Print and post your adaptation, and make a plan to remind each other that you are all *LOVED, no matter what*, always.

Then celebrate with your fun activity! And remember to find ways to remind each family member that he or she is treasured and valuable because God has lavished unconditional love on us through Jesus, with no strings attached!

POSSIBLE ADAPTATIONS:

- Talk about a recent family conflict; ask each person to speak about what he/she contributed (confessing only his/her own faults). Then discuss how none of this diminishes God's love for us or your love for each other.
- Do this separately with a child who's struggling with a specific issue.
- On a different evening, read about the prodigal son (Luke 15:11–32). Younger kids might act out the story; for older kids, discuss how each person in the story felt or might have felt.
- Consider joining another family (one with whom you are close and share values) for one or more of the above activities.

"You Are CALLED and CAPABLE."

I can find and build strengths in my child, even in misbehavior.

Correct — "You are RESPONSIBLE for your actions"

Coach — "You are CALLED and CAPABLE"

Connect — "You are LOVED no matter what"

Foundation — "You are SAFE with me"

CHAPTER 10

Finding and Building Strengths, Even in Misbehavior

The Bible tells us all children are created by God, called to the "good works" their Maker "prepared in advance" for them to do (Ephesians 2:10). This implies that they have the raw talent to do those deeds.

It strongly shapes our discipline when we embrace an unswerving conviction that every child is a miraculous creation, made in God's image, and uniquely designed to use their God-given gifts for His purposes. It's easy to lose sight of this in the turmoil of conflict or chaos. But the fact remains that discipline situations provide exceptional opportunities to breathe life into the truth that all children are called to and capable of those good works God already has planned for them. In other words, they give us opportunities to share with them the powerful message, "You are *called and capable*!" In this section we'll demonstrate how to put this idea into practice.

• • •

We did *not* start out with this unswerving conviction, especially related to the sibling conflict in our home. We just wanted peace and quiet, because the bickering and fighting between our youngsters was intense and frequent.

Frequently, I (Lynne) felt pushed to the edge of sanity. Daniel, who'd been picked on by older neighbor boys, used the social skills he'd picked up in that realm to intimidate and harass his little sister and brother. He also was extremely strong-willed (as we've mentioned!) and was determined to be in charge of his siblings . . . if not the entire family.

Bethany, three years younger, was very sensitive, and she'd perfected the victim role in their relationship. We each played a defined part in a thoroughly choreographed dance: Daniel bossed, taunted, or hit; Bethany whined, wailed, or screamed; I lunged in as Crazy Mama, ready to punish. I knew my kids were precious miracles created for God's glory, yet I completely lost sight of this when they fought. And fought. And kept on fighting.

From the basement I'd hear, "Bethany, stop it! You can't touch my Legos! You dummy—you broke it!" *SMACK.* Piercing shriek.

I'd swoop down the steps, a missile programmed to aim for the tyrant. Seeing Bethany unhurt, I'd grab Daniel by the shoulders and get in his face. "That is *not* okay! Go to the time-out bench for ten minutes. Why are you so mean to her all the time?"

Daniel would yell right back: "It's *her* fault—she broke my Lego Explorien Starship! *You're* the mean one. You always just protect her. It's not fair!"

His anger at us both would boil the whole time he served his sentence. Not long after, they'd be right back at it, and I'd have the same reaction ready.

I knew I had to change my responses. Here I was, wanting them to change, yet I was doing the same thing, to the same effect, again and again and again.

My first step in addressing these dynamics was to look below the surface at what was going on in my heart. I saw that part of this wasn't about the present; it had to do with my own past. When I was young, my older brothers teased and occasionally harassed me—not excessively, but still I hated how this felt, and it never really resolved well. I realized I was targeting Daniel with my judgments about big brothers who picked on little sisters.

I talked with Daniel about this, confessed to him that he was getting leftover resentment, and asked his forgiveness. I also started working at pausing to consciously set down that baggage before I engaged with my kids. This helped me come into conflicts with a little less anger and a little more emotional safety and love-no-matter-what. I began to develop deeper empathy and more understanding for the difficulties my children had in getting along.

The most significant change happened when I learned to enter the fray with this question foremost in my thoughts: *Lord, what's the opportunity here? How can I help build the skills they're going to need in life?* Jim and I wanted to discipline with the long-term view instead of just trying to eliminate the short-term behavior issues. We had a vision for our children to develop the affection, empathy, and conflict-resolution skills that would serve them well in their families, workplaces, and ministries.

We didn't stop using consequences, but we tried to find and strengthen whatever was right instead of just instantly punishing what we thought was wrong. For example, were the kids using "gentle hands" despite their harsh words? Were they standing firm and strong for what was important to them? I wanted to identify and affirm these traits and actions while also addressing the actions or words that needed correction.

We also started using questions and offering choices to guide the kids through resolving disputes: "Do you want to solve this respectfully now, or do you think you need to calm down first? How much help do you need to do that?" These questions and choices told them *You are capable* instead of *You are a problem.* (For other potential ideas, see section C of the appendix, "Growing True Respect and Reconciliation.") Inspired by this outlook and approach, our impulsive reactions slowly gave way to more thoughtful engagement.

There was a long process of ups and downs; on many days we wondered if we were getting anywhere. But the seeds we planted did bear rich fruit. Our kids grew to be great friends and even started a small business together. They learned to serve as peacemakers during group conflicts. As a college student negotiating life on her own, Bethany announced, "I get along with everybody and can resolve conflict with anyone—I've got Daniel to thank for that!"

MY RESPONSE

- What ideas in this section could I apply to sibling (or peer/friend) challenges?

No One-Size-Fits-All Quick Fixes

At parenting workshops we often ask, "What's a typical goal when you discipline your child?" Essentially, the two most common responses are:

- to make a bad behavior stop
- to teach them to do the right thing

Stopping what's wrong and teaching what's right are good goals, but they aren't corrective discipline's primary goals because they address only what's on the surface. Disciplining what matters most requires getting beneath the surface of behavior to the causes or beliefs that fuel the misbehavior itself.

Jesus looked beneath people's problems to see how they could serve God's kingdom; His goal was *inner* change. He didn't treat "misbehavior" simply with intent to correct the behavior but with an eye for the changed hearts of those He engaged. His method was almost always unique—there was no formula. His consistency in confronting sin was not in His methods but in His faithfulness to respond out of peace and oneness with His Father. Like Jesus, the goal of our corrective discipline ought to be changed hearts.

Consider how Jesus responded to sexual sin. He received a prostitute's anointing, her tears, and her love. He then forgave her sin without a word of rebuke, and she left transformed— saved! (See Luke 7:36–50).

He met an adulterous woman at a well and offered her "living water" (John 4:10; for the full account, see vv. 4–42). He gave no chastising, only a truthful, compassionate rendering of her failures. Amazed, she went back to her village, sharing her experience with Jesus and inviting her neighbors to come to Him. Again, a changed heart.

He protected a woman dragged from adultery against men's accusations and plans to kill her. After turning them all away— with the invitation, "Let any one of you who is without sin be the first to throw a stone"—He invited her to leave her "life of sin" (John 8: 7, 11; for the full account, see vv. 2–11).

No righteousness recipes. No magic mantras. Just wisdom and grace. Jesus looked at who people could become—who they were created to be. His goal: heart change. *Always.*

The lack of a quick fix for misbehavior might sound like bad news, yet it's actually good. This motivates us to be like

Jesus: watchful, prayerful, dependent on God, and discerning about what's truly going on with our children. Ironically, *this* approach brings potent influence into their lives.

That's why the ideas suggested in these pages can become valuable items in your toolbox. As a parent, you must determine which tool(s), and when, will most benefit your unique child in a particular situation. One child may first need empathy to know her parent understands. Another may benefit from affirmation before his misbehavior is addressed. Still another may simply need firm words followed by some reasonable choices.

Long-Term Motivation: Kingdom Purposes

The goal of heart change is enhanced when we parents focus on long-term, big-picture aims instead of merely punishing to halt misbehavior. Thoughtful discipline helps our children to realize God's purposes for them and builds the values and skills they need to walk a path that glorifies Him. Even in their faults and missteps we can find and build these strengths.

Consider the differences in the following two scenarios.

Typical Discipline

"Jordan, get your shoes on," says his mother, Lynette. "It's time to leave." She doesn't want to be late and is feeling rushed to get out the door.

Jordan, half buried in Duplo pieces, replies, "No, Mommy! I'm making a truck. I don't want to go."

Lynette, feeling challenged, puts her hands on her hips and raises her voice slightly: "You get your shoes on right now, or I take away those toys."

He knows she means business, so he reluctantly puts on his shoes. He's learned Mommy has more power than he does; he'd better do what she says.

While this isn't a bad lesson to learn, it's solely behavioral. So often the tendency is to stop here, thinking the "discipline" worked. But just as instant results don't prove our communication effective (that it "worked"), discipline is more than managing behavior. At the heart of discipline is *discipleship*.

Discipleship Opportunity

"Jordan, get your shoes on. It's time to leave."

"No, Mommy! I'm making a truck. I don't want to go."

Lynette looks at her son with a hint of a smile and says, "It's difficult to obey sometimes, isn't it? God sure made you both creative and persistent."

She pauses to pray silently, *Lord, how will you use these gifts in him?*

Then she makes this offer: "Hey, before we get your shoes, show me this cool thing you're working on."

Mommy feels safe to him; eager to please, Jordan proudly displays his truck.

"That's impressive! I love the huge wheels and the extra light on top. Know what? You can set it up here on the table so you'll remember to finish it later. Do you want to wear sneakers or sandals?"

Jordan still might return to defiance and end up with a consequence, but Lynette's approach is now that of a discipler. Her heart is with him, working to encourage obedience, not against him, leveraging authority.

In the first exchange, Lynette's goal was quick compliance, and she engaged with a posture of control. In scene two she remained conscious of the immediate situation but sought a way to mentor her son by bringing out the best in him, looking for and calling out the unique capability that is evidence of God's crafting.

Believing Jordan to be capable both of creating and of obeying, she noticed two details. The first was the abilities he showed—even in misbehavior—and how God might use those in the future ("God sure made you both creative and persistent"). Second, she facilitated his opportunity to make a wise choice ("Before we get your shoes, show me this cool thing you're working on" and "Do you want to wear sneakers or sandals?").

She made it easy for him to choose, not forcing but encouraging him to decide wisely. Even though she addressed how he first responded, she showed she was his teammate and not his opponent.

The time for firmer action would come if Jordan continued his defiance. We'll discuss this more in section 4 and in section C of the appendix.

· · ·

God disciplines us for our good, in order that we may share in his holiness. (Hebrews 12:10)

This verse compels me to follow God's example in two concrete ways. First, I'm challenged to discipline my children for their good, not for my relief or my desire to seize control. Second, I'm invited to consider how discipline can lead my child toward holiness—God's "set apart" or supremely distinct purposes for my child's life.

The key is to view my kids both as humans who still sin (like all the rest of us) *and* as beloved miracles created in God's image and for His purposes. Only then will I begin to see them first and foremost as capable of great things, no matter how they're acting or what they're saying right now.

MY RESPONSE

- What is a frequent struggle for one of my kids?
- How might I work with my child to encourage obedience and bring out the best in him/her?
- What beliefs about himself/herself do I want to strengthen?

CHAPTER 11

Discovering Diamonds in the Rough

Each and every one of us is created in God's image. Nothing can change that. However, this doesn't negate our most pressing problem: We're all born into sin, which affects every aspect of our lives and injects selfishness into our motives and choices. Becoming like Jesus is a lifelong process that won't be completed until we're in heaven. Even after we've become new creations in Christ, we carry sin baggage. (See 2 Corinthians 5:17.) Paul said of this struggle, "Although I want to do good, evil is right there with me" (Romans 7:21).

It is good to identify sin and help my children understand its influence. But if, when they misbehave, all I do is focus on and punish the sin without calling out the reality of God's very image in them, they'll begin to identify *themselves* with the sin, the misbehavior, or the problem they seem to be. If they develop shame and resentment, they'll increasingly want to hide sin from us and, ultimately, from God. This makes true repentance difficult and pushes many toward open rebellion.

To help my children truly repent and turn away from sin, they need a vision for what to turn toward, for living out their identity as God's own children.

Looking for the Hidden Gift

One of the most influential ways to encourage this true repentance is to look for "the gift gone awry"—a God-given talent that's coming out twisted by sin and selfishness. Because of the shifts and changes in developing brains, children and teens are frequently confused, and they struggle in the effort to figure out life and self. They tend to be markedly self-focused, using their gifts and strengths most often to benefit themselves. But their struggle can give alert parents insight into their potential strengths.

It takes skill to misbehave. Whatever the skill, in and of itself it's a gift from God. The way the skill is used gives clues about what that gift might be. When my child misbehaves I have a great opportunity to look behind the sin and identify a skill that, if used as God intended, will bring glory to Him. This perspective on misbehavior has helped many parents form new attitudes.

• • •

Kari, a single mom, shared about her own growth:

> Eli was whining for something over and over again. Realizing he was being persistent, I actually enjoyed wondering how God might use that strength someday. It helped me to be calm when I responded.

That insight enabled Kari to affirm Eli's strength of persistence and help him use it more and more in alignment with God's purposes as he grew.

Seeing and affirming a child's gift in the middle of stressful situations is no easy task. But doing so can be life-giving, truly inspiring.

The following are twelve common misbehaviors along with gifts/talents that we have found tend to drive children.

- Arguing/talking back ⟶ Honest with feelings and opinions; confident (Research has shown that argumentative children are less likely to lie or be deceitful. In the long run they're more likely to adopt their parents' values because they passionately exchange ideas instead of going underground with their views.)
- Yelling ⟶ Expressive; longs to be understood
- Stubbornness ⟶ Determined; intensely focused
- Bossy/strong-willed ⟶ Assertive; has potential to lead
- Lying ⟶ Creative; has a good memory; wants to keep the peace
- Stealing ⟶ Planner; courageous; able to take risks
- Irritable ⟶ Sensitive; a desire for God-given pleasure and joy
- Insecure ⟶ Attuned to the feelings and perspectives of others
- Impulsive ⟶ Lives in the moment; quick responder
- Whining ⟶ Persistent; insight into others (and what motivates them to make decisions, e.g., how parents give in)
- Complainer ⟶ Aware of problems; potential for problem-solving
- Defensive ⟶ Strong sense of right and wrong (Kids who have the hardest time admitting guilt are usually those who feel the worst about having done something wrong.)

The perspective on "misbehavior" (by parents or kids) is biblically grounded. Part of our calling is to search for any situation's treasure:

> Whatever is true, whatever is noble, whatever is right, whatever is pure, whatever is lovely, whatever is admirable—if anything is excellent or praiseworthy—think about such things. (Philippians 4:8)

This is exactly how God has responded to His children—He sees the potential He crafted in all of us. Moses murdered a man . . . but God saw a passionate defender of the Israelite people. God redirected that passion to lead them out of Egypt. Paul was using all his gifts of leadership, knowledge, determination, and passion to destroy the church . . . until God turned him 180 degrees to use all those talents to *build* the church. Then there's Peter, the impulsive ADHD-poster-child disciple, known for his failures and blunders. Jesus knew Peter's intensity, faith, and confidence were the raw materials of an effective leader.

Repositioning Moses', Paul's, and Peter's misguided gifts for God's purposes was holy work. It's the same for parents as they seek to identify their child's wayward gifts and channel them toward honoring purposes.

In our home, we understood that for all five of us, failure often was a manifestation of our "gifts gone awry."

I (Lynne) was the unofficial "family manager," the one most likely to handle household needs, follow through with details, hold kids accountable, etc. Unfortunately, I was also prone to nagging. Jim was spontaneous and expressive, but under stress could be a bit snippy. We had good conversations about these misguided traits with our kids and equipped them with specific phrases to respectfully confront us when our gifts came out awry. "Mom, I'm feeling micromanaged right now." "Dad, that seemed a little harsh."

This brought deeper grace into our relationships and more peace into the craziness. Over time we would see that this approach revolutionized the outcomes of our discipline.

● ● ●

Through most of his childhood, Daniel argued intensely to ensure he received whatever he perceived to be equitable treatment. "That's not fair," he would say. "I didn't get as much ice cream." "You're always on Bethany's side." "Bethany and Noah don't have to do this much work." He could present his case with all the logic, detail, passion, and persistence of a clever attorney, exhausting any adult who happened to be his caregiver. Lynne's brother once mused, "It's like arguing with a really ticked-off little adult."

Once we identified that one of his gifts gone awry was a strong sense of justice, we determined to help Daniel move away from its selfish expression to an honoring expression. This meant helping him understand other people's feelings and perspectives. Soon he began to be concerned about fairness for others and became an "Impulsive Champion of the Underdog," quickly assessing who was most at fault in a sibling conflict and administering "justice." One day, when Bethany accidentally stepped on and crushed Noah's Lego creation, Daniel yelled at and whacked her. As I comforted her, she said tearfully, "He was just protecting his little brother." We certainly dealt with his misbehavior, yet it helped that we all had come to understand its root.

As he matured in the Lord, that passion—which we learned to affirm even as it came out warped—eventually developed into a drive for justice and compassion for hurting people. As a twenty-one-year-old volunteer in Peru, Daniel raised thousands of dollars to help an impoverished clinic; he has forged values and aspirations centered on standing up for the oppressed.

We've seen this sequence in numerous kids whose parents have been willing to search below the surface to notice and nurture the good and thus connect with their kids' hearts. Usually the gift first appears selfishly or in misbehavior. Gradually its application is more under control and less selfish. Over time, it can become filled with grace and wisdom. Identifying these gifts not only connects with your child's heart but also turns discipline situations into discipleship opportunities.

MY RESPONSE

- What unique trait or "wiring" does my child possess that sometimes comes out in unhelpful or exasperating ways?
- What might be the "gift gone awry" driving misbehavior?

Addressing My Child's Gift Gone Awry

Here are two examples of how parents might typically address common misconduct, and then how parents might address it with a vision of their child as created in God's image, capable of accomplishing His purposes.

Common Misbehavior

Justin, angry about not getting to drive the car, vents loudly, "I've been telling you all week that this is really important to me. I just want to go out for a little while to catch this movie, and I hate your stupid 'chores first' rules. No other parents are so strict. Why don't you get it?"

Typical Response

"We've told you not to speak to us that way. Keep this up and you'll not only miss the movie tonight, you'll be grounded from the car the rest of the week."

A child usually feels attacked by a response of this kind. If he thinks he has a chance of winning, he'll fight harder; if not, he'll give up and take out his anger later or maybe on someone else. He learns his parent has all the power—for the moment. He may see he has to act differently to get privileges but isn't likely to internalize the value of doing right things for right reasons.

Affirming Response

"Justin, you're really being straightforward about some strong feelings, which is good. I do want to hear what you have to say when you're calm enough to use a more respectful tone. Maybe we can work something out. Do you want to take a break for a bit, or are you ready now?"

A child tends to feel heard and respected through a response like this. His honesty was noted; his disrespect was addressed, and he's still accountable for it, yet his parent didn't counter-attack. While he may not be happy, he'll likely choose to settle down and talk appropriately. Even if he doesn't, his parent's level-headed, respectful approach will make it easier for him to see that continued defiance would be about him, not an irrational or insensitive parent.

Justin learns he can negotiate only if he's respectful and he sees that his parents believe he can work it out. When he's calm, they can help him realize that his authenticity and strong will are abilities God has gifted to him.

Common Misbehavior

First-grader Hailey has just left a mess of markers all over the table and is headed toward the playroom. The rule has been frequently stated: "We clean up one mess before making another, or we lose the toys that we left."

Typical Response

"Hailey! Where are you going? Clean that up right now or I'll take them."

Hailey may or may not clean up the markers. What she learns is that her parent—not she—is responsible for keeping the rules. The threat becomes her impetus for following the rule. Instead of being allowed to learn from failing and then interacting about what happened and why, this reinforces a cycle of "child ignores ⟶ parent nags/threatens ⟶ child finally responds."

Affirming Response

When Hailey leaves the table, her dad waits to see if she'll remember to clean up before playing with other toys. When she gets out her dolls in the playroom, he goes to the table, begins putting markers in the "time-out bag," and says, "Hailey, I'd like you to come over here while I pick these up."

Hailey immediately objects: "No, Daddy. I want my markers."

"You really enjoy doing art, don't you? And you like having a lot of things going on at once." He affirms her gifts. "But it's important to be responsible with those abilities. So if you'll help me clean up now, we can make it a one-day consequence instead of two. Do you want to help?"

Hailey learns that her daddy believes in and supports her talents *and* that she's responsible to keep the rules; there will be a consequence if she doesn't. (We'll cover the message "You are responsible" more fully in section 4.)

Experiment with possibilities as you identify what might be a misdirected skill. Here are starter suggestions on responding with affirmation when your child is whining or being demanding:

- "You sure are a determined person!"
- "You really know what you want."

- "I can see that you like _____" (whatever it is they're seeking).
- "I appreciate your _____ , but how you're using that gift right now isn't very helpful."

When we learn to respond this way, kids tend to calm down. Perhaps they feel surprised, or maybe they're used to feeling criticized and this feels more encouraging.

Then, as they cool off, you can facilitate further success. For example:

- "Nice work calming down. Being calm makes it easier to talk."
- "It seems you also know some other ways to ask for what you want."

As such responses become more habitual, your kids will feel more respected and gradually learn more considerate ways of expressing their gift and navigating conflict. At some point you may even start receiving this same kind of respect in return from them.

By the time Daniel was in his later teen years he'd learned to stay cool—usually—in conflict. One day he confronted me (Lynne) respectfully when I was micromanaging again, reminding him to follow up with a customer of his budding photography business (who just *happened* to be a friend of mine). Instead of being defensive, he took a deep breath, smiled, and identified my "gift gone awry."

"Mom, I appreciate your concern about this," he said. "But how you're showing that concern right now is not very helpful."

I realized I was nagging a young adult in charge of his own life. "You're right. That wasn't my issue to manage. Thanks for the grace and your kind response."

With a grin he offered a hug and said, "I learned it from you, ya know."

It took us a while to consistently see our children's gifts beneath misbehavior—especially when things got intense. But when tempers cooled a bit, our focus on identifying strengths gave us a purposeful follow-up plan. Once we'd thought it through, we'd go back to the kids and say something like, "I've been thinking about our conflict. I really appreciate your [honesty, convictions, sensitivity, etc.] and would like to try that conversation again." We went through this cycle time and time again over the years and forged our way into a habit of leading efforts to resolve by naming "gifts gone awry."

MY RESPONSE

- As I consider the list of twelve challenging behaviors and their associated gifts on page 128, what gift gone awry might have been evident in a recent misbehavior of one of my kids?

- If I didn't acknowledge the gift behind the misbehavior, how might I have a conversation with my child, acknowledging the God-given strength that was evident?

Positioning the Gift for Good Purposes

Once a gift gone awry is identified, positioning it to be used for good purposes is the important next step. For example, if my child yells mean words, I can affirm: "Son, you are so expressive. I wonder if you could be expressive in a more helpful way." This doesn't excuse or justify what he said; it just offers a vision for how he can use his gift more constructively, and now he gets to choose. Many times, a child will calm down and try another way instead of escalating the conflict.

. . .

At the outreach center for high-risk teens where I (Jim) worked, many of those teens who ultimately decided to follow Jesus looked to the ways they were treated when they misbehaved as critical steps on their path to finding God. Christa was one whose life was changed by grace-filled redirection of a gift gone awry.

I once left a building to round up kids for a meeting and stumbled on Christa, who was yelling abusively at Hannah. Her string of profanities and expletives might have reddened a weathered sailor. My impulse was to yell at her to "stop the abusive language right now!" I could feel the heat in my face, and I knew that if I spoke I could be disrespectful.

So I prayed, *Lord, give me your grace.* Had she been physically threatening I would have acted quickly, but since she wasn't, I slowed my pace as I approached from behind. Hannah's eyes widened as she saw me coming.

Christa stopped, seeing the shift in Hannah's gaze. When she spun around, her expression transformed from anger to embarrassment, and she asked sheepishly, "Am I kicked out?" She knew the published consequence for her infraction was a one-month time-out from programs and an apology (to Hannah) before returning.

I'd have been justified in saying, "You know the rules. Yes, you'll have to take a break." Yet God's Spirit seemed to be whispering another option. (I've learned over the years to enjoy the treasure hunt of looking for the diamonds of His purposes revealed through the roughness of misbehavior.) "Christa, taking a break is one way we could handle this, but I need to tell you, I've never seen such a powerful and creative use of those words before. You are one amazing communicator."

This took Christa, Hannah, *and* me by surprise, significantly altering the tone of the interaction. What had been highly charged and defensive was now curious and open. Wanting to be sure Hannah felt supported, I said, "Christa will need to resolve things with you no matter what, Hannah. Then I wonder if it's okay with you if I offer a little different consequence instead of just booting her."

Hannah agreed.

"So, Christa," I continued, "I want to offer you a choice. We could follow the normal rules and give you a month's time-out from programs, or you could put that communication gift to use here—you could meet with me each week for a month to help prepare announcements and the promotional fliers we make for activities. I think that would be a much better way to use the talents God gave you."

She nodded in agreement. "I choose the second one," she said humbly. "And, Hannah, sorry for cussin' you out like that. I've had a tough week."

"It's cool," Hannah replied.

We went inside together, and the two of them were chummy thereafter.

Over the next four weeks I followed my plan to involve Christa in the center's communications, something she would then continue doing for several months. She grew to be much more protective of the environment of respect and emerged as a leader in the program. As she used her skills to serve the outreach, we noticed and affirmed how blessed we felt to have her help. Her sense of purpose increased, and she became more open to hearing about other ways God might use some of the gifts He'd given her.

Christa's heart opened to all that we taught—including the gospel. Today she's following Jesus and raising her children to respect and serve others.

. . .

That encounter illustrates the profound impact of finding ways to affirm God-given traits that show up in misbehavior, and then thoughtfully positioning those gifts to be used in alignment with God's purposes.

Whenever we can discover ways to affirm kids—not "You are great" but "Your gift/talent blessed me"—we remind them of the masterpiece they were created to be and of the good works God created them to do. This can only serve to open their hearts to God's greater designs for their lives.

One of our least effective responses to Daniel's bossiness toward his siblings was trying to control it. We'd done plenty of this, and it seemed to hold a double standard: "Daniel, if you boss them, we'll boss you." So we began to equip our other kids to stand up for themselves, and then got involved as minimally as necessary. (More on that in section C of the appendix, "Growing True Respect and Reconciliation.") This minimal response, ironically, was much more connective, because then, outside the skirmishes, we'd proactively encourage this creative, determined, persuasive kid of ours. "You have a strong personality and some solid leadership potential. We believe God has plans for those strengths, but how you often use them with your siblings doesn't seem to be preparing you well for those purposes." This perspective built a shared, hopeful momentum.

To spur further thinking we also asked, "What kind of approach do you want to practice to prepare you for leading in the future?" When he sensed we were truly trying to help him—not just control him—we could guide him with more questions that helped him learn to wisely facilitate group activities. It has been so rewarding to watch him grow as an effective leader.

Speaking to our kids in this way is not the difficult part; most parents can learn scripts and repeat the words. The difficulty is that to do this sincerely, we have to truly believe our child is a gift—a miracle—created for important purposes: He or she *is* God's workmanship, called and capable. Our work as parents is less about learning the right things to say and more about relentlessly nurturing a vision for God's purposes in our kids.

MY RESPONSE

As I consider a "gift gone awry" I identified in one of my kids while reading through this chapter:

- How might God use that gift in the future?
- How can I thoughtfully create opportunities for my child to use that gift for good purposes?

CHAPTER 12

Building the Wisdom Kids Need

In one of our favorite parenting passages, an angel tells Zechariah his son will have perhaps the most important role of any prophet. God will call John the Baptist to usher in the Messiah, with specific guidelines.

The heavenly messenger clearly lays out what John will do, and how.

> He will bring back many of the people of Israel to the Lord their God. And he will go on before the Lord, in the spirit and power of Elijah, to turn the hearts of the parents to their children and the disobedient to the wisdom of the righteous—to make ready a people prepared for the Lord. (Luke 1:16–17)

The "what" of John's job was leading people back to God and preparing them for the Savior's coming. The "how" was to turn parents' hearts toward their children and turn the disobedient to . . . (catch this, it's really important) . . . the *wisdom* of the righteous.

Surprisingly, there's no focus here on obedience. Disobedient people don't need to be taught obedience; they need wisdom to value God's righteous ways. Wisdom opens the door of the heart—to repentance and relationship with Christ, and *then* to obedience.

This is a life-changing truth that has major implications for parenting, for right in the middle of preparing people for Christ's coming is the relationship between parents and children. At its core is not teaching obedience, as so much Christian teaching suggests, but teaching wisdom.

Prioritizing quick obedience short-circuits the tremendous opportunity for growth that disobedience or misbehavior holds. Here's an example of the peace and learning that happen when the focus is building wisdom.

Eli lived with his mom in our house until he was three. At two, he began to whine and cry every morning at the bottom of the stairs. He wanted to be carried; his mom kept trying to coax him up on his own. She saw this entirely as an obedience problem: he was disobeying her command.

"You come up here on your own, Eli," Kari would say firmly. "I'm not going to carry you."

The whining persisted, and most days it escalated to screaming. To get to work on time, Kari often stormed back down, scolded and disciplined Eli, and carried him up. This gave big attention to his behavior and only perpetuated the problem. Warnings and time-outs did nothing to change his response.

We talked with Kari about the value of teaching him to make wise decisions and how to offer two simple choices. The next time they encountered the stairs, she shifted to a pleasant, relaxed tone: "Eli, you can stay there and whine as long as you'd like, or you can come up the stairs and be with me." She then walked upstairs and left her son to decide.

The first day he screamed loud and long before he came up. He was, after all, accustomed to the process that led to him being carried up the stairs. But Kari worked hard to stay calm and let him wail for a bit. When he paused for a breath, she gently reminded him, "You can come up when you're ready."

Each day the crying lessened, and by the end of the week the fussing and begging were completely gone. Eli happily came up the stairs by himself.

Kari realized that with her new approach, Eli was learning to make decisions, and wisely. He learned that his behavior was no longer controlling his mom's emotions, and that it was lonely and boring to fuss downstairs. He learned the helpful skill of self-calming. He also learned that he was responsible for and capable of climbing up the stairs, and that life was much more enjoyable when he did so without fussing.

By letting go of her immediate-obedience value, Kari could calm herself down, connect pleasantly with Eli, and offer choices that helped him grow. She was far less stressed, and he learned to self-regulate and be self-motivated without parental controls.

Calm → Connect → Choices

The process Kari followed diffuses most power struggles *if* administered calmly and wisely. Options offered with intimidation or coercion usually feel like snares or setups, which builds defensiveness and disconnection, not wisdom. So when you begin an interaction, *calm* down, briefly *connect* with your child, and then offer two reasonable *choices*. Take care that the choices don't feel like a trap. (For example, "You can either do what I say, or be grounded.") One child described this sort of approach vividly: "It feels like there's a trapdoor under one of the choices."

Considering and offering two appropriate choices shifts the parent's brain out of a highly reactive mode into a more rational thinking state. Reasonably offered, non-trapping choices then activate the child's rational processes as well. These elements combine to create an environment of mutual trust.

· · ·

Don came to a parenting class and then later wrote of an *aha!* moment:

> Every Friday in my son's classroom is Sharing Day, when each kid can bring in a favorite toy or stuffed animal to show the class. On this particular day Cameron excitedly grabbed his hockey stick. I said firmly, "Cameron, I don't want you to bring the stick. Go pick out another toy."
>
> I tried to explain that it might hurt someone, but he'd already started to wail and throw a fit. I decided to try your advice from the class I'd just attended. So I closed my eyes and took a deep breath, got down on my knees, looked him in his eyes, and told him I loved him. He stopped wailing and looked at me, so I knew I had his attention. I then explained he had two choices: one, he could leave the stick, pick out another toy, and then he could play with his stick the minute he got home from school, or two, he could leave the stick with me and not bring a sharing toy today.
>
> To my surprise, he stopped crying, put his stick away, and grabbed another toy. He was not happy with me, but we were then able to talk about why it wasn't a good idea to bring a hockey stick to a classroom with twenty-five other kids.
>
> The long-term effect of that single moment has been remarkable. In this last year, not only does Cameron listen better, but my wife and I are now much more aware of how we communicate with both our son and our daughter. I've also become more aware of his perspective.
>
> Looking back, I understood that all Cameron wanted was to bring his favorite toy and share it with his friends. This was a pivotal incident for me through which I learned that

parenting is not about forcing my will on our children but about giving them choices so they can be successful.

MY RESPONSE

- What are three common misbehaviors in my home?
- What are two reasonable choices I could offer my child for each one?
- How can I get calm and then connect so I don't interfere with his/her opportunity to make a wise choice?

"Doing Our Own Verse"

Parents love this passage, and many quote it often as the rationale for their focus on immediate obedience:

> Children, obey your parents in the Lord, for this is right. "Honor your father and mother"—which is the first commandment with a promise—"so that it may go well with you and that you may enjoy long life on the earth." (Ephesians 6:1–3)

However, this instruction for children does not stand alone. Right after it is instruction for parents:

> Parents, do not exasperate your children; instead, bring them up in the training and instruction of the Lord. (v. 4)

So before engaging your kids, ask yourself, "Which part of the passage energizes me more?" If you're sick and tired of your kids' disobedience, it would be natural to focus your efforts on the teaching to kids. But it could well be that what's needed is more focus on the teaching to parents. What could you do to be less exasperating? Are your kids safe with you? Do they know you love them no matter what? Do they know you hold in your heart a holy vision for the masterpiece that each of them is?

As you become parents who learn to "not exasperate your children" while raising them "in the training and instruction of the Lord," you'll have kids who trust you more and more and *want* to do their verse. They will *want* to obey you, *in the Lord*! Not out of insecurity or fear. This is how they best enter into the promise of their verse, "that it may go well with you and that you may enjoy long life on the earth."

Living by this admonition means learning to let go of our selfish *control* and instead walk in true God-given *authority* to teach and train our children. We've seen much exasperation and even bitterness in kids whose parents put a premium on obedience because of their desire to feel in charge, look good in front of others, and keep life smooth.

Ray, who was having difficulties with Carson, his intense twelve-year-old, said his own dad had often quoted the passage about obedience as he harshly disciplined. Now, years later, Ray was struggling to break that same habit of being demanding, reactive, and punitive. His eyes opened wide when he heard the command to train and instruct instead of exasperate. "I wish someone had told my dad that verse!" he said.

Ray's dad had mistaken compliance for obedience. Many parents also believe that getting compliance from their kids will teach them obedience to God. But control through intimidation negates the biblical foundation of love for obedience. Being treated this way prepares children either to blindly obey other intimidating people or to become intimidating for their own purposes once they leave their parents' care. Children raised in authoritarian homes often have difficulty comprehending that it's okay to struggle and make mistakes because that's part of life. They find God's love and grace foreign, and many wonder how intimacy with this guilt-inducing God could even be desirable.

. . .

Jana's parents loved her deeply and were passionate about giving her a foundation of faith. They believed requiring obedience was the way to teach obedience to God, so they resisted giving her choices and controlled her decisions. As a youngster, delayed or noncompliant responses meant a spanking; as she grew older, it was quick, stern confrontation. Though appearing compliant, she harbored a growing, simmering reservoir of anger, shame, and discouragement.

As is fairly typical of kids raised without freedom to question authority or consider options,[1] Jana hadn't learned true obedience. Appearances may have suggested otherwise, since she complied so well for so long. But when she left home at eighteen she rebelled against all the years of control, and against God as well. Tragically, this is an all-too-common outcome in families with parents who idolize obedience.

Jana was desperate to please others and "obeyed" what her boyfriends told her to do, resulting in some painful and lasting consequences. As a young adult she returned to faith but tearfully said, "I have no idea who I am or how to make a wise decision."

We can be assured that our heavenly Father is unimpressed by fear-based compliance and behavior that doesn't match our motives.

> These people . . . honor me with their lips,
>   but their hearts are far from me.
> Their worship of me
>   is based on merely human rules they have been taught.
>   (Isaiah 29:13)

Thankfully, God's priority is not rule-following but true honor springing from connected hearts. This takes the pressure off of us *and* our kids to "get it right." When parents embrace obedience as a natural decision flowing from love and trust—not control—different fruit starts growing and thriving.

● ● ●

Parenting with God's grace doesn't mean kids quit misbehaving; it means we can guide misbehaving kids toward holy wisdom. For a strong-willed child, obedience may initially mean respectfully selecting one of the offered choices. Parents set the boundaries and kids function within them, developing a sense of who they are, what's important to them, and how to make wise choices.

Linda is an example of applying godly authority toward the building of wisdom. Her story illustrates the long-term results of mentoring a bright, strong-willed child toward heartfelt obedience and responsible independence. (For more, see section C of the appendix, "Growing True Respect and Reconciliation.")

> Ali seemed to be born wanting her own way. We tried just forcing our will on her, but every little thing became a major conflict. She didn't like to be told what to do, but her life seemed filled with orders: put on clothes, brush teeth, get in the car so we can go. . . . Just getting her to put shoes on to leave the house was a major issue. We couldn't avoid asking her to do things, so life became a miserable struggle of the wills.
>
> This struggle helped us to see vividly that God had created her as a strong person with a will of her own. We didn't want to punish her into compliance, but we needed to find a way to have peace in our home while maintaining her inner strength. What we discovered was that by simply giving her options, we allowed her to use her intelligence and strength while not creating a conflict a hundred times a day.

So instead of telling her to put on her shoes, she could choose to put her shoes on now or when we were ready to get out of the car at our destination. She could play in the open with sunblock, or she could play under the umbrella without sunblock.

We felt good about this approach since when God parents us, He does not force us into submission but lets us know that we will reap what our choices sow. (See Galatians 6:7 NRSV.) Still, while offering choices sounds simple, the constant effort to think of reasonable options and consequences was exhausting. Every option for her had to be realistic and fair.

I remember one particular day when Ali was about five. I was so tired of thinking up realistic options that I pleaded with her to obey me just once. She quietly pondered my request, then looked at me and said sweetly, "What will happen if I don't?" I just laughed. Once I explained what her consequence would be for not cooperating, she chose wisely.

Given all our battles with her as a child, we worried we'd really have trouble later. We didn't. Over time it became clear that Ali felt responsible for her own life. She learned both by the fruit of making wise choices and the consequences of unwise choices. Sometimes it was so hard for us to follow through when she made a poor choice, but this was essential in keeping our authority with her.

During her elementary school years, she gradually began to do things simply because we asked her to, learning true heartfelt obedience instead of forced compliance. Our relationship with her grew stronger, and she grew more and more responsible to make wise choices in her life. Ali's strong character and intensity are now serving her well as she serves others. She's in a master's program with a strong sense of calling to help struggling youth.

148

MY RESPONSE

- As I think about my "theology of parenting," what would be the biblical basis for my beliefs about raising my kids?

- How have I gradually learned obedience to God?

- In what ways can I live out Ephesians 6:4 ("Do not exasperate your children; instead, bring them up in the training and instruction of the Lord")?

- How have I parented in ways that help my child grow in "the wisdom of the righteous" (Luke 1:17)?

CHAPTER 13

Problem-Solving and Skill-Building

Coaches of athletic teams know better than to try to teach new skills during games. The competitive brain is primed not to learn new skills but to put into play the skills it's already learned in practice.

Successful coaches also recognize that one essential aspect of preparing for the next game is to review the last one. What went well? What didn't? And then the team will practice whatever its players need to be better equipped.

Building problem-solving skills in our kids is similar. Taking time when the "players" have settled down and can think clearly is the best approach to teaching and training kids for future challenges.

Reviewing and Preparing a Game Plan

Parents often start planning for the next "game" of their children's challenges by asking themselves, "What can I do to keep that from happening again?" The best answer lies in reviewing with the players what happened in the first place.

This can begin as soon as everyone has calmed down enough to be able to learn well. First, ask questions to help your kids identify their feelings and thoughts. When they feel heard, they're far more open to working collaboratively to solve past conflicts and prevent future problems. Here are some open-ended questions that tend to help children learn to work through conflict and feel joined and understood rather than accused and judged.

- "How would you describe what happened?"
- "What was the most frustrating part for you?"
- "What do you wish you had done differently?"
- "What are your ideas for avoiding this problem in the future?"

Let the kids answer, even if your views differ. Avoid questions that invite mere yes or no replies or that might make them feel trapped. Also, questions like "What were you thinking?" or "Why did you do that?" or "Did you consider how the other person was feeling?" feel blaming or discouraging rather than interested and hopeful, so they lead to closed-ended exchanges.

When you've listened well, respectfully share your perspective and your own answers to those questions. If the viewpoints vary greatly, don't simply tell the kids they're wrong. Find *something* in what they said that you can validate, and acknowledge that people's perceptions can have differences. Focus on working toward future solutions you can agree on rather than on past blame.

With each person's thoughts and concerns on the table, brainstorm possible resolutions. Work together to establish common goals: having fun (instead of fighting) at bedtime, developing a fair system for sharing chores, finishing homework on time most nights to play a game together, and so on.

This process strengthens the message, "You are capable (of wise choices and actions)." Children gain confidence and hone skills when they can articulate their concerns respectfully and reach a creative solution or mutually acceptable compromise with you.

We followed this coaching process when our vacation conflicts during car rides became disrespectful. Questions focused on both the last and the next "game."

1. *How does each person feel as a result of the conflict?* We modeled listening to kids and asking questions first. (Family vacation drives often left us feeling irritable, frustrated, and disconnected when we arrived at our destination. Kids wanted attention, freedom, and to just get there! Adults wanted peace and quiet.)
2. *How does each person want to feel about the situation?* (To arrive feeling peaceful and connected, ready to enjoy fun times.)
3. *How could we work together to achieve that?* (Each person assembled a little personal bag of favorite stuff. The kids worked together to build a lap desk and collect art supplies. Lynne got audio books from the library. Jim led entertaining car games. We brought a Frisbee for vigorous get-out-and-run-around breaks.)

This process helped us to share many enjoyable multi-day trips with school-aged kids.

MY RESPONSE

- In what ways have I carefully listened to my child's perspective in an area of repeated conflict?

- In what ways, or at what times, have I not carefully listened?
- What questions might I ask so I can better know what it's like to walk in his/her shoes?
- What can I do to facilitate a problem-solving approach (rather than a power struggle)?

Four Skills to Practice

Perhaps you've asked or heard someone ask, "Don't you know any better?!" The truth is, much of the time, kids truly don't know any better. They haven't been taught or given opportunities to practice the skills they need for real-life challenges. Somehow parents expect that telling their kids *not* to act in certain ways will translate into the kids knowing the expected way *to* act. But they won't be able to act in new ways under stress until they've been taught and practiced new skills.

The best way to prepare for future challenges is to practice. The following are four skills and suggestions for teaching them.

1. Identify and give words to feelings.

The more kids are able to express how they feel, the less aggressive they are. Start by naming different common feelings they experience. For younger kids, you can play a game by making demonstrative expressions; see if they can identify the emotion you're representing and think of a situation that might cause it. Invite them to picture the situation and imagine themselves in it. Then have them say the feelings out loud, as if they were in the situation.

Kids young *and* old benefit from this practice because it helps them learn the words they'll need to shift their "game-time" mental activity from right-brain self-protection to left-brain language and logic.

Then make a habit of regularly discussing and even rehearsing feelings. At or after dinner, talk together about specific emotions (not just highs and lows) that each of you experienced that day. This will equip your children with helpful insight they can steadily learn to access in stressful times.

2. Make a plan.

Help your child to step out of the immediate moment and think ahead. For instance, asking, "What do you need to do to be ready?" is more helpful than saying, "Brush your hair and put your jacket on." Regularly ask questions designed to make your child stop and think, e.g., "What's your plan for doing this?" "How will you accomplish that?" "What's the best way to make this happen?" You'll be helping her brain to develop organization and problem-solving. Learning to plan well when she doesn't feel stressed serves to shape and strengthen her skill for thinking her way through tougher circumstances.

3. Consider natural impacts.

Natural impacts are simply the results of an action. Helping kids to see this increases their sense of responsibility for their behavior. Basic questions will expand their understanding: "What do you think will happen if . . . ?" (that is, if "you do this" or "do that," or if "you were to decide this way" or "that way"). Ask this question frequently about choices or plans your child might make. Affirm his insights, and guide him with more specific questions as needed. You can even talk about the impact of choices made by various characters in a story or movie. When he chooses wisely, be particularly diligent to help him see the natural benefit or blessing to all involved. (We'll look at misbehavior's natural impacts in chapter 15.)

4. Delay gratification.

Kids who can delay gratification are more competent when handling stress and frustration. You can help your young child learn healthy waiting when you intentionally delay granting a request for a few seconds or minutes. Add a little encouragement (a smile or a thumbs-up) while she's waiting. Compliment patience. As kids are becoming older, help them learn to save up for things they want. (Also see section C of the appendix, "Growing True Respect and Reconciliation," for ideas on teaching flexibility.)

In general, keep an eye out for any instances in which your child uses self-control or flexibility or delays gratification, and affirm her success.

● ● ●

The possibilities for practicing with kids to help them avoid misbehaviors are endless. When we use misbehaviors or failures as learning experiences to proactively guide growth and practice better ways for the future, children become more invigorated and hopeful, and parenting becomes more fun. It's like the difference between pulling weeds and planting flowers.

Guiding practice for success, instead of just giving consequences when kids misbehave, resoundingly says, "I am for you, not against you." It's the *yes* after the *no* of discipline. After the *stop*, it's the *go* to help my child get back on a path of wise behavior. The apostle Paul often uses this pattern when confronting sinful behavior: no, yes, and why. Consider these examples:

Anyone who has been stealing must steal no longer [*No*], but must work, doing something useful with their own hands [*Yes*], that they may have something to share with those in need [*Why*].

Do not let any unwholesome talk come out of your mouths [*No*], but only what is helpful for building others up according to their needs [*Yes*], that it may benefit those who listen [*Why*]. (Ephesians 4:28–29)

Next time you find yourself focused on a *no* for your child, consider how to teach them the *yes*, and help them value the *why*.

MY RESPONSE

What are one or two action points from the ideas above that I would like to try, to help my child build the following skills:

- Identify feelings
- Make a plan
- Consider natural impacts
- Delay gratification

KID CONNECTION: Gifts Gone Awry

Give each family member a sheet of paper and markers.

1. Read aloud the list of twelve misbehaviors (in chapter 11) and ask each person to pick the one he/she relates to the most. (Modify any of them as needed to fit a particular person.) Parents, model this: Pick first, then explain why you relate to that particular behavior and share how you feel when you act that way. Acknowledging that we all misbehave is a good starting point. (See 1 John 1:8.)

2. Next, talk about a gift underneath the misbehavior each person chose. Give each other feedback about ways in which you've seen him/her use that gift for good purposes. Share how good it feels to apply a gift of your own in a helpful way.

3. Have an older child read Ephesians 2:10: "We are His workmanship, created in Christ Jesus for good works, which God prepared beforehand so that we would walk in them" (NASB). Explain how God has created each person's unique gifts (even if we sometimes misuse them) to be a blessing to others. God has ways planned out for us to accomplish this.

4. Share how you think God might use each person's gift in the future to bless others. (A little creative imagining is fine!) Ask each person to draw a picture of himself/herself using their gift for God's purposes.

"You Are RESPONSIBLE for Your Actions."

Effective discipline puts responsibility on children to right their wrongs.

Correct — "You are RESPONSIBLE for your actions"

Coach — "You are CALLED and CAPABLE"

Connect — "You are LOVED no matter what"

Foundation — "You are SAFE with me"

CHAPTER 14

The Goal of Biblical Discipline: Restoring Hearts

Repentance. Reconciliation. Restoration. These are at the heart of biblical correction of sin. As agents of reconciliation, we guide a person to

- recognize what he has done wrong. (See Matthew 18:15–16.)
- embrace God's mercy and kindness (see Romans 2:4), which lead him to turn from sin (*repentance*) toward the wisdom of God's righteous ways. (See Luke 1:17 and Romans 12:20.)
- *reconcile* with others, to *restore* wounded relationships. (See Genesis 33:4; 45; Proverbs 14:9; Galatians 6:1; Matthew 5:22–23; 18:15; Ephesians 4:32.)

Bringing grace and truth into our homes means following this same process with our children. It takes a gentle, humble spirit to facilitate heartfelt *repentance* and true *reconciliation*.

In guiding our kids to make right (*restore*) what they've made wrong, we seek to use consequences not to shut down misbehavior but to show kids they are responsible for their lives and actions.

• • •

"If you talk to me that way again, you're grounded for two weeks!"

Probably, in a desperate moment, we've all barked something like this, a sign of two common problems with how parents might impose consequences. The first is responding impulsively rather than thoughtfully—being motivated by short-term solutions while neglecting to consider long-term impact.

That quick-fix approach is fueled by the second problem: a belief that if a consequence is painful enough, the behavior will stop. Sadly, there's truth to this: Behavior can indeed be stopped by inflicting pain. But stopping behavior and shaping a child's heart are different matters altogether.

When emotionally driven parents hammer out quick-fix solutions and painful punishments, little to no long-term heart change occurs in kids.

These are some additional possible examples:

- "If you don't get off that computer right now, you'll be in your room for the rest of the night."
- "That's the last straw—time for a spanking."
- "Eat those vegetables, or you go to the time-out chair."
- "You're not getting away with treating your sister like this. No video games this weekend."
- "I've had it. You are not using my car!"

Such consequences are convenient to impose, don't take much thought, and sometimes curb the immediate behavior. However, they usually do little if anything to facilitate true reconciliation or grow the convictions and qualities that parents actually desire their children to embrace.

Other pitfalls related to this approach:

- If my child is overly focused on something, my frequent confiscation of it will tend to increase his obsession as he defends his right to it.
- My child will probably resent what she perceives as my unfair control, which over time lessens my real influence and closeness with her.
- My child loses valuable learning opportunities. Not learning to desire wise behavior for good reasons, he may simply learn to get sneakier.

In short, consequences have consequences. Parents who realize this will give them more thoughtfully, with consideration for long-term learning.

● ● ●

When we think carefully about consequences we use, we tend to be more respectful and reasonable. We'll follow through with what we've administered, knowing that we're gaining the influence and heart connection with our children that helps them *want* to restore what they've made wrong.

Scriptural Perspectives

The way God disciplined *His* children throughout Scripture provides a diverse assortment of creative, purposeful possibilities to consider. Covering this theme in detail would require a large book on its own. But exploring a few principles here can give some food for thought and prayer.

Natural Impacts

In what may be the most encompassing principle for consequences, Paul wrote, "Do not be deceived; God is not mocked, for you reap whatever you sow" (Galatians 6:7 NRSV). The metaphor is that our choices and actions are like seeds planted in the ground of our lives. Whatever we plant *will* grow. In other words, there are automatic results of, or consequences for, our choices of all kinds. We call these "natural impacts," and helping kids understand them has nearly unparalleled effect.

Do-over / Practice a Right Response

When Peter sinned by denying Jesus three times, instead of scolding him or casting him out of fellowship, Jesus invited him three times to answer a question that counteracted Peter's lies: "Do you love me?" Three times Peter said yes. Then Jesus said, "Feed my sheep." (See John 21:15–19.)

In other words, "Peter, you blew it, and I know you feel pretty bad about that. But I believe in you. So I want you to make it right. Let's try again." Peter's do-over showed Jesus he was ready for the next invitation—not really a consequence in the common sense. Jesus asked him to make right what he'd made wrong by calling him to leadership in the church. Peter gladly obliged.

Encouragement

Moses, called to lead Israel out of Egypt, reacted with terrified defiance: "*No.* Somebody else. Not *ME*." Three more times God extended the call; Moses dug in his heels with excuses. God didn't punish him or tell him he'd lost his chance. God progressively calmed Moses' fears with encouragement, help, and guidance until Moses finally agreed to go. (See Exodus 3:4–4:17.)

Similarly, Jesus encouraged those struggling with sin (except self-righteous legalists like the Pharisees, whom He rebuked repeatedly). Jesus' dealings with sin often short-circuited impending punishment. He compassionately exhorted those stuck or caught in sin with forgiveness and an encouragement to go and leave one's life of sin . . . essentially inviting them to a do-over. (See John 8:11.)

We walk in God's footsteps when we reassure our children, "I will be with you to help you if you want to make a different choice."

Losing Privileges

Adam and Eve sinned in the Garden and lost the privilege of staying in the Garden, from which they had stolen. (See Genesis 3.) Moses dishonored God while leading Israel toward the Promised Land, so he lost the privilege of entering the land. (See Numbers 20:1–12.) The consequence of the loss of kids' privileges, if respectfully and reasonably administered, can compel them to do what they need to do to make things right and to reconcile.

Make Restitution / Reconcile

Many of us weren't taught as children to make restitution or reconcile conflicts. Rather, we were told to go to our rooms and not come out until we could speak the words "I'm sorry," regardless of the condition of our hearts.

Within the church there is much unresolved conflict and division, but God has shown us how we're to go about seeking to right our wrongs and repair our relationships. Jesus said, "If another believer sins against you . . ." but He didn't continue, "tattle to your leaders and get them to punish her."

First, we're to "go privately and point out the offense" (Matthew 18:15 NLT). And we're to repeatedly attempt to reconcile, with gradually increasing assistance in the process before church discipline may be needed. (See Matthew 18:15–20.)

This principle compels us as parents to actively encourage our kids toward true reconciliation. No sweeping unresolved sins under the rug. No quick-and-easy "I'm sorry." At the heart of this effort is the message of the gospel, which ultimately teaches us that true reconciliation is only possible through confession of and repentance from our sin and receiving the restoration Christ provides.

Possible Applications

This wide variety of biblical examples compelled us to broaden our approach to putting consequences in place. We developed a flexible, biblically informed sequence to help our kids be restored. And we applied these general principles with the goal of communicating the four Discipline that Connects messages (You are *safe*, You are *loved*, You are *called and capable*, and You are *responsible* for your actions):

1. *Understand the natural impact.* We found that when we helped kids discover the automatic (no adult intervention) results of their behavior, they were often compelled to repair or restore what they'd done.

2. *Make-it-right consequences.* Once the kids felt moved to make things right, we would help them figure out how to do it. For example, if you used your hands to hurt, you can make things right by using your hands to help. So the child might make a card asking forgiveness from or affirming the one they hurt.

3. *Identify and reposition "gifts gone awry."* We often saw that whatever gift was behind misbehavior could be used to make things right. If expressiveness was used to tear

someone down, a consequence was to find ways to use the gift to build the person back up. This also helped kids develop their own vision for using their gift in honoring ways.

4. *Do-over/practice a right response.* If a child did something in an unhelpful or hurtful way, we sometimes asked them to repeat that response in a right or honoring way. If they continued to struggle, we'd invite them to repeat it several times in hopes they'd learn a helpful habit.

5. *Losing privileges.* When the privilege that is suspended is clearly related to the specific misbehavior, the consequence is purposeful and much more likely to help kids get back on track.

There's no one "right way" to administer these principles. Let's consider how to adjust the sequence and adapt the ideas for options when a child is whining or demanding.

1. *Note the gift gone awry:* "You know what you want and are very persistent to get it! That's a good gift from God."

2. *Understand the natural impact:* "However, whining is draining for whoever has to listen. And it's a disrespectful way to try to get what you want—that's just not a good habit."

3. *Do-over/practice a right response:* "Before I answer your request, you can practice patiently waiting for a while and then ask respectfully."

4. *Make things right/reconcile:* "Dealing with lots of whining takes me away from the things that I'm responsible to do. You can make this right by apologizing when you're ready and then doing something extra to help me out."

5. *Lose the privilege:* "You've lost the privilege of [the thing you whined for] today, but I think tomorrow you'll ask much more respectfully."

MY RESPONSE

- What is a common misbehavior in my home?
- How might I implement some or all of the above five principles in response to that behavior?

What About Spanking?

Many parents ask about spanking. There are a few biblical accounts of strong physical consequences for an individual's sin. For instance, God afflicted Azariah with leprosy for not eliminating places of idol worship. Ananias and Sapphira lost their lives for attempting to deceive God and His church. (See 2 Kings 15 and Acts 5, respectively.) Yet compared to the frequency with which the Lord used other types of natural and imposed consequences—especially with individuals—physical punishment seems to be the exception.

On interpreting Proverbs verses about using "the rod," Christian leaders disagree. Some believe the verses support the act of spanking as a primary tool for disobedience and defiance of all kinds. Others believe Jesus taught a nonviolent approach to life and that such references to corporal punishment are figurative, calling parents to be strong in their authority without inflicting physical pain.

We (Jim and Lynne) are not dogmatic about whether or how to use spanking as a general form of discipline. But we do believe spanking is not a biblical mandate.

There's no word for *spanking* in Scripture, and neither is any young child struck on the rear end with a hand or small object. It's well known that certain children are absolutely harmed by spanking (traumatized kids, sensory-sensitive kids, kids with developmental imbalances, etc.). It stands to reason that if God truly meant spanking to be a universal mandate, these kids would benefit from the discipline.

What we are quite dogmatic about is that, regardless of chosen discipline methods, it's the parent's responsibility to be growing in grace and truth and in discernment about what consequences effectively reach their children's hearts.

A primary problem we see with spanking—and we see it a lot—is parents relying on it as their primary discipline tool without working toward gaining a variety of creative approaches. This may explain why, though research is varied on spanking, it usually appears to be counterproductive and likely to increase a child's tendencies toward aggression.

Many parents believe spanking is "working" when their kids respond with apparent remorse and obedience. But we've heard from numerous young adults from "good Christian homes" that their quietness and obedience was mostly shame- and fear-based compliance. Great discernment is needed.

MY RESPONSE

- If I employ spanking as discipline, how do I determine what my child has learned from it?
- What messages would my child say he/she receives when spanked? (Perhaps you could ask.)

No Single "Right" Consequence

Parents often want an easy, plug-and-play consequence. But as we consider God's example of creative discipline, it's clear that with the complexities of each unique situation and the nuances of each parent/child relationship, there is no consistent, same-consequence-every-time right answer.

A question in one of our workshops illustrated this principle: "How does all this work when, no matter what you've done to get your seven-year-old to put on her shoes, she keeps going outside in socks? She must have wrecked ten pairs already this spring!"

"Great question," I (Jim) said. "Who knows *the* right answer?" No hands went up.

This opened a door for us to illustrate both what a creative adventure integrating the Discipline that Connects principles can be, and also how any number of consequences might help our children learn to take responsibility.

To the gathered parents I said, "Around your tables, assume you've done your work to be a safe parent. Assume you've let your child know she's loved despite this behavior. And assume you are helping her know she is God's workmanship, called and capable.

"What consequences might you then put in place to help her begin to realize she is responsible—in this case, more responsible for taking care of her socks? Make a list, and then decide which answers are your table's favorites."

The groups spent the next few minutes in energized conversation. Here are some of the possibilities they developed:

- Have the girl go to her piggy bank and get money for new socks each time she ruins a pair, or have her pay for more socks at the next store visit.
- Put her in a time-out chair and stay with her until she has put on her shoes, explaining that she can't go outside without them.
- Teach her to do the laundry and have her help each time she dirties her socks.
- Help her understand the natural result of her actions. Put all the wrecked socks in a box to show her when she

runs out of them. When she sees them, ask her what she wants to do about them. Use this opportunity to teach her about money, socks, and honoring the resources and possessions God has provided.

- Take away her socks until she's motivated to have them. Then figure out how she can be more responsible—maybe she buys her own socks.

All these good examples of thoughtful consequences may help kids learn to be more responsible when they have disobeyed. Some may seem fitting for you and your children, while others may not; you—as the parent—know best.

• • •

What's clear is that when we take the time to think, we'll find there are numerous constructive possibilities for discipline that can help children take the reins of responsibility for their own lives. As we learn to think like this, we can test various consequences while staying calm and well-connected.

That's what this section of the book is about: learning as parents to think through effective consequences that can help our kids see they are ultimately responsible for themselves and their actions. We build a helpful identity in them as we communicate the message, "You are responsible!"

MY RESPONSE

- What helps me do my most creative thinking?
- How might I apply that to discipline situations?

CHAPTER 15

Reaping and Sowing: Natural Impacts

The leveraging of natural impacts is possibly a parent's most potent teaching tool, so they merit a deeper look. As Galatians 6:7 says, "Do not be deceived; God is not mocked, for you reap whatever you sow" (NRSV). This simply means, *If we do bad things, bad stuff naturally happens.* Conversely, *if we do good stuff and don't give up, we'll harvest good things.*

Parents sometimes forget this important truth when it's time to discipline. We tend to rush past or altogether forget about God's ready-made natural consequences by imposing *unnatural* ones. There is a time for imposed consequences, but only if the natural results aren't compelling for a child.

For example, taking away a daughter's iPod because she was sassy is an imposed consequence. Imposing it may give the parent a sense of control, but if in so doing he or she doesn't address the behavior's natural results, the child won't learn anything about sassing's impact on her and those around her.

Once, after a workshop, a mother described to us this situation:

> I was working in the kitchen while listening to my children play in the next room. Things were going well until my three-year-old daughter started wailing the kind of wail that could only have been caused by my four-year-old son's aggression.
>
> I rinsed my hands and rounded the corner to see him leaning over to pick her up. It looked like he had shoved her to the floor. But by the time I reached them, he was hugging her and telling her he was sorry.

Then her voice became stern. "So what should his consequence be for pushing her down?"

Here is a parent's dream come true—a child showing sincere remorse and making it right on his own by comforting the younger sibling he's just hurt. The natural impacts (her pain and sadness, his remorse and desire to repair the relationship) had played out beautifully. Based on her question's tone, though, this seemed clear: If the mom had been able to respond sooner, she'd have intervened and imposed consequences, thus negating the powerful moment of her son's self-motivated restoration.

If she'd taken over, instead of experiencing his sister's hurt and sadness and his own sorrow, he'd have instantly focused on his mom's anger and his fear of her reaction. The opportunity to initiate reconciliation based on his own feelings of guilt would have become complicated or maybe even lost.

Letting Natural Results Teach

A threefold process can guide us in helping kids to learn from natural impacts (what happens automatically, without adult intervention).

We can get out of the way.

As just illustrated, experiencing natural impacts helps kids focus on learning from actual results. Not only do we parents too frequently jump in and start scolding or punishing, we also sometimes even shield our kids from such outcomes. If when my son forgets his lunchbox on the kitchen table I rush it over to the school, I prevent him from seeing the practical outcome of overlooking his responsibility. Which child is more likely to learn to remember: the one whose parent brings the lunch without fail, or the one who has gone hungry? It can be difficult to let our kids face the music of their choices, but this is how they learn.

We can explain the natural impacts without lecturing.

In the example above, the son's learning could have been enhanced if Mom had said, "I can see you feel bad about what happened. And it looks as if she felt bad too. That's what happens when big brothers hurt little sisters. I can also see that you want to comfort and take care of her. That's why God made you her big brother. Doesn't it feel good to take care of her that way?" A response like this can help motivate him to care even better for his sister in the future. It truly does feel good to do something right!

We can ask questions to help kids discover the natural impacts of their actions.

For example, you could gently ask, "What happens when sisters punch each other?" or "How does he feel based on how you acted?" or "What might happen if you left that mess on the floor?" As kids' brains engage to seek answers, they both settle down *and* learn the basic cause/effect thinking that develops wisdom.

* * *

Toni, our daycare provider, shared with me (Lynne) her experience of helping our son Daniel understand a natural impact. One day he was playing carelessly with a ball near her glass-front cabinet. She came over to him, showed him the glass, tapped on it gently, and explained how it can break into sharp pieces when something hits it.

Then she asked, "What might happen if kids play right here with a ball?"

"It might break," Daniel said.

"That's right," Toni affirmed. "Where do you think would be a good place to play with a ball?"

"Over there, on the other side," he answered.

He felt trusted to make a wise choice, and he played appropriately with the ball from that point forward.

For me this episode was a bit of an epiphany. The idea was so simple, yet I'd never considered doing anything other than tell Daniel the rule about where to play and what the consequence would be if he broke it. On a good parenting day, I might have remembered to explain the reason for the rule. At times, a "state the rule with a rationale and a consequence" approach suits perfectly. But Toni saw an opening to teach wisdom, self-control, and respect instead of just compliance.

Other common natural (not imposed) impacts might include:

- **When a sister hits her brother:** His body and feelings are hurt. He might not want to go on playing with her. She may feel sad.
- **When a child is interrupting:** It's hard for others to talk; they get frustrated and may not want to be near him when they talk.

175

- **When a child grabs a toy:** The other child's feelings are hurt. He may grab it back. The toy might be broken if they fight over it.
- **When children leave messes:** Other people can trip over the items or feel disrespected. Things may be difficult to find.
- **When a child doesn't do her homework:** She (not her parents) gets a bad grade, falls further behind, and may get discouraged. The teacher faces extra challenges when some students don't keep up. The child doesn't learn study skills that would help her later.
- **When a child steals:** The person he steals from loses what's hers, which costs money to replace; she may become angry or worried. The child who stole feels guilty and may develop a hard heart.
- **When a child is verbally abusive or disrespectful:** There are hurt feelings that cause distance in the relationship. The receiver of the mean words may avoid the hurtful person, come to believe untrue things about herself, or even seek revenge.
- **When a child lies:** Trust is broken. If no one finds out, the lie stays inside; guilty feelings (e.g., knot in stomach) can become a hardened heart. The person who was lied to doesn't trust the one who lied.

MY RESPONSE

- What is a misbehavior for which I often impose consequences?
- What are natural (not imposed) impacts of that behavior?
- What might be a natural impact that I inadvertently interfere with by over-helping?

Communicating With Encouragement

Learning to talk with our kids about natural impacts in a relaxed, nonjudgmental way equips them to take more responsibility for their behavior.

Benny was an extremely sensitive kid, physically and emotionally. Every day after kindergarten he would yell at and pound three-year-old Emma just for saying a wrong word or accidentally bumping into him. What bothered his mom, Julie, was that he seemed to have no remorse. He'd even once told her, "Emma deserves it because you don't punish her enough."

One day Benny threw a hard toy at Emma and she burst into tears. Julie took a deep breath, got down on the floor beside her kids, and reminded herself to stay calm. "Hmm. Benny, would it be okay if I told you a story?"

"I guess."

"There was a day, long, long ago—last week, I believe." (This playful beginning was connective and calming for them both.) "You were walking through the living room, and Emma bumped you by mistake. It wasn't a very hard bonk, but you were upset because that didn't feel good to your body. I think that's how Emma feels right n—"

"I'm sorry, Emma!" Benny interrupted. "Would you like to build Legos with me? We could take turns. You do some and I do some."

"Okay!"

They started building; Julie sat there . . . stunned. She realized her previous "That is not okay! How does Emma feel?" confrontations had contained so much rejection and judgment, they'd shamed Benny into defiance, not insight. When he felt safe and loved, she could help him discover the natural impact of his actions *and* the true heart God had given him for his sister.

This incident was a turning point for all of them. Several months later Julie said the conflict and aggression had decreased dramatically and the kids were having so much more fun together. "They're really good friends now."

Before going straight to imposed consequences (particularly with ages four and up), try engaging the logical/learning part of your child's brain by saying something to this effect: "Let's see if you can learn from your mistake and make a plan to keep it from happening again." You might ask, "What was the impact on everybody, including you? What could you do to solve the problem that happened because of what you did? Would you like to talk about it with me?" If the child is willing to have this conversation, an imposed consequence isn't usually needed.

The Fruit of Focusing on Natural Impacts

If parents are diligent in planting seeds of effective teaching about natural impacts, they're likely to harvest the following outcomes:

- Children will feel bad about what they should feel bad about instead of bad about the way Mom or Dad treated them.
- Judgment, conscience, and internal motivation to correct poor choices will come more naturally for kids, as parents talk through the positive and negative results of different choices.
- Children's social skills and compassion will increase as they come to better understand the feelings within various interactions.
- Even if an imposed consequence is necessary for your child, understanding the natural impact of his misbehavior will help him see the purpose of the imposed consequence.

- Children will be ready to take responsibility for their own lives when the time comes, because natural impacts (not imposed consequences) will follow them out the door of your home.

Imposed consequences are an important part of discipline. But, as in Benny's case, the natural-impacts approach may help your kids take responsibility for their actions without needing any further consequences.

MY RESPONSE

- What is a misbehavior that may have triggered me to inadvertently lecture or shame my child?
- How could I help my child understand a behavior's natural impacts with a gentle, encouraging approach, a story, or lighthearted questions?

KID CONNECTION: Reaping and Sowing

Re-read Galatians 6:7 (NRSV): "Do not be deceived; God is not mocked, for you reap whatever you sow."

For younger kids, open a favorite fruit that has seeds or a pit. Show them the seeds/pit inside, and then show them a weed seed, or print a picture of a thistle seed. Ask, "What would I get if I planted this (fruit) seed? Could I get a dandelion? Could this thistle grow a peach?"

Then share: "Our actions are like seeds that grow different results in our lives. Wise or kind seeds grow helpful results, and unwise or selfish seeds grow hurtful results." Talk about how the natural impact of what we do affects us and those around us—helpful and hurtful, right now and over time. You might discuss the seeds of sharing, name-calling, serving, whining, and more.

As kids get the idea, see if they can contribute examples. Share your own experiences of good and of bad seeds you've planted. Finish with the kids drawing a picture of themselves making an honoring choice—"planting a good seed"—and the immediate impact on those around them.

For older kids, look for teachable moments to share some of your life lessons about the results of various different choices you've made. Kids will often be more open if you start with a painful lesson from a poor choice and then share how you responded differently over time.

For all kids, Philippians 4:8 ("Whatever is true, whatever is noble, whatever is right, whatever is pure, whatever is lovely, whatever is admirable—if anything is excellent or praiseworthy—think about such things") guides us to focus on anything worthy of praise. Highlight times you've seen your child planting good seeds!

CHAPTER 16

Understanding *Why* My Child Is Misbehaving

Neither a surgeon nor a mechanic tries to fix a problem without knowing the cause. Likewise, discipline ought to have great consideration for underlying causes of misbehavior. It seems that the unique reasons children misbehave can be grouped into four primary categories. (As these almost never stand alone, testing out various possibilities requires discernment and patience.)

1. The Sin Problem

"We all, like sheep, have gone astray" (Isaiah 53:6). Through Adam and Eve, we each—parents and kids—bear sin's imprint, or DNA. In the words of Facebook, "It's complicated." While we're on this earth, sin will entangle and chase us around. That's why at the very heart of this book is the belief that *grace is needed.*

Grace is unmerited favor. Grace is irrationally positive. Grace gives the benefit of the doubt.

It reframes our every effort to address our kids' misbehavior when we recognize that sin is at the core of all misbehavior, and that only by God's grace through Christ do we have the ability to fulfill our calling to become like Jesus. So be sure to keep grace at the forefront of your thoughts, words, and deeds in the same way that "God demonstrates his own love for us in this: While we were still sinners, Christ died for us" (Romans 5:8).

While sin will always complicate things, three other underlying factors often contribute to misbehavior. We've found that considering these can be enlightening and even transforming.

2. Identity (negative self-concept)

Children who consistently struggle to control their behavior often are discouraged or anxious. They may have developed an identity as, for example, a troublemaker, a whiner, an angry child, or a black-sheep family member. This template says, "This is the kind of kid I am, so this is how I respond to this kind of situation."

Certainly, self-perceptions can fluctuate—we all relate to feeling like a wise parent one day, when everything goes smoothly, and a failure the next—but overall we have predominant self-perceptions that factor significantly in the behaviors we choose. As a growing child's actions become challenging and the struggles between parent and child become more volatile, she can begin to form entrenched negative identities that can snowball into resentment, discouragement, and even despair.

It isn't easy to remind a misbehaving child of who she truly is: loved no matter what, called and capable, and responsible. Although our kids don't need a theology lesson whenever we discipline, we can weave this perspective into our interactions. (Helping kids grow a healthy, Christ-centered identity is the basis for the many practical, proactive strategies. Read more about this throughout the appendix.)

Consider some specific ways you may want to strengthen your child's identity, even in misbehavior, as someone who

- is learning self-control
- is forgiven and loved
- enjoys serving others
- often makes wise choices
- loves his siblings no matter their skirmishes
- has a heart to love God and others

After giving Daniel "reconciliation consequences" for an aggressive conflict, we would occasionally observe, "You seem a lot happier now than you did after you hit Bethany. That's because when you're kind to your sister, you're living out of the true heart of love God gave you for her. You can recognize it by the joy you feel." This helped him grow to value his role as a caring older brother.

The apostle Paul knew the importance of identity as a foundation for behavior. In his letters he strongly argues for the believer's identity in Christ as the foundation for how to live. Even in more confrontational letters to churches immersed in sin, Paul started with his identity and authority as an apostle, a line or two of blessing in grace and peace, and then solid teaching about their identity in Jesus. Only then did he confront the sin issues.

As parents, we too can respond from a God-given authority to bless our children and teach them about their true identity when they misbehave. If Paul was adamant that behavioral change flows from an identity anchored in faith, we can incorporate this as our kids begin understanding simple faith concepts.

Scientists have further clarified the importance of identity in making choices. According to Chip and Dan Heath, experts in human behavioral research, "Because identities are central to the way people make decisions, any change effort that violates someone's identity is likely doomed to failure."[1] It's crucial to work at a heart level, reminding children of our love and God's love. This encourages them to build skills based on who they truly are, not merely to do this or not do that because Mom or Dad said so.

* * *

Lila, a nineteen-year-old woman, was repeatedly making poor choices with sex and alcohol use and feeling a great deal of shame. Her decisions were rooted in the firm belief (identity) that *I have an addictive personality type, therefore I have no self-control.*

I (Jim) informed her that lots of people—myself included—have a personality prone to addiction, but this does not obligate *anyone* to damaging choices, including those she felt stuck in. We discussed times when she'd used good self-control and the factors that had enabled or encouraged her to make those decisions. We also talked about what gave her true joy.

Lila's entire countenance changed as she began sharing about how much she loved to serve people. And she left that session significantly encouraged. Shortly thereafter she found a job as a server in a high-class restaurant and began walking a challenging but hope-filled road toward better choices.

MY RESPONSE

- How might my child's identity contribute to frequent misbehavior?

- What truth do I want to convey to him/her instead?
- In what ways could I do this?

3. The Payoff (perceived cost/reward)

People also choose how they will act by simply considering the benefit: What could I get out of doing this, or what might it cost me? To kids, a big emotional response from their parents is usually a big payoff—they feel powerful, in control. When teaching the Discipline that Connects principles to parents, we do spontaneous skits, one with typical/reactive discipline, and then the same scenario with our approach. When a class participant plays the role of a child, that parent often has an *aha!* moment as he or she experiences what it's like to be a kid getting big attention and power for misbehaving, contrasted with a kid receiving thoughtful, connective discipline.

One dad said, "In the first skit it was quite entertaining getting your goat. You gave me lots to swing at. In the second skit I didn't even want to misbehave." Though the skits are obviously staged, we've found the dynamics remarkably similar to real life. Making a similar shift from reactive to connective in your own discipline will avoid the feeding or fertilizing of misconduct (see section 1, especially chapter 5).

Sometimes, of course, kids get a payoff for misbehavior if they get what they want or get out of what they want to avoid. It's helpful to consider this and plan accordingly. For example, when my child knows that if she argues loudly and disrespectfully to get what she wants, she (A) gets no big attention or sense of control, and (B) loses the possibility of getting the item that day, then the behavior's costs and rewards likely won't compel her to continue to argue this way. Many parents have learned the helpful script, delivered from a "safe" posture, "I love you too much to let you learn to get what you want that way. If you try again more respectfully, we can at least talk about it."

MY RESPONSE

- What might be the payoff that's fertilizing a certain frequent misbehavior in my home?
- How could I adjust my responses to make sure my reactions aren't tempting my child to misbehave?

4. Physical Factors (body/brain)

Sometimes kids misbehave because their bodies are working against them (e.g., through fatigue, low blood sugar, under- or over-stimulation, etc.). Randy was a thirty-year-old pastor when he told us how hypoglycemia, discovered in his twenties, had driven his out-of-control emotional outbursts as a child. His voice quivered as he shared painful and shame-filled memories of ruining numerous family gatherings and vacations due to "misbehavior."

These physical factors can also include difficulty with processing sensory information. Any of these reasons can make it difficult for kids to learn the skills they need to manage their own behavior wisely. Kids need our assistance to learn and practice these abilities. This perspective has helped many parents find new and hopeful ways of dealing with challenges they'd previously treated with conventional discipline.

* * *

Eight-year-old Raul's body worked against him in challenging situations. He struggled to focus, was always moving and making noise, and could erupt at fairly minimal provocation if over-stimulated. His flare-ups were paying off with power over his peers and intense attention from concerned adults.

His parents, Jose and Bella, contacted us for coaching after Raul had been suspended from their church's Wednesday night Bible program because of wild behavior and impulsive aggression toward other kids. They were concerned Raul was building an identity as an "angry kid" and that this self-perception was driving even more aggression.

With these aspects in mind, we carefully planned an approach. Raul's mom and dad dealt with the physical factors that made self-control difficult. They provided regular massage and big-movement activities to calm his body. (You can find a video of sensory input techniques as well as other sensory resources at disciplinethatconnects.org/links.) They taught him how to recognize his energy/anger levels and apply practical self-calming strategies.

He also got help learning to better plan out his actions, telling his parents when and where he was going, how he would play with others, and what adult he could go to for help if he got upset at church. This planning decreased his impulsiveness and, as a result, his aggression.

Raul had already experienced a strong but appropriate consequence for his aggression by losing the privilege of participating in Wednesday night activities. His parents also helped him understand the subtler natural results of his actions: how his behavior made others feel, and how *he* felt when he was disrespectful or aggressive.

Jose and Bella strengthened Raul's God-given identity: You are loved even when you struggle; you are capable of learning to make wise choices. They taught him how to reconcile with others when he got angry or hurtful. They looked carefully for examples of his kindness and gentleness, affirming and encouraging him about the impact of his positive choices.

Raul's parents and siblings noted numerous changes in him over the next several months. The highlight was when he announced, "I'll be fine going back to church on Wednesday. I'm not an angry kid anymore." Clearly Raul's identity had changed in the process. Our final coaching session focused on channeling his God-given energy and intensity into healthy leadership skills.

This effective discipline took into consideration all of the behavior's possible causes. Throughout the journey Raul received priceless messages: "You are *responsible* for your actions," given by parents who'd first shared, "You are *safe* with me—I'm for you, not against you," "You are *loved* no matter what," and "You are God's creation, *called and capable.*"

MY RESPONSE

• What ideas does Raul's story give me for helping one of my children who might be struggling in a similar way?

Rebuilding and Reconciling

Correct — "You are RESPONSIBLE for your actions"

Coach — "You are CALLED and CAPABLE"

Connect — "You are LOVED no matter what"

Foundation — "You are SAFE with me"

CHAPTER 17

Rebuilding: What to Do When It Falls Apart

We hope you are inspired and equipped to be emotionally safe with your child, communicate love no matter what, recognize and affirm your child's calling and capability, and impose consequences that truly grow a sense of responsibility. Having these principles etched in your heart and mind will guide your vision for connecting with your child's heart when you discipline.

However, we must confess that even with this inspiration and vision in place, and having learned many skills for engaging constructively with our kids' misbehavior, we've blown it. A lot. We've reacted impulsively instead of responding thoughtfully through the lens of vision. We've disciplined for our comfort rather than our kids' best interest. We've made demands that had no sound basis, simply because "we're the parents," exerting our power to control.

We sometimes had selfish, sinful motives behind masks of authority, logic, and even "spiritual" guidance. As a result, on numerous occasions we did not obey the first part of the

Ephesians 6:4 command. We exasperated our children. Our discipline methods would "provoke [them] to anger" (NASB).

We give thanks that even when our parenting was out of alignment with His purposes, God was still present and active. He established in our hearts and minds a vision anchored in the Discipline that Connects principles. We worked diligently to talk about these guiding ideas—with each other and our kids—and even wrote them down.

The result was that when we blew it, we knew it, and we knew what to do about it. When we exasperated our kids, we were inspired and equipped to rebuild in a way that "unexasperated" them and also honored the second part of Ephesians 6:4, to "bring them up in the training and instruction of the Lord." We'd compare our actions to our vision, recognize what hadn't lined up, and then go back to confess and restore.

When parents really blow it with a child and hurt the relationship, they often feel a mixture of guilt for their own actions and resentment of their kid's behavior. It's tempting to offer a quick "drive-by apology," maybe mumbling something like, "Sorry I was kind of harsh." This is like slapping a little plaster on a crack—it's a temporary cover on a problem that will reemerge under stress. It may ease the guilt a bit but does little to truly restore the relationship or work out the recurring problem.

Instead, we can rebuild. Rebuilding brings our vision to life. It's in life's messes—the crises—where our beliefs and convictions become real.

Remember from chapter 3 the day I (Jim) came home to find my kids fighting over a magazine? I walked in and yelled at them, firing off harsh demands dictated by selfish desires. I did not prepare myself before speaking. I was angry and unsafe. Between the lines of my spoken words was the unspoken message, "What's wrong with *you?*"

My son's astute response ("Where's the love?") jarred me.

After requesting a do-over and stepping back outside, it was easy to reflect on what had just happened, because I'd memorized and practiced a set of simple principles to guide my thinking. I prayed and asked for the grace to be truly safe with my kids. I reentered the room and communicated love. They settled down, and I asked if they could solve this on their own or needed help, conveying the message, "I believe in you and your ability to work things out."

I gave them the responsibility for solving the matter respectfully and asked them to relocate the conflict if they still needed time. What only three minutes earlier had been torn down was now rebuilt, and all of us were more encouraged and aligned with the joy of the Lord.

Sometimes resolution takes longer. I (Lynne) had a similar experience that took more work to bring to a constructive conclusion.

Guests were coming, and we were all stressed from cleaning up our messy house. As one child took out frustration on another, I grew irate with the aggressive behavior. Feeling pressed for time, with commando zeal I sent them both to a bedroom with a scathing order to quickly resolve the conflict. My glare at the aggressor left no doubt as to the focus of my anger.

As soon as they were alone, that child fired a load of hurtful words at the other, resulting in an explosion of tears. Hearing the screams and sobs, I realized I'd contributed significantly to the outcome—the aggressive child had followed my example quite well.

This was a true rebuilding opportunity. I asked Jim to finish preparation and engage the guests, then went to the children and began with an apology: "Kids, I felt a bunch of pressure to be ready, and I took my stress out on you. You didn't deserve that. I'm sorry. Will you forgive me?"

They settled down immediately, and both nodded. I invited them to sit near me on the bed, and I put my arms around each of them, reconnecting. This reseated me as trusted mentor and removed me as angry bully. I then sought their ideas about how to reconcile while adding my own perspective. It took longer than I'd have liked, but they apologized and forgave each other, and we engaged our guests with true joy.

What goes around comes around. When we're intentional about rebuilding, what often comes around is kids who follow our lead.

MY RESPONSE

- What is a "rebuilding" story of my own?
- What brought on the incident, and how did we work through it together?

Heartfelt reconciliation sometimes takes prayerful, humble persistence. And it's worth everything it requires, for our faithful efforts to rebuild can help open our children's hearts to God's redemptive purposes and model for them how they can repair damage in their future relationships.

Here are some practical steps.

Confess and Apologize

Confess your sins to each other and pray for each other so that you may be healed. (James 5:16)

Admit to your child that your own attitudes and/or actions weren't good, then apologize and say what you'd like to do differently. This demonstrates your own true repentance. You could say something such as, "I know I was harsh with you. I'm sorry. I wish I'd been more thoughtful." Then ask for forgiveness and say, "I will work on this, okay?"

This simple rebuilding step will likely set a much more constructive tone for further conversation about the incident. Whether a child is three, thirteen, or for that matter thirty, a parent's contrite heart and apology can smoothly pave the way for restored relationship and a child's ensuing repentance.

Reconnect

Prioritize the message of love.

When a child has been harshly disciplined, she tends to feel rejected or unwanted and receives the message, *You are a problem*. Counteracting this is as simple as reconnecting. Whatever the behavior, even in appropriately firm discipline, kids needs to know they are loved.

Say, "I know this is hard right now, but nothing you do can keep me from loving you." Then act on it. Spend time together— do something fun; share hugs; give a back rub; pray together, thanking God that His love never leaves us.

Engage and Enlist

A parent's apology sets the stage to engage the child in the rebuilding process. An honest confession of what you did and what you wish you'd done opens the way to ask, "What did you do?" and "What do you wish you'd done?" Your child can now follow the example you set. This doesn't necessarily make the rest of the conversation easy, but it opens the door.

Instead of pronouncements or judgments—"You know better than that!" or "How many times do I need to tell you?" ask helpful questions: "What were you hoping for?" or "Tell me more about what you want." Your child may still not be on board with you, or he may have a difficult time putting words to his feelings. He might respond, "What do you think I was hoping for? You *never* listen to me!"

This can be difficult to hear. In fact, it can be easy—even natural, when you're working hard to rebuild—to get frustrated if your child responds in this way. But this is what you can expect when he feels hurt and upset—view it as a potent opportunity to model a new way of responding.

Instead of saying, "How dare you!" continue with the goal of engaging and enlisting your child and say gently, "I can see you're pretty frustrated with me. It seems to you that I never pay attention. Tell me more about that." There are no judging statements, just a gracious reframing of what you heard and an invitation for more. If you persist with this goal of engaging, your child will eventually begin to respond in new ways too.

You'll know the child is engaged in rebuilding when she starts to work with you instead of against you. With older kids, this can be a slow process because we may have lost their emotional trust over a long period of time. Stay patient, and note subtle differences in responses and body language. She may say things like, "I just feel so stupid" or "I don't know what to do" or "I wish I could figure it out." These suggest she's now focused on her choices and actions rather than on you and your "energy" about the misbehavior.

Once she begins to engage, you can enlist her in the process of determining a better future (*not* assigning blame to the past). Questions to assist might include: "How would you like to see this go if it happens again?" or "What do you want me or you to do differently if this comes up again?" or "What was the best thing we did to try to make this work out well?" Based on her answers, you could even invite her to practice a respectful response.

When consequences are needed, if your child is old enough (perhaps five or six), you can even help her to "own her growth" by inviting her to think of a consequence. For example, if she angrily threw toys or got sassy about picking up before bed, say,

"I really want to help you learn to clean up and be responsible in more respectful ways." Then ask, "What consequence do you think will help you learn?"

She may or may not have ideas. If not, you can offer, "I have some ideas." Name two or three and ask, "Which of these do you want to try?" Let her choose, and then follow through.

MY RESPONSE

Which of the "rebuilding aspects" is most difficult for me?

- Confess and Apologize: "I can see you are really hurt by what I did. I'm sorry."

- Reconnect: "Even when we have a difficult time, I still really love you."

- Engage and Enlist: "I believe we can figure out some ways to make this go better next time. Let's think about it and talk later today."

What are some key phrases to memorize that could help when I'm recovering from a difficult interaction? What "rebuilding script" could fit a typical challenge?

Here's an example of rebuilding, shared with us by Vicki, mother of eight-year-old Haley.

Haley was at a neighbor's house playing for much of the morning. When I went to get her, she was very upset about leaving. As her objections grew stronger, I grew sterner. She finally relented and begrudgingly followed me outside. On the short walk to our house, Haley kept up her verbal assault and finally kicked me hard in the back of my legs, almost knocking me down.

Haley is a very intense child, but this was new. I was furious, and I let her know it! Our strong reactions to her intensity were backfiring more regularly lately, but my anger kept me from seeing my way clearly out of this one. So I called my husband, told him what happened, and insisted he spank Haley. Josh was shocked and angry at what Haley had done. Because spanking often made matters worse with Haley, he didn't feel good about it, but he spanked her anyway. This threw Haley into a screaming, explosive tirade. We were at a loss. All we knew for sure was that we didn't want this conflict to end this way. As we reflected on what we'd learned in coaching sessions, we decided we needed to rebuild.

So Josh convinced Haley to go for a drive with him, just to connect through some car games and maybe talk a little. I took this time to pray and ponder what had happened and how to rebuild. When Josh and Haley returned, we gathered the family and I shared what I'd learned from God's Word and through prayer regarding my own anger. I also apologized for times when I had reacted in anger to different issues. I shared that with God's help I was going to make an effort to set anger aside in my parenting. I said that I love each of my children very much, and that we're a family that loves each other and wants to encourage and build one another up with gentle words and loving actions. We affirmed that it's good we're a family of grace and forgiveness.

We then asked Haley if she wanted a do-over. We asked her what she could do differently when she was asked to stop doing something she enjoys. She gave her answer, and we practiced responding that way. We clearly established that if she was disrespectful like this again, she would lose the privilege of going to a friend's for a while.

She had an opportunity a few days later to go to a friend's house. We reminded her of the respectful response she had practiced, and when we called her home she did very well. It seems our rebuilding approach opened her to both our love and our teaching about respect. We have a long way to go, but this experience anchored our commitment to connecting and rebuilding well.

KID CONNECTION: The Duct-Tape Approach to Reconciliation

For a fun illustration to help kids understand true reconciliation, use plain paper and a pen or markers. Little kids might use colored or heart-shaped paper; for teens, just talk about the concepts. Kids (or parents) can write down answers to this question: "What strengthens your love for _____ [a certain family member]?" Answers might be that we share our Legos, he's my brother, we giggle after Dad tucks us in at night, we ride the same bus together, etc.

As you fill up the paper, talk about how valuable this love is. Keeping it strong helps us become people who will have loving relationships throughout our lives.

Then ask, "What hurts that relationship sometimes?" Grabbing toys, hitting, calling the person bad names, etc. Say: "When we do selfish or hurtful things to each other, it's like putting a rip in the paper [demonstrate with a rip a few inches long]. If we kept ripping the paper [do another rip] without fixing it, what would happen?" (There's damage; the relationship gets weaker, etc.)

Demonstrate as you describe different ways to fix the rip: "If we just smooth the paper flat and pretend the hurt didn't happen, it doesn't fix the rip. If we just quickly say *sorry*, it's like putting a little clear tape across it—it only helps a little. But putting duct tape the entire way along the rip makes the love stronger than ever. How can we fix our hurts like duct tape?"

Kids love duct tape. Make a rip for each child to fix as they share their best ideas. Write down shared ideas as guidelines for how to resolve conflict.

At a level your kids can understand, talk about how true reconciliation in families reflects the gospel. For young kids:

"Jesus fixed the rip between us and God when He died on the cross, and we believe in Him. Now Jesus helps us fix the rips with people we love."

For older kids: "All this is from God, who reconciled us to himself through Christ and gave us the ministry of reconciliation" (2 Corinthians 5:18). The sin that was between us and God is taken away when we receive Christ's sacrifice for us. This frees us to keep our hearts connected with others as Jesus lives in us and gives us strength. "Anyone who loves God must also love their brother and sister" (1 John 4:21).

Next time you have a conflict, gently help your children calm down until they are ready to truly repair the relationship. Then celebrate the results and how they protected and strengthened the love in their relationship.

CHAPTER 18

Conclusion: A Lasting Fix

Bill and Layna were chasing the American dream. They both had good jobs; they lived in a nice house; they had two elementary-aged daughters and a dog. The kids were doing well in school. They went to church on Sundays and were involved with several additional activities.

However, certain challenges with the girls and a slow-growing negative energy in the household were leaving the couple with an ache in the back of their minds, a fear they somehow were missing God's mark for their family. So they signed up for a Discipline that Connects workshop at their church.

They learned the connective-discipline principles and felt convicted. Afterward, Layna came and confessed, in tears, "We have things completely backwards. We thought we were doing just fine, but we've realized we have no vision and have taken our blessings for granted. This has impacted us deeply. We now feel God's sense of calling and purpose for parenting."

That was ten years ago. While the children and families around them kept going and growing in typical fashion, Bill and Layna's family began to change, little by little, as they did their best to deliver to their kids the messages *You are* safe, *you are* loved, *you are* called and capable, *and you are* responsible. At first glance, the family didn't look a whole lot different. However, a closer look revealed some significant changes.

Instead of taking Disney World vacations or cruises, they went on family mission trips for three years. Sydney, their oldest, started a small business, collecting donated old jeans, sewing them into cute little purses, and selling them to raise money to build homes for Native Americans on reservations. Their youngest, Hannah, started saving allowance money so she could give it away.

While many of their peers started to chase boys at young ages and fell gradually into troubles and pitfalls common to American children, Sydney and Hannah stood apart. They were friends with boys but not obsessed. They didn't use drugs or alcohol. They grew to be faith-filled, self-confident, and responsible.

In ninth grade, where peer relationships tend to be strongest, Sydney recognized that the pressure she was feeling wasn't healthy and felt God was leading her to switch schools. Hannah soon would make the same decision.

Sydney, continuing to grow in her faith, became a light for Christ on her college campus. As she listened to the family stories of struggling college friends, she wrote her parents a letter of deep gratitude for how they'd raised her and for the solid foundation that had led to a life of faith.

This family would say they still have a long way to go. But with Bill and Layna's primary parenting goals firmly in place, Sydney and Hannah are flourishing as young followers of Christ. Their lives were transformed because of their parents' vision and passion to bring grace and truth into one of life's toughest arenas: the discipline of their children. You can join them!

Encouraged, Inspired, and Equipped

We write so that even during the toughest times parents will be encouraged, inspired, and equipped to dive into discipline challenges with a vision to connect with their child's heart. Knowing that how we discipline our children when they misbehave is perhaps our most potent opportunity to demonstrate grace and truth, we extend this invitation: If you haven't done so already, change the primary reason for disciplining your children. Instead of seeking to stop, change, or control behavior, make Discipline that Connects your goal.

With this as your target, you can consider the effectiveness of your discipline through new lenses. Instead of asking, "Did it get my kid to do what I wanted?" or "Did it work?" you can first ask, "Was I safe? Does she know she is loved? Do I have a vision for my son's calling, and do I believe he's capable of learning the wisdom that will prepare him? Does she feel a true sense of responsibility?"

As you make answering these questions with a resounding *Yes!* your primary goal, you have discipline objectives for which you're entirely responsible. If you miss the mark, you can confess, regroup, and rebuild accordingly. If you hit it, you can celebrate God's work. You'll be freed from the power struggles that come from focusing predominately on behavior.

As you lovingly guide your children to take responsibility for their own lives, they can more freely come to understand that God is at once just and compassionate, merciful and true. They will know they have been blessed and are invited into rich relationship with Christ. They'll understand they are called and capable as His handiwork, His workmanship, His masterpiece, "created in Christ Jesus to do good works, which God prepared in advance for [them] to do" (Ephesians 2:10). They will know they're accountable to God alone for their faith and for their choices.

We pray that your kids will see a brighter and more attractive light than they have seen before—and that they will choose to receive what God has to give, and grow in Christ to become a blessing to the world.

Note: Be sure to look at the appendix that follows! In it you'll see dozens of practical applications of the Discipline that Connects approach for common behavior challenges. If you want to dive into these ideas in a fun learning format (great for individuals, couples, or small groups), you can sign up for the Discipline That Connects online course at disciplinethatconnects.org.

MY RESPONSE

- How has my style of discipline demonstrated what's truly important to me?
- What has changed in me through reading this book?
- What stands out to me about drawing my children closer to Christ through the ups and downs of family life?
- Who might I share these thoughts with to encourage and support me?

APPENDIX

Wisdom for Specific Challenges

This appendix applies the Discipline that Connects approach to the most common challenges of family life. For each topic we note practical/biblical perspectives, thoughts about long-term vision, and ideas and stories about how to communicate "You are *safe* with me, you are *loved*, you are *called* and *capable*, and you are *responsible*."

Nothing in the following sections is intended to be "the answer" but merely an idea starter for you to prayerfully adapt as desired to your own family. Think through your own biblical perspective and vision statement for the areas important to you. Let the concepts and suggestions here feed your custom-crafted strategy. Make this content the subject matter for conversations with kids old enough to give input. Keep wondering, learning, and growing—that's how your discipline will connect with your child's heart.

Self-Motivated, Responsible Kids

Messes

Practical/biblical perspectives: The Bible does *not* say cleanliness is next to godliness. However, cleaning up our messes decreases stress, honors those we live with, makes it easier to find things, and helps us welcome others into our home. Perhaps you can help kids think of other good reasons to clean up.

Long-term vision for my children's lives: to develop a value for and habit of cleanliness that will facilitate hospitality and maximize effectiveness in God's calling for them.

"You are SAFE with me": What's going on in me that affects how I engage with my child?

Ponder these questions as you seek to become safer with regard to your kids' messes:

- Am I taking their messes personally/feeling taken for granted?
- Am I worried I'm raising a future slob?
- Am I unloading frustration that's actually about a messy spouse or my own cleanliness shortcomings?
- Do I dislike cleaning but somehow am expecting my kids to have a different attitude?

"You are LOVED": How can I connect or empathize with my child?

We can join our kids in cleaning or chores, aiming to build connection and teamwork. After all, "Two people are better off than one, for they can help each other succeed" (Ecclesiastes 4:9 NLT). Empathize by letting them know you understand feeling overwhelmed by a task, and share an example.

One day I (Lynne) was trying to think of a new consequence for messes, a real zinger that would solve the problem once and for all (as if there's such a thing!). But I dared to pray, "Lord, what would you do if they were your kids?" And the phrase came into my mind, "I'd clean with them and enjoy the results." My immediate tongue-in-cheek response was, "Rats, you would, wouldn't you!" I made it a goal to shift from stern commander to encouraging co-worker, and the kids became far more responsive. When we make cleanup fun and then gradually fade our help over time, children will be more likely to enjoy and value the endeavor.

"You are CALLED and CAPABLE": How might I acknowledge and redirect a gift gone awry?

Messy kids usually have good traits that contribute to messiness. They may be relaxed (not anxious about order), creative, spontaneous, or distracted by other interests. Find ways to validate and incorporate those gifts. For example, capitalize on a playful nature by saying, "You're a fun-loving kid! Want to clean up quickly before you move on to something you consider more fun, or do you want to figure out how to make the cleaning fun?"

How might I nurture capability in my child?

Kids often resist cleaning when they are overwhelmed. Help your child break down the job into whatever size he can manage. Designate a specific, manageable area (e.g., put a circle of string around a section of mess) and have him come find you as soon as it's done. Help him to feel good about his accomplishment; offer a little help as needed to keep up momentum. Try to call it quits before he gets distracted or discouraged so that he finishes feeling successful. Even if it's a small success, it will build more over time.

Eventually kids themselves can break down the task or figure out what else they need to help them finish (music, a snack while they work, periodic parent visits, etc.). Ask, "What do you need so you can be successful with this?" To engage their problem-solving and increase their ownership, bring them with you to select the supplies needed to make the task easier and more rewarding.

It's helpful to build cleaning into a routine by letting go of our efficiency goals and taking the time needed with younger kids. Kari, the single mom who lived with us, would tidy the toy area with Eli every evening before they came up to eat. It was second nature, there were no arguments, and since the mess didn't accumulate, cleanup wasn't overwhelming. One time, when Eli was two, Jim went down to say dinner was ready and Eli started putting toys away on his own.

"You are RESPONSIBLE": What consequence best teaches my child responsibility for his actions?

Do-over/make it right: What normally prompts kids to clean up is their parents' reminder. Want to work yourself out of a job? If a child drops an item in a common area, have her practice putting it away several times, starting from what she was doing *before* she dropped it. This whole-sequence do-over helps her practice a neatness routine to gradually learn independence. For example: "Put your jacket back on, please, walk through the front door again, and this time hang it on the hook. Tomorrow, if you forget, you can practice two times." Then encourage her with the natural benefits of her responsibility: "Now it won't get dirty, and you've learned a good habit!"

One "make it right" consequence we used flowed from our vision to maintain a quickly hospitable home. We knew the kids would need the skill of noticing and spontaneously cleaning messes. If they left a mess in a shared area, the consequence was to find and take care of a certain number of things that needed putting away or cleaning and then report back to the parent. This gave us an opportunity to affirm and value their noticing and their diligence.

Lose the privilege/item: When children misuse or don't clean up their own things or things they're privileged to use, they lose the privilege of using them. If toys, you can take them away by calmly saying, "You didn't take responsibility to clean up your toys, so you have lost them." Set a time frame as well as clear expectations about what he must do to get the toys back. For instance, "You can get these back once you show you can take care of your other toys by cleaning up after yourself well for the next two days."

If they complain, validate their feelings: "It's hard to lose your favorite things, isn't it? Can you tell me what you need to do to get the toys back?"

Other ideas: Helen, the mom of twins, valued a neat home. Every night she'd tour the house, pick up any left-out kid stuff, and put it in a box to be ransomed the next day with a quarter from their allowance. She did this calmly and kindly. The twins often scrambled to clean up just before bedtime, and gradually they made a habit of putting things away.

If a child just can't clean up after herself, then store most of the toys away, and work with fewer toys. Help her learn to organize what's still available to her. She can earn other toys back incrementally by keeping the play area clean.

Noah loved Legos, and Gramma loved giving him Legos! In our house, they were everywhere. They often carpeted the playroom like tiny landmines prepped to injure any unwary barefoot adult. After perpetually struggling with the issue, I (Lynne) gave Noah the option to pack them away for quite a while or to organize them. We set aside some windows of time, and I guided him as he developed a system of categories, using containers with little drawers and labels. As we sorted, he realized he had more than he needed, so he gave away some and sold some. His new scheme helped him find pieces he wanted and design even cooler creations, so he was eager to maintain it.

Chores

Practical/biblical perspectives: In a family, we all need each other. We're a team, sharing in the household's responsibilities. Each child has a special contribution to make to the body of Christ and to whatever groups to which she belongs, including her family. When all contribute, all benefit. One child's service to the family blesses other family members.

Long-term vision for my children's lives: to learn to work diligently and joyfully as part of a team for the common good, preparing for faithful service in the body of Christ. (See Colossians 3:23.)

"You are SAFE with me": What's going on in me that affects how I engage with my child?

Ponder these questions as you seek to become safer regarding your kids' tasks:

- Is my family's pace of life so intense that expecting growth in cleanliness and responsibility routines isn't realistic?
- Do I feel resentful and alone in taking care of the house?
- Do I enable a lack of responsibility because it's easier to do things myself than to guide others to follow through?
- Am I nagging more than I'm encouraging or affirming?
- What might I do to develop a more peaceful and affirming approach to chores?

"You are LOVED": How can I connect or empathize with my child?

If one or more of my kids has a short attention span or struggles to focus on routine tasks, how can I best help him learn to do the chores? How can we enjoy chore time together? If my kids complain about and avoid chores, an essential part of the solution is to nurture a culture of joyful teamwork.

This was graphically illustrated in our interactions with two different moms. Michelle had been required to do chores when she was young and faced strong consequences if she protested or refused. She shared her discouragement about the impact of this with Lynne over coffee. She generally dislikes housework now and quickly feels resentful and critical if she thinks she might be doing more than her share.

A few days later we joined our friend Jodi at her cabin. After joyfully welcoming us, she refused to let us put fresh sheets on our bed: "Oh, no. You have no idea how fast Gaby and I are at this!" Her twelve-year-old grinned—she knew the drill. The two of them whisked off the old sheets and had the new ones on in no time, laughing about their amazing speed and skill.

Jodi had been widowed with young children, but she nurtured joy in teamwork as a family, even to the extent of getting three used lawnmowers so she, Gaby, and her son, Patrick, could all mow the cabin's large lawn at the same time. Their motto is, "If we all work together, we'll get it done in no time!" She never has need for discipline or consequences for avoiding chores; each of the kids serves eagerly and diligently.

"You are CALLED and CAPABLE": How might I acknowledge and redirect a gift gone awry?

Some misdirected gifts regarding chores struggles are similar to those of messy kids—creativity, spontaneity, or distraction by other loved interests.

Others that feed resistance to chores can be a strong will, determination, and leadership. By nature, these intense kids have difficulty following a plan in which they've been given no input. In one family we coached, the teenagers felt such a lack of ownership in the list of chores presented to them, they took it out to the garage and shot it full of BB gun holes. The parents restructured by inviting one of the older children to lead and another to take notes at their next family meeting, and the family tone was much more positive and helpful.

Let your strong-willed child put that leadership to good use. "I love that you've got strong ideas about stuff. What are your ideas about this question: What would a reality show camera see in our home if no one served anyone else?" Have some fun imagining and describing it. "What would the camera see if we worked well as a team?" "How do we want our family to be?"

How might I nurture capability in my child?

Strong-willed or not, when children have choices and input into how chores are distributed, their engagement and cooperation increase immensely. Chuck and Korrine's family had a weekly Sunday-night time to eat a special meal, have fun together, and brainstorm any challenges, including chores.

We made a list of all the things that needed doing to make sure the family would run in a way that everyone got at least some of the things they thought were important. Laundry, dishes, and cleaning rooms were important for Mom and Dad. Playdates, eating, and free time were the important kid issues. Attendance of these meetings wasn't required, but since decisions applied to everyone, kids chose to come and give their input. We'd reevaluate weekly until we found something that worked for everyone.

At one meeting it was brought up that the kids were not putting dirty laundry where it needed to be when it was supposed to be there. We asked what ought to be done about this, and several of the kids had ideas. After hearing them all, the family agreed that for one week there would be a warning ten minutes before the laundry deadline. After that week, whoever was late needed to fold the laundry for the rest of the family. This rapidly solved the problem and eliminated nagging and lecturing.

Family meetings give kids healthy ownership in issues as well as practice at compromising and problem-solving. Sometimes they even develop their own consequences. (For information regarding family meetings, see disciplinethatconnects.org/links.)

Equip children with clear training. I (Lynne) had been frustrated by ten-year-old Noah's lack of thoroughness and seemingly poor efforts in cleaning the bathroom. Then one day it dawned on me: I was expecting him to just know how to do it without ever actually breaking it down for him. So we started over and cleaned together while I guided him in understanding and writing a step-by-step checklist of tasks that he taped inside the cupboard. He felt invested instead of ordered around, and he became a faithful bathroom cleaner.

Once a child shows he knows how to clean, engage his problem-solving by challenging him to figure out how to do it faster without sacrificing quality.

Enlist ownership of results. When you've given a child a task, ask, "How will you know you've done a good job?" Invite her to be as specific as possible in describing what a good job will look like. If the description does not meet your expectations, graciously clarify what you expect.

When Noah was sixteen, we paid him to do a few handyman jobs around the house—almost but not quite worthy of hiring a professional to do. Noah's workmanship was haphazard, and our impulse was to point out deficiencies in his effort and pay a reduced wage as a consequence. But we wanted him to be more thoughtful about his expectations for himself. So Lynne said, "Looks like you've gotten most of today's list done. I want you to evaluate how it went. What do you think are the characteristics of a diligent worker? What would an employer be looking for in someone who does a really good job?"

He answered, "Someone who works efficiently and doesn't get distracted," then continued, "and does careful, high-quality work."

"Those are good ones," Lynne said, adding, "and probably doing thorough cleanup after a job is done. So on a scale of 0 to 10—worst job possible to best job possible—how do you think you did?"

On each characteristic he rated himself about how we would have rated, averaging about a five. We told him the "salary range" we'd considered and said we would pay what he honestly thought he deserved based on the quality of his work. He chose an amount slightly below what we were thinking.

A few days later we gave him another list of jobs. This time he recorded work times for each job far more accurately. He told us he worked pretty hard and got distracted only once to check emails. He rated his work a six or seven and asked for a wage $1 per hour higher than for his first list. He seemed to feel much better about his job performance on this second try.

Connect well at transitions to a chore. When a child is engaged in a favorite activity, it's difficult to transition into chores—the more fun the activity and the tougher the chore, the more overwhelming. Alter your daily routine to avoid this problem, or consider what can be done to ease the transition. For example, connect with a brief shoulder rub while you explain the chore, or offer a quick snack before the kids get started. You can even say, "It's time to get the dishes loaded now. What will help you get started?"

"You are RESPONSIBLE": What consequence best teaches my child responsibility for her actions?

Do-over/make it right: If kids don't follow through on a chore, a logical consequence is, "Because you didn't complete the last one as expected, you'll have your usual chore and also this other one as an extra chance to practice responsibility." I can remind my children that learning responsibility is an important part of doing what they were built to do.

Lose the privilege: Of course, it's reasonable to withhold immediate general privileges if tasks aren't completed. "You may go outside *after* your chores are done." Loss-of-privilege consequences directly related to the chore are even more effective: "It seems your phone distracted you a lot today. It will be off-limits tomorrow until you contribute responsibly to household duties" or "Since you didn't do your part to clean the dishes, you'll be responsible to take care of your own meal and cleanup tomorrow night" or "Since you left your laundry all over the couch, I picked it up; you'll get it back when you show responsibility for your other chores."

Other ideas: Chores come before privileges. Mason, age ten, was perfectly capable of feeding the dog but always procrastinated. Either his mom, Rachel, badgered him into doing it or got so fed up with his dramatic excuses that it was easier for her to feed the poor pooch. She made a plan to clearly affirm teamwork was essential to keep the household running smoothly; they all had chores before dinner. Hers was fixing the meal, his was feeding the dog, and his sister's was emptying the trash. Each person could eat when that job was done. Rachel lightheartedly quoted, "'The one who is unwilling to work shall not eat'" (2 Thessalonians 3:10). Mason begged and argued to do his chore after dinner, but Rachel calmly stood her ground and the problem was solved. And once into the routine, Mason felt good about being responsible.

Chore systems: You can search online for a chore chart that is well-suited to your family. We recommend one that uses pictorial descriptions; even kids who can read do better with pictures. And it helps kids stay on track if they can physically remove the chores they have completed from their list.

Poor Listening and Follow-Through

The listening issue can represent a real challenge. Sometimes kids hear what we say and choose not to do it—this is ignoring, which usually is about defiance (addressed in section C). Sometimes they hear what we say and intend to do it but get distracted by something more fun—this is distractibility. Sometimes kids have poor auditory processing and truly do not understand what's expected of them. Other kids simply become extremely focused on a visual task.

Many parents treat distractibility and poor listening as defiance. At best this is unhelpful, and at worst it's hurtful; children who struggle to listen and follow through aren't necessarily defiant. Treating them as if they are tends to discourage them and form beliefs that they're actually bad kids. Children who believe that usually act it out.

While it may be hard to learn whether kids are ignoring, listening and forgetting, or not hearing or understanding, the key to discerning is to work with distractibility and listening issues first. If you work through the following ideas and the kids still don't follow through, it might be a defiance issue.

Practical/biblical perspectives: Careful listening honors the speaker and is a helpful skill for school, work, and family. "Everyone should be quick to listen, slow to speak and slow to become angry" (James 1:19).

Long-term vision for my children's lives: to be thoughtfully responsive to the words of others, whether related to tasks, ideas, or emotions.

"You are SAFE with me": What's going on in me that affects how I engage with my child?

Questions to consider:

- Am I modeling the listening I want from my children?
- What would my kids say about me as a listener?
- Do I make it hard for them to really listen because I'm too stressed to communicate clearly and respectfully?
- Do I feel invalidated or like a failure when my kids don't listen?

As a homeschooling mom of teenagers, Sharon gave her children many instructions and requests and often felt frustrated and disrespected in this role. After going through our class, she began getting in touch with some emotions under the surface of her mom/child interactions. She realized that one reason it was hard to get kids to listen and respond was that she didn't feel worth listening to. She saw that much of what she said was delivered with shame, and that she lacked the confidence needed to enlist good listening.

Sharon started on a path of learning God's value of her, which significantly improved her confidence, her relationship with her children, and her ability to confidently give instructions that more effectively enlisted them.

"You are LOVED": How can I connect or empathize with my child?

Help the child struggling to follow through on chores with simple statements of compassion or empathy: "It seems you really want to keep playing." "This is pretty hard, isn't it?" "I bet you'd rather be doing something more enjoyable right now." Said with sincerity, these show kids that you understand them, possibly opening the door to further encouragement or constructive conversation. Then the instructions you want your child to hear will fall on much more fertile soil. This helps kids to stay engaged and also prepares parents to respond more calmly and respectfully if they don't.

"You are CALLED and CAPABLE": How might I acknowledge and redirect a gift gone awry?

A "gift gone awry" for kids with poor listening is often a high-intensity focus on a preferred activity. Stopping to savor and comment on that interest honors God's gifting in them. "Peter, you sure love building stuff. I can see you've really worked hard on this. What a creative spaceship!" This helps my child feel valued before I ask him to focus on something I value.

In addition, if Peter is the kind of kid whose strong will makes following instructions difficult, I can encourage the honoring use of that strong will by changing a command into a question that shows his capability: "What needs to happen now, before dinner? I'll bet you can figure it out."

How might I nurture capability in my child?

Consider: What is the intensity of attention I give my child when she listens? How does that compare to my intensity when she doesn't? Typical parenting tends to focus on correcting non-listening, which feeds a child's self-perception (identity) of "poor listener." Instead I can proactively build her identity as a good listener. One way to build that identity *and* listening skills is to play games like Simon Says or hide objects around the house and give her verbal clues to find them. The next time I give a task request, I can remind her of her success at listening during the games.

Once I've given a warm but clear instruction, asking her to repeat it back to me helps build her habit of good listening. Then I have an opportunity to affirm her for listening well and hold her accountable to follow through.

Family meals and conflict resolution situations are also opportunities to proactively develop thoughtful listening. (See appendix sections B and C for details.)

"You are RESPONSIBLE": What consequence best teaches my child responsibility for her actions?

Do-over/make it right: When a child doesn't follow instructions, I can ask him to repeat the forgotten or disregarded instruction a certain number of times (maybe one for each finger), which helps ingrain the task in his mind, or even ask him to keep saying it aloud till it's completed. I can also have him write down whatever task(s) he'd been told to do, or draw a quick picture of it that will remind him. This puts the focus on learning a strategy for being responsible rather than on making him feel bad. If he's still struggling, I can problem-solve with him a unique strategy to help him stay on track—maybe making up simple songs for regular sequences of tasks.

I can also use practice as a consequence for poor listening: "Now you get an extra chance to practice listening carefully. Do five jumping jacks and then put the crayons away." Or, "Put all the clean forks into the silverware drawer, and then the spoons." Then, "Can you repeat what I asked?" When he can do so, "Nice job listening!"

Another make-it-right option is to explain that it takes extra time to follow up with a child who hasn't listened well. Then I can ask her to help me complete one of my tasks or chores to make up for that time.

Lose the privilege: If there's an activity/item (screen time, toy, phone, etc.) that often hampers listening and following through, it can be a privilege that's lost until she can demonstrate growth toward better listening habits.

Homework and Grades

Practical/biblical perspectives: Education is a privilege that deserves our passion and diligence. Good work habits with homework pave the way for future opportunities and practice the diligence children will need to "do [the] good works . . . God prepared in advance for us to do" (Ephesians 2:10).

Long-term vision for my children's lives: curiosity and a love for learning that lasts a lifetime; a sense of responsibility for their lives that helps kids persevere through difficulties.

"You are SAFE with me": What's going on in me that affects how I engage with my child?

Questions to consider:

- What shame might I have about my own school performance?

- To what extent am I getting my value from my child's achievement?
- Do I have anxiety about his future academic or work success?
- Are any of these factors making me more intense and reactive about my child's homework?

"You are LOVED*": How can I connect or empathize with my child?*

Consider Mitch and Andy's math-homework story from chapter 7. Ask yourself, "What's my attitude when dealing with homework issues? Is my child convinced that I truly love her no matter what her grades are? If not, what can I do to remedy that?"

One autumn there was huge variation in our children's report cards. Bethany's and Noah's were of the "Ya make me proud, kid" variety, while Daniel got quite a "variety" of grades. I (Lynne) was ready to have a firm talk with him about improving the low ones. It probably would have been about as productive as most of my other "firm talks" (aka lectures).

Jim wisely recognized the disparity in grades as a great opportunity to communicate to all three children that our love for them is unrelated to their success. We got them together and announced, "We're having a Report Card Party to celebrate the fact that we love each of you absolutely unrelated to your grades or success!" They were a little surprised but delighted. We had a special dinner and then ran around the house like loonies, whooping and hollering and firing Nerf guns at each other. Popcorn and a game rounded out the evening. We all had a blast, and of course the child with the lowest grades seemed to have the most fun.

The next day we sat down with Daniel and asked him how he felt about his grades, starting with his strong subjects. When we got to the lower grades, he felt safe to express his discouragement and join us in making a plan to improve them. He learned two big lessons: first, that *he* was responsible for his grades, and second—and far more important—that our love for him is rock solid, not fluctuating with his performance. This helped him cling more tightly to God's unconditional love. More than a decade later he said, "Sometimes when I fail at something and get really discouraged, I remember, 'There's a Popcorn Party of Grace for this.'"

"You are CALLED AND CAPABLE": How might I acknowledge and redirect a gift gone awry?

Kids who aren't motivated to complete assignments may be independent thinkers about what's really important or relevant for them. Honor that as a potentially good trait, especially when combined with a little wisdom. Savvy adults learn to focus energy in support of their values and reduce effort toward unimportant or distracting tasks. Many highly successful people didn't do well in school, including Bill Gates, Steve Jobs, Keira Knightley, Frank Lloyd Wright, Anne Bancroft, Tom Hanks, and James Cameron. Their diligence and passion about what *was* important to them enabled them to soar. Lots of not-so-famous people have done okay in life without stellar grades. I (Jim) got through high school and college by doing well in classes of high interest to me, and not so well in those that seemed insignificant (code for "didn't hold my attention"). Focusing fully on all my classes was far too stressful.

Instead of nagging your child to do his best at every class, tap into his independent thinking to help him identify what matters to him and what his steps might be to achieve it. Then ask questions like, "What kind of grades will support what's important to you? How much work will that take? What help can we give?" Enlist a mentor in his area of interest to give input if needed.

Another idea to help an unmotivated child is to work together to make a different "report card." Together, make a list of essential character traits that will help her live out who she was created to be: e.g., perseverance, creativity, relational skills, integrity, diligence, compassion. Highlight strengths or progress you see; brainstorm how to strengthen those qualities even further.

How might I nurture capability in my child?

Children trying to do homework in a busy, noisy household is a setup for frustration and distraction. Quitting and complaining often get more parental attention (which acts as a fertilizer) than working hard. So sit across the table from your child in a quiet environment and do your own "homework"—read, work on bills, etc. Your modeling is apt to focus and calm her, and you can give a quiet comment or thumbs-up as you notice her working hard.

Children often are fatigued and unfocused by homework time. Help your child figure out what his body and brain need to prep for the task. Focus improves with simple adjustments like vigorous physical activity beforehand, or sitting on an exercise ball for constant gentle movement while studying. Provide a sport bottle to hydrate with, or chewing gum or a crunchy snack. Plan short movement breaks to keep energy up—an around-the-house jog, jumping jacks, swinging, etc. (For more info about helping your child regulate his energy level, go to alertprogram .com or zonesofregulation.com.)

"You are RESPONSIBLE": What consequence best teaches my child responsibility for her actions?

We have seen many grade-control efforts backfire. Kids inherently know, "These are *my* grades—why are my parents acting as if they're theirs?" When we put more energy into kids keeping up grades than they do, they tend to either rebel to keep a sense of control, or comply without internal motivation. Learning to support them to take responsibility in this realm can be tricky, because this is one of few discipline areas where there are regular reports and progress updates. The ultimate aim is to have a child hold up her report card and say, "I am fully responsible for these grades." Parents play a significant role on the road to this goal. Walking the tightrope between too much and not enough engagement requires skill.

Brandon, the oldest child of a highly successful doctor, felt a lot of pressure from his parents about homework and grades. Brad and Rochelle nagged him to get homework done and punished him for low grades (mostly Cs and Ds) by eliminating phone privileges. Infuriated, he "punished" them by arguing and manipulating incessantly and getting even lower grades. In his mind, if he got good grades, they would win. They were in a tailspin, and the three of them came in for some coaching.

The process started by helping Brad and Rochelle get to where they could let their son's grades be *his* responsibility and not theirs. As we began to discuss some of the reasons for Brandon's difficulty with focus and organization, Brad realized he'd had similar issues as a kid. His empathy definitely encouraged his son.

We then focused on family strengths: What was going well in their relationship? What did helpful encouragement for him look like? In what areas was Brandon working hard? How could his strengths in those areas help his homework challenges? We also worked together to develop strategies for organization and regulating his energy level while studying. Brandon agreed to check grades online once a week and let his parents know if he needed any help. He decided to pursue assessment and help for possible ADHD issues.

Because Brandon felt understood and supported, he was able to admit that he'd been discouraged about his grades and truly did want to do better. I asked about his goals for his next report card and he said confidently, "Bs." His mom immediately chimed in, "Don't you think you could get an A in music or art?" I reminded her that it was important for him to own his grades and that if he achieved his goal, he just might feel encouraged to shoot a little higher. She agreed that Bs were a good goal, and the family implemented their plan. Brandon's next report card was his best ever, averaging right around a B.

This doesn't mean parents totally give up expectations about homework and grades. Hard work earns privileges. It's quite reasonable to have a family rule about responsibility before privileges, like "No screen time before chores or homework." If a child consistently gets glued to a screen while "forgetting" homework, parents can reserve screen activities for weekends.

Sometimes the problem with homework is getting it done; sometimes it's turning it in. Working with teachers can be critical to helping kids learn to take responsibility. Chuck and Korrine monitored but didn't try to control their daughter's school performance. They determined as much as possible to let her own the problem and experience the pain from her actions. Adrianne was a delightful but scattered child who needed daily reminders to bring her backpack to school. One morning, after explaining to her that she was very capable of remembering her backpack and would no longer get reminders, they let her race down to the bus without it. Even though he knew it was the right strategy, Chuck had a knot in his stomach as he watched his daughter go.

The teacher called and was unsupportive of this approach—missing assignments were a hassle and essentially made a student's irresponsibility the teacher's problem. She insinuated it was the parents' responsibility to make sure children brought their backpacks. Chuck empathized but said, "How could we make this Adrianne's problem?" Together they agreed that when she forgot her backpack, she'd be held in from recess to complete assignments due that day. This was necessary only a couple times; she began to bring her backpack regularly. Adrianne learned that she, not her parents or teacher, was responsible for her schoolwork.

Screen Time

Most parents have frustrations with their kids' interaction with technology (electronic games, social media, TV, texting, etc.). Some condemn the activities, "pulling the plug" or policing their use and butting heads regularly on the matter. Others have given up and allowed their youngster free rein.

Practical/biblical perspectives: While a Bible word search for *technology* comes up empty, Scripture gives wisdom about making decisions, particularly about pleasurable activities that can be addictive. Paul quoted the boasting of the pleasure-seeking Corinthians ("Everything is permissible!") and wisely responded. They'd misinterpreted their freedom in Christ to mean they could do whatever they pleased—not unlike dealing with a glued-to-screen child who essentially says, "Don't interfere with my fun. I can do what I want."

Paul addressed a question we might ask: "What's the quality of my activity, and is it truly good for me?" He answered the statement, "I have the right to do anything" with "but not everything is beneficial" and "I will not be mastered by anything" (1 Corinthians 6:12). What we dwell upon impacts us, and we're called to focus on what's true, pure, and admirable. (See Philippians 4:8.) Years after we clashed with Daniel about video games, he looked back on those days and reflected, "Single-player games were a soul drain. When you guys would get me off the computer, it took a while for real life to regain its relevance."

"I will not be mastered by [addicted to] anything" poses the question, "Am I in control of my screen time, or is it controlling me?" We can't expect a child to see or readily admit her screen time is out of control. Many times, though, we've seen kids feel much better about themselves after their parents have worked in positive ways to bring their screen use to a healthier level.

Long-term vision for my children's lives: to have a significant vision for three-dimensional life in God's kingdom and the wisdom to use technology to support, not derail, that vision.

"You are SAFE with me": What's going on in me that affects how I engage with my child?

Technology is a key area for getting in touch with my own anxieties. Do I feel out of control because I don't know enough about my child's show, game, site, or text content? Do I have shame about my own technology use that prevents me from engaging wisely? Am I fearful that my child is getting addicted or engagimg in harmful activities? Do I feel overwhelmed by the danger that's just a click away?

There is a lot to be concerned about related to kids' technology use. It has tremendous power to lure them into experiences they are not prepared to handle. If we abandon them in it, they're almost sure to get hurt.

But if it's fear that drives my interaction, it will probably do more harm than good. Overwhelmed, fear-driven parents often have critical, black-and-white judgments that draw fighting lines in the sand right from the start. Research actually has shown that moderate amounts (up to two hours a day) of nonviolent, nonsexual screen time can be beneficial for social, academic, and/or coordination skills.

Let's learn to come alongside our kids with wisdom, grace, and safety, and keep an eye out for the opportunities inherent in technology. The older a child is, the more asking curious questions combined with a problem-solving approach should help to build this safety.

"You are LOVED": How can I connect or empathize with my child?

Discipline that Connects finds ways to use current technology as one way of staying in touch with—even encouraging—our kids. They're usually pretty easy to approach (even defensive kids will let us near when nose-deep in their screen). Take advantage; just be with him while he plays, and say, "I'm going to hang with you awhile." Ask curious, safe questions to find out what he really likes about his technology and how he thinks it's good for him. Have him show you his favorite parts and see if you could join in the activity with him. Observe and make a list of what's cool about it or what he learns from it. This puts you in the role of learner, not critic, and lowers his defenses.

In the early days of texting and social networking, I (Jim) coached a dad who believed his teen was out of control. "She sends at least a hundred texts a day," he said, irate about what he called her addiction. "And that's just the start—she spends at least two hours a day on Facebook and 'talks' to people she doesn't even know. Or worse, to people faking an identity just to talk to her! She and I have no lines of communication at all."

With a harsh and condescending tone, he added, "She doesn't know how to communicate the good old-fashioned way."

I empathized with him about how challenging that can be but encouraged him to view this not as a problem to fix but as an opportunity to explore. Then I asked, "So what would be the chance she'd communicate with you through text messaging?"

"I don't know how to text message," he said.

"Know anyone who might teach you?"

"Really?! Do you think she'd teach me?" His face lit up; he hadn't considered this and was plainly hopeful.

"I don't know. But you could ask."

Two weeks later I talked with him again. He told this story:

> It was so cool. My daughter taught me to text. We had fun together for the first time in a long time. Then we went to a school basketball game together. She ditched me ASAP, but I kept my eye on her and her pack of friends. I texted her, "I luv u." She didn't respond. I tried again. "Tx for teaching me 2 text." Still there was no response. I was tempted to get angry, but I remembered that you said it would likely take persistence to truly connect with her. Then I got a surprise. When I went up to the concession stand, my daughter sent her first text of the night: "Where r u?" She'd been watching me—actually paying attention. I texted back, "It's a secret." We had fun playing a subtle game of hide-and-seek that allowed her to stay with her friends. The drive home was pleasant, and things have been much better ever since, just because I took away my judgment and joined in her way of communicating. The coolest thing is that we actually talk voice to voice again too. I think I'm learning not to be so judgmental of everything she does, and she feels safer talking to me. Now I text her when I think of her. I just send simple things, not judging things or prying into her life.

There is no quick fix for troubled relationships, and parents can still address the complex negative potentials of technology. Even so, letting go of "technology judgment" can create opportunities to begin to reconnect.

"You are CALLED and CAPABLE": How might I acknowledge and redirect a gift gone awry?

As you connect with your kids about technology, you can begin to realize what they love about it. Then affirm and honor those passions and gifts by giving them an even more exciting expression. One dad of teenage boys shared what he learned:

> Unplug computer games and just do real life with your kids! If they want to race cars, buy remote control cars or build some makeshift cars and go race for real. If they want to shoot stuff, get a bag of rubber bands or some airsoft guns and go shoot stuff for real. If they want to golf or bowl on a console game, then take them golfing or bowling for real. Do whatever you can to give them real-life experiences in these things. Only then will they learn to conduct themselves in real life!

How might I nurture capability in my child?

We laid down the law with our strong-willed teenager in an escalating screen-time conflict; Daniel continued defying us. We installed a lock on the computer room door; he deftly broke into the office after school, played his favorite game, relocked the door, and smugly told us about it when we got home. This approach was going nowhere. We were stuck.

Then we got serious about forming a vision for this issue in our family, and we found it in Ephesians 2:10: "We are God's handiwork, created in Christ Jesus to do good works [in His real-life, three-dimensional kingdom], which God prepared in advance for us to do."

We connected with Daniel and expressed sincere conviction that we did not want his potential to walk in God's calling limited by excessive or unhealthy screen use. We were willing to make sacrifices to help him develop his real-life gifts that would enable him to bless others.

We shared many discussions about balancing screen time with creative alternatives that were a fit for his unique bent. He gradually saw screen time as "dessert for the brain" and realized he needed a healthy real-world diet of varied activities in order to thrive.

For our vision we paid the price both literally and figuratively, getting Daniel tools like a used camcorder, a digital camera, tree-fort supplies, and golf lessons. These provided the real-life, 3D fulfillment of adventure, creativity, and conquest he'd been seeking in computer games. They also provided opportunities to bless others. He took free family portraits for a single mom. He organized groups of kids to make videos, giving lead roles to those who were insecure or struggling. He built forts for younger kids who admired his three-level "mansion in the maples."

Each activity required parent involvement—for instance, Lynne helped with video props and logistics, and Jim worked alongside on the tree fort and coached the golf team—but all was well worth it. Our engagement said, *"Your life is well worth my time and effort!"*

Research shows that children who truly connect with God's love and are involved in serving others are at much lower risk for unhealthy behaviors.[1] They need persistent guidance and a positive focus on developing purposeful, alternative interests that fit their unique gifting. When children realize we're on their side and want to help them become all they can be, they are much more likely to work with instead of against us. What's the *yes* behind your *no*?

This perspective has been helpful for numerous families with technology challenges. For the complete story of the insightful, connective approach that changed the life of a Minecraft-obsessed fourteen-year-old, as well as other screen time resources, go to disciplinethatconnects.org/links.

"You are RESPONSIBLE": What consequence best teaches my child responsibility for his actions?

Unlike the rest of our world, screens don't reflect but rather emit light. This difference—a big issue for kids' sensitive, developing brains—can make transition from a captivating screen back into real life almost torturous. Kids typically ignore, ignore, ignore our escalating requests and then either explode or sullenly comply. In neither case have we helped them learn self-control.

Kids need clear expectations and the "exit strategy" ahead of time. For example: "I'll give you a five-minute warning and set the timer. I will ask for eye contact from you confirming that you understand and will get yourself off the computer within that time. When the timer goes off I'll come in; if the computer is turned off, great, you'll have earned the privilege of all your time tomorrow! If you're still on, I will shut down the screen, and you will have twenty minutes less tomorrow. Is this clear?" Ask her to repeat the expectation.

If the expectation isn't followed, follow through. If the problem persists the next day, it's fully reasonable to remove the privilege altogether the next day. Be sure to work at administering the consequence calmly and firmly, without forgetting to convey, "You are loved" and "You are called and capable" (i.e., "I believe you can learn this").

● ● ●

Jason was a typical third-grader who manipulated and intimidated his overwhelmed single mom, Lynette, into way too much access to computers and TV. Most of his screen time ended with howls of protest at turning it off. Through some coaching, Lynette started thinking about the challenge at a deeper level and made a new plan for constructive discipline.

She told Jason that all this screen time was keeping him from developing the great potential he had and that it was important to her to help him develop it. She gave him some ownership in deciding what hours he could have screen time and what hours were off limits. For him to earn the privilege of each session he had to do two things:

1. Creatively use his time in between screen sessions (no whining about being bored). Together they developed ideas for creative or athletic activities and obtained the needed supplies.

2. Exit respectfully from the previous session. When it was almost time to get off, Lynette would give a five-minute advance notice and then return at that time to calmly offer the choice: "You can argue and stall and lose your next session, or you can get off quickly and respectfully and keep your next screen time. Which would you like to do?"

It took a couple of sessions, but Jason quickly learned that his mom was determined and would follow through. Of course, when he exited quickly, Lynette encouraged him with how helpful his wise choice was to both of them. She made more of an effort to connect with him and sometimes played his game with him. Eventually he felt pretty good about all this and even told his teacher how well he was doing with his computer use.

Screen conflicts can get even more intense when there's inappropriate content involved. Both parents and kids feel anxious, ashamed, and defensive. When this is the case, avoid any statement that communicates, "We're angry at you, and we're going to stop this behavior" or "How could you do this?" Kids need parents to convey, "We love you. We understand that this is a difficult issue at your age. We want to work with you toward some good, long-term solutions. It's important to us that the screens we provide our family are safe." Though far from easy, this approach keeps the nonnegotiable of safe Internet use in place without a volatile or controlling tone.

SECTION B

Peaceful Daily Routines

Mornings

Practical/biblical perspectives: How we start our mornings as a family often sets the day's tone. Being aware of God's love and our love for each other in the morning helps us all to be encouraged and responsible as we get ready to face our day. "The LORD's lovingkindnesses indeed never cease, for His compassions never fail. They are new every morning; great is Your faithfulness" (Lamentations 3:22–23 NASB).

Long-term vision for my children's lives: to develop the lifelong habits, values, and faith to start their day responsibly and joyfully.

"You are SAFE with me": What's going on in me that affects how I engage with my child?

Consider:

- What feelings and expectations do I have about mornings with my children?
- Do I feel responsible for every aspect of getting them ready to go?

237

• Do I begin each day by seeking God's mercies for our family? Or, do I let my stress level set the day's tone? "C'mon, hustle!"

"You are LOVED": How can I connect or empathize with my child?

Many families who have challenges with morning routines benefit significantly from a little creative connection with their kids before voicing any "time to get moving!" prods. This can last from a few seconds to a few minutes and may be anything a child enjoys, like snuggling time, a back rub, a short story or joke, or a quick hug. One dad said, "I learned that if I could get my son laughing, everything went so much better."

David had particular difficulty helping his son Jack take responsibility to get out of bed and be ready for school on time. The usual drill of alarm clock, nag, nag, nag, was leading to more power struggles and missed buses. David decided *he* would become the alarm clock. He made sure to stay light and pleasant as he quietly sang to wake his son. Once Jack began to stir, David began to rub his shoulder gently. Soon Jack was awake enough and David tickled him, which led to a pleasant skirmish. David made a game of getting Jack out of bed and then giving pleasant instructions, which Jack promptly followed. David reported months later that this connective approach had permanently changed the tone of their mornings.

"You are CALLED and CAPABLE": How might I acknowledge and redirect a gift gone awry?

For some kids, the downside of morning routines is they're "borrrrring," the same old drill. Behind their resistance might be God-given desire for novelty or a challenge when instead of brushing their teeth they'd rather irritate a sibling (which can be entertaining) or find a screen activity.

Taria, eight, hated getting ready but loved a good challenge. Her mom often hid one shoe before Taria was up and then progressively gave more specific clues to find it. This started the day with fun and got her moving.

If your child has this intensity and thrives on challenge, see if she can complete her getting-ready routine on one foot, sitting on an exercise ball, using only one hand, or with her eyes closed. Then challenge her to think up the next day's challenge.

How might I nurture capability in my child?

Kids' bodies working against them can factor into morning routines. Scientists have found real differences in brain function that affect how various people get going each day. Parents can help slow-moving kids to wake and be responsible with energizing sensory experiences—lively music, a brisk back or shoulder rub, gradually brighter light, etc. Or bring a bottle of chilled water or a sports drink. The combination of hydration and sucking on something cold really increases alertness.

Problem-solve with your kids what will best keep them on track. Maybe it's a simple list of pictures or words to remind them of their sequence. If your child loves music, put the list into a simple melody. Or the night before, set out a line of his "supplies" across his bedroom floor, starting with all his clothing in the order he puts it on and ending with a tube of toothpaste.

"You are RESPONSIBLE": What consequence best teaches my child responsibility for his actions?

Avoid reminders (nagging) as well as rescuing your children (doing their work for them). Both of these approaches communicate to kids that they are not responsible to get themselves out the door—and that you are! So what are some possible solutions to the pitfall of frequent reminders?

Establish clear-cut rules ahead of time about getting ready, and then stick to them. The family meeting format (see Chores, appendix section A) is really helpful for this. Here are some examples of rules families have developed:

- No breakfast till you're dressed and ready.
- Alarm clocks will be set earlier if kids aren't ready on time.
- Parents will stand behind any school tardiness consequences.
- If kids aren't ready and a parent must leave to be on time for her obligation, then kids, ready or not, go into the car as is.
- Last-minute rides due to missed bus/carpool or poor planning cost the child a predetermined taxi fee.

The key to effectively enforcing any rule is the parent being peaceful and sympathetic, not angry or lecturing. Follow through when a child chooses not to get ready on time.

Lose the privilege: When little, our kids were notoriously distractible dawdlers. So we requested they get ready a half hour or so early, so they had time to play before we left. We'd check in a few minutes later. Any child not ready went to the time-out bench with clothes, away from all those enjoyable distractions, until dressed and ready. The motivation to regain the privilege to get back and play drastically improved dressing speed. The privilege of any game, toy, or item can be lost if it distracts a child.

Another privilege loss could be bedtime-related. If a child just can't get going in the morning, she's probably too tired and can't handle the privilege of her current bedtime; fifteen minutes earlier might help her. Similarly, if she doesn't respond to the warm greeting of a parent in the morning, she can lose that privileged way to wake and learn to rely on a less-pleasant alarm clock.

Meals

We asked a wise mentor who'd raised five outstanding, faith-filled children how he did it. "We shared our lives together around the table," he answered without hesitation. He described the richness of their commitment to family meals focused on shared responsibilities, stories, prayers, laughter, and tears.

This experience is far from the reality for many families. Why?

In an informal survey we took with young moms, mealtime won the "Most Difficult Time of the Day" contest. Everyone's cooped up together, movement is restricted, various sounds can aggravate anyone (our daughter still gets irritated by a brother's noisy chewing), and smells and tastes mix into the sensory barrage. It's no wonder kids often rock in their chairs, make loud noises, complain about food, antagonize a sibling, or just climb down and try to escape. Stressed parents (probably wishing they could leave the table too) often demand or control. Add in everyone's emotional baggage and conflicts from the day, and the volatile formula for mealtime mayhem is complete.

Practical/biblical perspectives: Mealtime habits can become powerful shaping rituals. Throughout Scripture, meals are often celebrations meant to strengthen family, faith, and community. Jesus shared joyous connection at meals with such a variety of people that the Pharisees accused him of being "a glutton and a drunkard, and a friend of tax collectors and sinners" (Luke 7:34). His early followers continued this practice: "They broke bread [shared meals] in their homes and ate together with glad and sincere hearts, praising God and enjoying the favor of all the people" (Acts 2:46–47).

So how can we bridge the gap between what God intended for meals and the everyday experience of many stressed families?

Long-term vision for my children's lives: to value meals as a gift from God to nourish our bodies and spirits.

"You are SAFE with me": What's going on in me that affects how I engage with my child?

Consider:

- How do my experiences at my family table growing up affect my expectations now? (Was it stressful? Peaceful? Was I forced to clean my plate and eat my broccoli? How did I feel about that?)
- What anxieties do I have about meals with my own family?
- What expectations do I have about mealtime, and what do I do to set the tone for having those expectations met?
- To what degree does my tone draw my kids to look forward to mealtime?

"You are LOVED": How can I connect or empathize with my child?

Discuss together how God has designed meals to be a relaxed time for connection, not a feeding frenzy or a time for TV. Make a conscious effort to set a positive tone. After a prayer of blessing and thanks over the food, intercept potential chaos or conflict by structuring positive connection:

- Share a simple verse or "faith thought" of the day.
- Read from a joke book or science fun-fact book.
- One family taught values and kept a positive focus by routinely asking, "When did you bless another person today?" or "What are you thankful for today?" Another family designated one person each night to have a "special person placemat," and others took turns saying something

they liked about that person or something cool they noticed that he/she did that day.

- Focusing on what each person felt good about accomplishing sets an encouraging tone. You might ask, "What did
you do or learn today that you feel best about?"
- Play the "Question Game"—each person thinks up a question to ask another family member until all have asked
and answered one. (Or utilize online resources for fun
connection questions.) This is also a great way to build
social and listening skills.

If children struggle with sitting still or behaving appropriately, let them know that you understand how difficult it
can be. Just this empathy may help them settle down. Don't
use the mealtime to address and try to solve problems from
other parts of the day, or to reprimand or lecture about unmet
expectations.

"You are CALLED and CAPABLE": How might I acknowledge and redirect a gift gone awry?

Mealtimes may disintegrate into mayhem because a sensitive
child is overwhelmed by the experience. These kids tend to cope
by having strong ideas about how meals should go—who sits
where, what's served, etc. Make opportunities for them to have
some "healthy power" related to their ideas.

Enlist your children's ownership and involvement in various
aspects of the meal. Have them take turns choosing one side
dish. Kids as young as three can help prepare food, set the table,
and serve. Working side by side, express appreciation for your
child's helpfulness. In doing this, he's likely to feel good about
the meal before he ever gets to the table. Bonus benefit: Studies
show that kids who share family responsibilities more strongly
adopt their family's values.

Suzanne's daughter often had morning difficulties, including decisions about breakfast. One Monday Katelyn refused the simple choices offered and began screaming at Suzanne to cook pancakes. Suzanne's first impulse was to firmly say, "When you yell like that, you won't get what you want." But she knew the transition from weekend to school day was hard for Katelyn and that an escalated conflict would be a bad start to the week. So she said, "If you ask me in a calmer voice, I'll make you pancakes. But you will need to cook breakfast for me one day later this week." Katelyn asked more respectfully, enjoyed her breakfast, and had a good day at school.

Later that week Katelyn insisted that her mom should choose a breakfast that would be a challenge to make. Katelyn appreciated the grace she had received and wanted to do a good job of serving her mom in return.

How might I nurture capability in my child?

Children are responsible for what (and if) they eat. This is an important part of their learning to care for their bodies. Parents are responsible to serve a variety of healthy food. Research shows power struggles over food are highly counterproductive in helping kids learn to eat healthy selections and amounts. For practical tips on helping picky eaters expand their diet and settling squirmy kids at the table, see disciplinethat connects.org/links. (Said one mom who did, "I was amazed at how much more peaceful our meals were and how much better my daughters ate!")

Each family will have unique challenges at meals and unique ways to solve them. We had quite a list of family rules hanging on the nearby wall, including "No singing at the table," "No pounding," "Sit flat . . ." (You can imagine what our pre-rules meals were like!)

Help everyone contribute to a simple list with the goal of enjoying meals together. Find out how your kids want mealtime to be. Some possibilities:

1. **Eat what you want.** At each meal have at least one food you know your kids will eat. This helps eliminate both complaining and "cooking on demand" because your child dislikes all the food. Each child puts a little bit of everything on her plate and then decides whether or not to eat it. You can reinforce this by having a "No nagging kids to eat" rule and letting them respectfully bust you if you break it.

2. **Honor the cook.** Complaints decrease dramatically when parents don't pressure children to eat. Kids should learn that complaining about food dishonors the one who worked hard to make it. A more concrete "Honor the cook" variation is, "You don't have to eat it, but don't complain about it." Be sure to model honoring the cook by thanking God for providing and the cooks for preparing the meal.

3. **Respect others at the table.** Have a child-friendly discussion about what it means to be respectful at mealtime and why it's important. Ask your kids what makes them feel respected at the table. Use conversations like these to establish your family's mealtime rules.

Once you decide on rules, you can rehearse what they are and how they work. Parents can pretend to break the rules; kids can remind them of the rule; parents can correct their "misbehavior" and show appropriate behavior. You can switch roles and have the kids practice. This makes the rules clear and builds capability. When you notice respectful interaction at meals, call kids' attention to it and talk about its benefit in helping everyone enjoy the meal.

"You are RESPONSIBLE": What consequence best teaches my child responsibility for his actions?

Lose the privilege. If a child complains about the food, you can slide his plate out of reach for a break and gently say, "You can eat or not eat whatever you want, but to keep your plate, you must be respectful." After a short time he can respectfully ask for it. If he repeatedly complains, invite him to work with you to plan and prepare a whole meal. Ask him to imagine how it would feel if several people complained about it.

If a child violates a specific "Respect others at the table" rule, she can take a break on a designated spot until she has a plan to be respectful. Or she might complete the after-dinner chore for the person she has disrespected.

Kids can know ahead of time that if they're seriously disrespectful at the table, parents will calmly let them know they've lost food privileges for the night. They may be hungry, but they'll probably be wiser by the next morning.

Transitions/Leaving

Practical/biblical perspectives: Some kids find it tough just to come to a meal or in from outside, let alone get organized to get into the car. The busier your schedule, the more times kids go from one thing on to the next. These transitions become the bookends of each daily activity, and so tend to create repeated patterns of either teamwork or power struggles.

Long-term vision for my children's lives: to learn the flexibility and responsibility that will serve them well in various future changes/transitions.

"You are SAFE with me": What's going on in me that affects how I engage with my child?

How a parent enters these transitions makes a huge difference. Here are three ideas to help:

1. Prepare ahead. Change equals stress for an immature brain, and stress shuts down your child's frontal lobe (which handles rational thinking), so make sure not to add your anxiety and stress by procrastinating! Set a timer to trigger you to get ready first before engaging the kids. When it rings, announce loudly that you're getting ready to go. This models responding to a timer, and you'll also be much more equipped to approach them peacefully.

2. Walk in their shoes. Wise engagement starts with insight into my kids' experience. How would I feel if every day a cranky, stressed person told me repeatedly that I had to follow their timetable . . . even when I was engrossed in a favorite book or thoroughly enjoying coffee and a deep conversation with a friend? What would be my attitude and response?

3. Nag-proof your thinking. If you subtly believe, "It's my job to herd you little rascals to the car," your child likely believes, "It's my job to artfully dodge being herded," and it's game on. Recognize that your kids are capable and responsible, and stay tuned for lots of practical ideas to help them learn this!

"You are LOVED": How can I connect or empathize with my child?

How often might your child's resistance to leaving be a result of feeling uncared about? From her perspective, "Why should I value your need to leave if you don't seem to care at all that I'm doing something important to me?"

Join her when it's time to prepare. Take a few moments to sincerely find out what she's doing, why it's important, and how you can reassure her she'll be able to do this again sometime.

Be specific. For example, if trying to leave a playdate: "I see you're working on lovely bracelets with Ava. Let's take a picture of them so you can show Dad! What cool thing do you think you'll make next time we're here?"

Even just gently putting a hand on her shoulder or rubbing her back can build connection and ease a transition. Megan was just beginning to embrace the Discipline that Connects principles when she emailed this story.

> Nate, my four-year-old, pitched a fit yesterday when we were leaving Papa and Nana's house. He insisted he was going on the airplane with them to Arizona today and was not coming home with me! Normally I'd have angrily demanded he obey me and get in the van and come home, and I'd have spanked him for the attitude he had as we were leaving. This time, I kept calm and let him get out some of his rage. I found him with his head in a corner and sweetly put my hand on him as I looked him in the eye. I gently said, "Nate, it's really hard to say good-bye to Papa and Nana, isn't it?" He looked at me and then ran out the door and into the van with a tearful good-bye to my mom as he ran. It was amazing.
>
> He cried all the way home, releasing his sadness about Papa and Nana. When we got inside, he ran into my arms for a hug, and I told him I loved him. He squeezed my arms and said, "Thank you, Mommy." What a transformation in me, and what a beautiful ending to a really hard time for him. Praise God!

"You are CALLED and CAPABLE": How might I acknowledge and redirect a gift gone awry?

In addition to your children's gift for whatever interests them (a knack for Legos, love for dress-up, etc.), if they have difficulty transitioning, they're usually also gifted with intensity, determination, and/or focus. You just might have some kids who will take the world by storm someday! From this vantage you can say, "I love how determined you are about your dolls. Let's see if we can use that determination to solve our problem about leaving the house."

How might I nurture capability in my child?

Engaging kids with questions to solve the problem helps them feel both capable and responsible. "How do we usually feel when we leave a favorite place?" ("We all get pretty frustrated and crabby. . . . The day doesn't always go well after that, does it?") "What does Mom/Dad do that's the most helpful when leaving? What do we sometimes do that makes it harder, that we should avoid? What do you kids do that makes it either easier or harder to get where we're going? What could we do differently so when we get in the car we're not cranky with each other and have more fun when we get there?"

Some possibilities you could discuss along with your kids' ideas:

- Timers—how much of a warning do your kids need? Would it help to put a favorite song on loudly when it's time to go, and see if they can make it to the car before it ends?

- Would it help if your family set aside time at the start of the week to review the week's schedule? One mom printed off a basic family activities calendar for each of their rooms. It went much better when they knew what to expect for the day.

- What older child might share some of the responsibility? A child with more intensity and difficulty with leaving may thrive when given responsibility to help with a younger child.

A transition item provides continuity from one environment to the next and can reduce "leaving stress." (Sensitive nervous systems easily can be overstimulated by changes and transitions, especially when intently focused on an activity.) What might your kids take along when it's time to go? Examples:

- A backpack filled with favorite small toys to fidget with, a drawing pad, or simply a favorite blankie or stuffed animal can help little ones feel safe and comforted.
- A juice box or a little snack bag of something crunchy can work wonders to calm and focus kids as they leave a park or other favorite place, especially if they're wound up or excited.
- A playdate friend can also serve as a "transition item": "Max, would you walk with Jack and me to the car? We'd love that!"
- A fun activity can serve as a transition focus—a piggyback ride out to the car, march and sing a favorite song together, see who can hop out on one leg, and so on.
- Whatever helps the transition go a little better—talk about it when you get to the car, e.g., "Thanks for getting your coats on quickly!"

"You are RESPONSIBLE": What consequence best teaches my child responsibility for his actions?

Questions and timers are nag-prevention tools to help you empower your kids. Questions give a chance to remember the strategies they developed and state the expectations: "What do you need to do to get ready?" Timers provide the expectations' objective measurement: "We're leaving in ten minutes."

Do-over: Kids who don't make it out to the car in time may have favorite privileges suspended when they get home until they practice the process: stop playing, get ready, and get into the car. Time them so they can figure out how much warning they need before leaving. This "dress rehearsal" also gives parents an opportunity to affirm the child's effort and responsibility.

Make it right: If kids make the leaving process harder for everyone, they can choose a way to make it easier next time, e.g., be the one to get coats out of the closet, or go around and let all kids know "ten minutes till be-in-the-car time." He might do a chore for anyone inconvenienced by his dawdling.

Lose the privilege: Whatever distracting activity is contributing to the problem can be timed out. For example, the iPad privilege is lost until a child gets out to the car quickly the next three times you have to leave, or playdates are on hold until a child's ability to do transitions has improved.

Bedtime

To help kids with the difficulty of falling asleep, it's important we understand it from their eyes.

It's your child's last shot for attention, and perhaps she's anxious about being alone in her room. She can sense the urgency and frustration in a parent's voice, which she may interpret as, *Mom/Dad is tired of me.* This makes her more anxious for Mom/Dad to stay with her. It also may be hard to ignore noises, lights, and other input that keeps her awake. Or her schedule and daily rhythms might be out of whack, and her body has trouble shifting gears to gradually calm down. Or maybe she's simply learned that by creating chaos at bedtime she gets more attention and stays up longer.

If bedtime is a persistent challenge and you've done everything you know, the first step is to understand what's going on with you and your child. The three basic goals of bedtime management are to calm the child's body, calm his spirit, and avoid fertilizing or rewarding any attention-getting or manipulative behaviors. (If getting to sleep and staying asleep is a significant challenge, Mary Sheedy Kurcinka's *Sleepless in America* is an excellent, thorough resource.[1])

251

Practical/biblical perspectives: Solomon wrote, "He grants sleep to those he loves" (Psalm 127:2). Trust in a God who loves us and helps us to sleep peacefully. In the same way, children sleep more easily when they feel secure and loved. Peaceful connection with a parent is an important bookend for their day. Of course, a good night's sleep is right up there with diet as a foundation of both physical and emotional health, so helping kids develop and learn healthy sleep patterns is a huge gift for life.

Long-term vision for my children's lives: to finish their day with a peaceful spirit and good sleep habits that prepare them well for healthy days.

"You are SAFE with me": What's going on in me that affects how I engage with my child?

Parents and kids alike tend to drag their stress and baggage from the day into bedtime interactions. Helpful questions to consider:

- Do I have chronic resentment at my kids for how tough they make bedtime?
- Am I feeling alone in this bedtime challenge, and resentful of that?
- What specific leftover stress from my day might I be bringing into this?
- How can I refresh myself with God's mercy for all of us before starting our bedtime routine?

"You are LOVED": How can I connect or empathize with my child?

Children love it when adults understand how frustrating bedtime is for their active bodies and minds. When our kids were little we sometimes stomped off to bed, marching to a silly song we made up: "I hate bed, I hate bed! It makes me want to throw up. I wish that I could grow up. I hate bed. . . ." It helped us all to release some tension before the kids hit the sack.

Some key messages can help set an encouraging "I'm for you, not against you in this" tone at bedtime:

- "I absolutely love you no matter how you sleep."
- "I can't stay with you at night because husbands and wives need to sleep together. That's very important for strong families, and we really want our family to be strong." Single parents: "I can't stay with you at night because we sleep so much more soundly in our own beds."
- "Let's figure out what helps you be a successful grown-up sleeper so we'll both get the rest that helps us feel good and have fun."
- "I'm confident we can figure this out together."

Heartfelt connection goes a long way to calm anxiety at bedtime. One dad made a discipline of finding something from the day to compliment his kids about. They got a journal for each child to keep a record of these affirmations, and soon his kids began making suggestions of things they each felt good about. Not surprisingly, bedtime became much easier.

It's also a great time to put a hand on your child and proclaim a strong blessing of God's love, presence, and faithfulness. (See *The Blessing* by Gary Smalley and John Trent.[2]) You can make up a simple song about your love for your child, or sing a familiar lullaby, hymn, or worship song.

If a child brings up irrational fears, validate the emotion without substantiating the reality. "I remember when I was afraid of monsters. It seemed really scary at the time! As I got older I learned there wasn't really anything to be afraid of. You'll learn that over time too." A silly name for the monster makes him seem less scary. If children insist on talking about it, make a date to chat about it the next day, and be sure to keep the date.

"You are CALLED and CAPABLE": How might I acknowledge and redirect a gift gone awry?

Kids who have trouble falling asleep often have sensitive bodies. They may flop around on their beds, trying to wind down, and they can be irritated by small sounds, need to have the light and covers just right, etc. You can acknowledge that sensitivity and utilize it for calming. "God has given you a really sensitive body. Some things feel really good to you, and some things feel kind of yucky. What can we do to help your body feel really good when it's time for sleep?" Many parents find that firm massage (or sometimes light stroking) is a wonderful final activity to calm those little bodies. It can also help to provide something interesting to focus on—lava lamp, fish tank, relaxing music, etc. One little girl went to bed much better when the cat was placed on her bed as Mom exited, providing soft, furry, purry company.

Because of the importance of daily body rhythms, one of the most helpful things for a sensitive child to sleep well is a consistent day-to-day schedule and bedtime routine. If a family's life is out of control, it's likely the child will be out of control at bedtime also. Sunshine in the morning and strong physical activity anytime up through late afternoon set a child's biological clock to be ready for bed. Most kids need a predictable, gradually less active routine to calm their bodies after dinner. Falling asleep requires a drop in internal body temperature, which roughhousing right before bed is unlikely to accomplish.

How might I nurture capability in my child?

A key skill for young kids to fall asleep is the ability to wait peacefully alone in bed. During the day, help your child build an identity as being good at waiting. Ask him to wait when you grant a request, and then compliment him on what a good job he did waiting. Refer back to this success at bedtime.

If a child is quite anxious, check on him as often as needed to empower him to stay in bed. Return for a visit before he normally starts to fuss, yell, or get out of bed, even if initially this is only a few minutes. Compliment him for the nice job of staying in bed quietly. Once he feels successful and secure that he isn't abandoned, intervals can gradually lengthen. If he gets out of bed, a relaxed, gentle statement like "I can help you get back in" avoids a power struggle and creates less anxiety or negative attention than "Get back to bed!"

With older children who struggle with bedtime, problem-solve bedtime conflict together. Discuss the natural impact of the conflict on everyone involved: "How does everyone feel by the end of the night? How does the stress at bedtime affect everyone's sleep? When it goes better, what does each of us do that's helpful?" Brainstorm ways to have peaceful, connected bedtimes, including establishing rewards or penalties that the kids develop.

Bedtime was a regular household problem for us. Typically the kids were wired, but Lynne was fried, especially when Jim worked late. We had chronic conflict till we all agreed we didn't like ending the evening angry at each other and wanted to do something about it. We started by talking about the frustrations we wanted to solve. Together we forged a system of consequences for lateness or arguing and rewards for getting into bed on time. Every minute late translated into three minutes of earlier bedtime the next night. A week with five out of six respectful on-time nights earned each child a later bedtime with popcorn and a movie on the seventh night (usually Friday).

It wasn't a flawless system, and sometimes there were still rough nights, but it was definitely better. Our collaboration helped everyone to own the problem and build creativity and conflict-resolution skills.

"You are RESPONSIBLE": What consequence best teaches my child responsibility for his actions?

Do-over: It can help a child to practice her bedtime routine in the middle of the day, when no one's tired or crabby. "You had a pretty hard time last night, so today before you get your next privilege you'll need to practice going to bed appropriately." When she does, affirm her success and talk about the natural impact of cooperating at bedtime. Then, when it's time for the real evening performance, remind her of her dress-rehearsal success.

Make it right: Children who exhaust their parents with long, drawn-out bedtimes can make restitution by lightening their parents' load the next day doing some extra chores. We told our kids that if they challenged us about bedtime and drew our energy away from our final cleaning for the day, we would leave the kitchen mess (or another mess) for them to clean the next day and would make sure to follow through to have them clean it.

Lose the privilege: Whatever a child's current bedtime, it's a privilege compared to the earlier bedtime he might have. Poor cooperation at bedtime may show that he's too tired and needs to start earlier each night. Consistent cooperation probably means he's getting enough sleep. So if he continually challenges you about bedtime, an earlier bedtime may well be called for.

Putting it all together: When anxious three-year-old Rachel had to kiss her beloved pacifier good-bye, she also bid *adieu* to peacefully falling asleep on her own. Her screaming and demands for her parents were intense, despite Lila and Matt's determination to soldier on with the bedtime routine.

They were at the end of their rope. With Rachel's intensity, a cry-it-out approach would have likely been a disaster. Lila wrote,

> We tried putting her back in bed without talking to her (one night we did that thirty-two times). We tried doing bed checks (she would scream bloody murder and kick her

closed door). In desperation, we began lying on her floor while she fell asleep, which could regularly take well over a half hour.

Lila came for parent coaching, and we developed, tweaked, and re-tweaked a plan to help Rachel fall asleep without screaming and crying. It was an integrated approach of strong connection and affection together with a solid routine of calming activities. The routine ended in a "calm and color" time with markers on the floor near a parent, before getting tucked into bed with one book and some relaxing music. At a set time, a parent would briefly visit. The visit intervals started at every three minutes and slowly increased with each successive check-in.

The final piece that moved them forward was when Lila used a gate on Rachel's door to motivate her to work hard at her "sleep manners" (lying quietly in bed). It was lovingly explained that if she had trouble remembering her sleep manners, the gate would help her remember and be successful. Notice the underlying messages of "You are loved, even if you have trouble falling asleep. We are for you, not against you." How different from the "You are a problem" message of threatening, "Stay in bed or we put up a gate!"

Since Rachel strongly disliked the gate and wanted to earn the privilege of an unrestricted door, she worked hard to use her sleep manners. Matt and Lila were careful to encourage her hard work each night.

Lila later wrote,

> Rachel is falling asleep much earlier than before (around nine o'clock vs. ten) with fewer visits. She seems to be relearning how to lie quietly and let sleep come. Matt and I feel less like we're being held hostage, and I think she's comfortable with the arrangement. I cherish the time and mental energy I've gotten back!

Growing True Respect and Reconciliation

On the day a child is born, he cries and fusses to make known his needs. He's rewarded as his parents work hard learning to soothe the distress that prompts all the noise. It's the only thing he knows how to do, and it's an essential part of building a trust-based bond with his caregivers.

It will be the parent's job to help him unlearn infantile communication and progressively replace it with more mature skills. If we reward fussing when he's old enough to use respectful words, he will persist and become skilled at whining and tantrums. Toddlers have intense emotions (they're heavily immersed in right-brain development) with limited ability to express and self-regulate them (left-brain functions). Yet even much later, during the teen years, the stresses of rapid brain growth and hormone fluctuation can compel older kids to revert to more primitive behaviors.

All kids need grace and growth instead of condemnation and control. That means we've got our work cut out for us. But it's vital, rewarding work as we persevere at equipping them for a lifetime of rich relationships.

Whining

Practical/biblical perspectives: It's tempting just to focus on stopping whining. But God has a more important, overarching desire for His children: that we learn to thoughtfully and respectfully ask for what truly matters to us and have a peaceful response to whatever is the answer.

> Do not be anxious about anything, but in every situation, by prayer and petition, with thanksgiving, present your requests to God. And the peace of God, which transcends all understanding, will guard your hearts and your minds in Christ Jesus. (Philippians 4:6–7)

Paul exemplified contentment whatever the answer or the circumstance: "I have learned the secret of being content in any and every situation, whether well fed or hungry, whether living in plenty or in want" (Philippians 4:12).

This passage gives us a context for both acknowledging a child's feelings and validating what's really important to her, while also encouraging skills for respectful requests and contentment regardless of the answer. In addressing whining, validating and training are two essential goals.

Long-term vision for my children's lives: to learn to articulate their feelings and true needs respectfully, and to grow skills of resilience and contentment.

"You are SAFE with me": What's going on in me that affects how I engage with my child?

Consider:

- Do I know how my child's whining makes me feel? (Angry? Anxious? Discouraged? . . .)

- How do those feelings contribute to my response? (For example, Do I become anxious or tense if he's upset with me and I fail to set firm boundaries? Or do I let anger drive us into a power struggle?)

What's your first thought when your child whines? It's helpful to identify these: *She sure knows how to push my buttons* or *This needs to stop!* or *That sound drives me crazy.* Reactions based on these will saturate our responses with frustration and control. Thoughts like, *Her mood doesn't determine mine* and *What does he truly need right now?* and *How can I help her learn a wiser response?* will lead us to better outcomes.

Also consider: Am I attentive to her first attempts to get my attention so I can guide her into a respectful request, or do I wait to respond till she whines or escalates to a tantrum? Do I do "grown-up whining" to get her to stop?

When two-year-old Garrett said in a fairly normal voice, "Wanna get down," his mom, Corrie, was deeply engaged in dinner-table conversation. He began to whine repeatedly and got louder and louder until he finally started pounding the high chair and yelling, even smacking her on the arm. She turned to look at him for the first time, glared, and angrily said, "That is *not* how you get my attention!" Actually, that was exactly what he had to do for her attention, and he got lots of it. Her response was a reward, not a chastisement.

If we don't have a strong, purposeful determination *not* to reward these behaviors, it's easy to end up teaching kids that these are effective ways to get what they want. Rather than a focus on eliminating whining, we can develop a clear vision to teach respect and self-control for their benefit, not our relief.

Some friends of ours used humor to remain calm and light-hearted when a child whined. They explained to their kids that they'd be playing a little game to help them learn to ask for things in a better way. When their daughter next began to whine, Linda turned and said sweetly, "Mike, can you hear what she's saying? Her lips are moving, but I don't hear anything. She must be whining." Mike joined in. "You're probably right; I don't hear anything either. I wonder what she's saying." Ali caught on quickly and made her request in a regular voice, which received attention and encouragement. Even though she was fairly intense and strong-willed, whining would not remain much of a problem in their home. The keys to effectiveness were the advance notice about the "game" and the wholly playful rather than condescending tone. (When Mike and Linda could see that their children were truly upset, they wisely chose empathy instead of playfulness.)

"You are LOVED": How can I connect or empathize with my child?

It's helpful to simply eliminate "Stop whining!" from our vocabulary, for those words are loaded with a couple of really unhelpful messages that pit parents and kids against each other and increase the problem:

- Your whining has a lot of power over my emotions.
- I don't care about you or what's important to you.

We can convey the opposite messages as we smile and say, "Remember, when you whine you won't get what you're whining for, but you will get my love—just as much as ever." (And if you say that, make sure you mean it.)

Empathizing with a whining or crying child powerfully expresses love without giving in to demands. It is also an essential way to help her learn to communicate respectfully when she's upset. "Put words in her mouth" as you restate what she seems to be feeling and wanting: "You're really *mad* that you can't have this cookie right now. I love cookies too." This encourages her self-awareness and communication and can help keep you calmer so you stand firm (no cookies right now).

From toddlers to teens, we've seen repeatedly that when empathy is sincere and a child feels truly understood and validated in what she wants, she's much more likely to calm down, ask respectfully, and, if necessary, accept "no" or "later" for an answer.

Here's an example of how the empathizing approach might look when your child is demanding you buy him some new treasure:

> "I can see why you really want [desired item]; it is cool. I like that it's _____ [positive details about it]." This connective language tends to deflate his negative energy and prepare him for some instruction. "I can't give it to you when you ask that way, so when we get home let's talk about a plan to get it."

"You are CALLED and CAPABLE": How might I acknowledge and redirect a gift gone awry?

What's a good gift gone awry in whining? If this seems difficult to answer, consider a contrasting behavior, e.g., indecision, a lack of confidence, a lack of trust in his caregiver, or giving up easily. Next time your child whines, you can consider his strengths, smile, and say, "You sure are _____ [persistent, confident, expressive, determined, aware of exactly what's important to you . . .]. We can talk later about how to use that in a better way."

When you do talk later, reflect back on and share about times your child used one of these qualities in a positive or honoring way. Then figure out how he might use his gifts to work toward what really matters to him or to bless others. For example, confidently expressive kids could help you teach Sunday school or visit elders in a nursing home.

How might I nurture capability in my child?

Whining to get ("I waaaaaannnt it"): Parents can usually predict some of the times or issues over which our kids will start to whine. Anticipate these, and set kids up to make a respectful request rather than waiting for them to fail. Maybe it's at the mall when they pass a certain toy store. Maybe it's that before-dinner cookie-begging hour. Set them up to succeed by saying something like, "It's about that time when you'll want a snack. What are our rules, and how do you want to ask about this?" Given this opportunity, they'll almost always ask appropriately.

Simply asking kids to wait for requests builds delay of gratification and decreases whining over time. "If you'd like a snack, I can get it for you in a couple of minutes, *if* you wait patiently. I bet you'll do great. What can you do while you're waiting?" They might draw a picture for you of their desired object to help you remember. Their patience gives you a chance to affirm their waiting and tell them what a grown-up thing that is to do. If your kids are old enough, you can even share a verse on contentment or waiting (e.g., Philippians 4:12 or Psalm 27:14) to help them see they're beginning to learn something of great importance.

Whining to avoid ("I don't waaaaannnna"): When kids are whining to get out of basic tasks, it's easy to default to whining back at them. This is not the time for a long discussion about why their chore is necessary or why kids need to accompany us to the grocery store. The Discipline that Connects messages can guide our approach:

- You are *loved*: Make a solid *connection* (instead of barking an order).
- You are *responsible*: Make sure they know your *expectations*, stating a clear consequence if they choose not to comply.
- You are *capable*: Add a couple *choices* if your child needs some "healthy power" (see Defiance later in this section).

- You are *safe*: *Walk away*, to pause, if needed (so that you stay peaceful and don't tempt your child with a power struggle).

For example, "Hey, [child's name], looks like you're working on something special here. If you get ready quickly to go to the store, we can leave it out for you to finish afterward. If not, we can put it away until tomorrow. Do you want some help getting your coat on, or do you want to do it yourself? I'm gonna go get mine on now."

"You are RESPONSIBLE": What consequence best teaches my child responsibility for his actions?

Whining was fairly infrequent in our house because the kids knew that was a quick way to come up empty—no attention, no stuff. With a no-expression and no-eye-contact response from Mom or Dad, they heard, "I know you really want _____, but how you asked for it wasn't helpful. Go set the timer for five minutes; when it rings you can have a chance to practice asking nicely a couple of times." This wait-and-practice approach incorporates the "lose the privilege" and "do-over" principles and teaches skills of quiet waiting and respectful asking. It also makes sure that a parent's anger and attention don't reward and fertilize whining.

Once your child asks respectfully, help her see the wisdom in how she asked. Make sure your facial expression and eye contact celebrate her success.

Tantrums/Meltdowns

Consider the Father's response in Psalm 73, throughout most of which the psalmist was on an "It's not fair!" rant. Do verses

21–24 sound like any of the tantrums in your house (yours or your kids')?

> When my heart was grieved and my spirit embittered,
> > I was senseless and ignorant; I was a brute beast be-
> > fore you.
> Yet I am always with you; you hold me by my right hand.
> > You guide me with your counsel,
> > and afterward you will take me into glory.

It appears that:

- God was unfazed by and not condemning or controlling of the outburst.
- He did not give in to the psalmist's demands.
- He was present, loving and guiding the psalmist through his difficult emotions.

When we respond this way, we help our children understand the depths of our love and God's love for them in their worst moments. After the above verses, the grateful psalmist passionately declares his love for God: "Whom have I in heaven but you? And earth has nothing I desire besides you" (Psalm 73:25–26).

In addition to this spiritual perspective, it helps to understand what's happening in your child's brain during tantrums. Her fight-or-flight centers and right brain (emotional, sensory) are raging out of control, while her frontal lobe (with all its guiding functions) and logical left brain (including language skills) are offline. Thus, reasoning during these events is futile; attempting to overpower the screaming with demands to "Calm down! Stop yelling!" only aggravates her fight-or-flight state. The messages we want to convey—"You are capable and responsible to make a wise choice" (left brain)—will land on deaf ears until she truly receives the calming messages "You are safe and loved" (right brain).

Some kids' meltdowns are mostly based in power struggles and opposition to adult requests (see again Defiance for additional strategies). For other kids they're about inflexibility and poor frustration tolerance (losing control when things unexpectedly don't go their way).

Long-term vision for my children's lives: to redirect intensity and passion toward God's purposes; to manage intensity through learning practical skills like self-calming, identifying feelings, flexibility, and problem-solving.

"You are SAFE with me": What's going on in me that affects how I engage with my child?

When parents struggle with giving helpful responses to their child, their approach usually falls into one of three categories:

Condescend—Sometimes parents mock or imitate tantrumming kids for their over-the-top emotional display or simply invalidate their big feelings ("C'mon, this is *not* that big a deal"). Other times the condescension is internal, as in Ryan's unspoken judgment that his explosive daughter was a "train wreck" (see chapter 6).

Control—"Calm down" or "Stop this" usually are a way to compensate for feeling stressed, out of control, or even ashamed of a child's behavior. Internal thoughts might be similar to, *This is ridiculous—this ends now!* or *This kid is just trying to get my goat and run this family.*

Cower—Other parents walk on eggshells, waiting for the next unexpected event to trigger a meltdown, and tend to try to fix it or placate the child as quickly as possible. Thoughts might be, *Oh no, here we go again. I can't take this anymore.* Their anxiety adds to their child's anxiety.

Avoiding these responses can be truly tough. But let's step into our kids' shoes for a minute. Picture yourself having a little meltdown of your own after a really rough day of parenting. I (Lynne) can remember the night I went into the garage and screamed at the top of my lungs. And hurt my voice. So I kicked a tire . . . and hurt my toe. Jim's big parenting meltdown started with a panic attack and ended with him throwing rocks as hard as he could at a sign.

How about yours? Almost all parents get to that crazy place, just like their children. To build some insight, let's imagine how you'd feel if your spouse or close friend had one of these responses:

Condescend—"Well, aren't you on a rant. Don't have a heart attack. They're just being kids."

Control—"Settle down and get a grip, would ya?"

Cower—"Umm, I'm gonna check email" (quickly disappearing or changing the subject).

What we need is *compassion*—someone to just listen and be peaceful, or to empathize. How can we prepare our hearts to respond to a child's meltdown with confident compassion instead of condescension, control, or cowering?

Helpful self-talk as your child ramps up can include:

- We'll get through it. This too shall pass.
- I'm not a bad parent. My child is not a bad kid. We're just having a hard time.
- I can handle this. Just take some deep breaths.
- My child needs help managing his intensity.
- God's not fazed by this. Jesus is here and He loves us.
- My child's behavior is not my report card. Jesus is my report card (our Jackson favorite).

"You are LOVED": How can I connect or empathize with my child?

Peacefully not responding takes stress off a child's fight-or-flight system so he has a chance to self-calm. So does simply "naming" the emotions he might be feeling, using simple sentences to describe what you perceive he wants.[1] This helps him feel understood and begins to engage his left-brain language and logic. (You've probably experienced feeling a lot better after figuring out what you're really upset about too.) Use basic, repetitious statements: "You loved that balloon! You *really* loved it. It was so big and bright. It's sad when it pops!"

● ● ●

Julia and Greg were exhausted and hopeless. They felt overwhelmed by their intense, anxious five-year-old's tantrums. It seemed that Abbie would kick, scream, and hit for two hours straight about almost anything.

Julia began parent coaching and worked on expressing empathy. She was elated with the result of this effort. "I knew it was probably gonna be a two-hour blast based on how Abbie started. I stayed calm and kept repeating in simple phrases how I thought she was feeling: 'You're mad right now. You didn't want to come home!' Abbie calmed down in only forty-five minutes. I was so proud of us!" (This was the start of much growth for them. Their story continues below, in the "How Can I Nurture Capability" section.)

When kids have specific things they want to resolve but are too upset to do so, try writing it down to solve later. One family had a recipe box on the kitchen table, and when their teenage son started to wind up and get out of control, they helped him write what he was upset about on an index card to put in the box for a later, calmer discussion.

"You are CALLED and CAPABLE": How might I acknowledge and redirect a gift gone awry?

This principle was the turning point for one extremely explosive six-year-old. Kyle's strong emotions would erupt in strong, hurtful, or colorful words. His mother, Brenda, shared:

> Our efforts to curb this were totally ineffective, despite having read numerous parenting books on strong-willed children. I was desperate. When I read *Discipline That Connects With Your Child's Heart*, the concept that struck a chord was identifying my son's "gift gone awry" in the midst of his misbehavior. I realized Kyle's intense, colorful tirades were partly a reflection of his love for and curiosity about words. I determined to get down on his level, as Jesus did for us, and call out that good gift when he struggled.
>
> At his next hurtful verbal explosion, I set aside the old resentful recording in my head, *Here we go again. . . .* Instead, I got down on my knees, looked deeply into his troubled eyes, and gently said, "Kyle, you're really angry right now! Your strong words come from a gift of a big vocabulary. I believe it's a good gift God has given you. Let's work together to figure out how to use that awesome vocabulary in a more honoring way."
>
> Kyle's discouraged heart soaked up this outpouring of love when he most needed it, as both of our hearts melted in tears. I thought, *Wow, this is safe. We're gonna do this differently than we have in the past.*

As Brenda started down this path, she also realized what a gift Kyle's intensity could be. She told him, "I love how you always tell me what your feelings are. It's a gift to recognize those strong feelings in yourself, and it's even a greater gift to recognize them in someone else, so you can help them." The more she helped Kyle share his big feelings accurately, the more he began using those verbal skills with self-control.

How might I nurture capability in my child?

Dr. Ross Greene, author of *The Explosive Child*, has said that meltdowns are a result of lagging skills and unsolved problems. We have seen this to be true: The kids who make the greatest progress overcoming tantrums have parents who are committed not to stopping the meltdown but to solving problems together and building the child's skills to stop their *own* meltdowns.

Brenda also helped Kyle learn specific coping phrases to stay more rational when he was upset.

> We all began to grow in an identity as a family of learners: "You're so great at learning, and we're all learning here together." We helped Kyle learn that when he is mad he can angrily and loudly say, "I'm so mad! I'm gonna go take a break" or "I have some really strong feelings that I don't know what to do with."
>
> We were careful to model such statements ourselves, and sure enough, he began to use his words in wiser ways.
>
> We also talked about how wonderful it is to use words to honor and build up. We learned and discussed 1 Thessalonians 5:11: "Therefore encourage one another and build each other up, just as in fact you are doing." Now most of the time after tempers have escalated, we walk away feeling really good about the way we handled it, and he feels good about who God made him to be. He often makes statements like:
>
> - "This is really hard and I'm feeling nervous, but I'm gonna give it a shot."
> - "Even if I make a mistake I'm probably gonna learn something from it."
> - "I had a strong feeling but I showed some self-control."
> - "I did my best."
>
> Kyle even told his teacher what an expansive vocabulary he has!

• • •

After Julia made strong progress with Abbie through empathy, she began helping her learn to self-regulate with sensory activities and a quiet space. Abbie chose her bed for her calm-down spot and picked out a stuffed animal that was for holding only when she was angry or sad. They picked calming music for those times, and Abbie helped her mom make a "calm-down jar," a plastic bottle filled with colored water, glitter, glow-in-the-dark stars, and other sparkling things, to shake, swirl, and look at when upset. (You can find ideas about making this on Pinterest.)

Julia also taught Abbie to close her eyes, clench her fists, and then count to ten. "That helps me with my sad and mad feelings," Abbie said. After she calms down, they talk about her feelings, the reasons beneath them, and how much better she feels when she doesn't hit or yell. Julia summed up the impact: "Now sometimes she may start to stomp or yell, but she closes her eyes for a moment and goes and sits on her bed until she feels better. What a transformation from two-hour meltdowns."

Even little tykes can learn sensory-calming strategies. Callie's two-year-old, Maddie, had speech delays, sensory issues, and a lot of frustration. Frequent meltdowns got longer and louder with Callie's exasperated attempts to get her to stop. Since they both loved music, one day Callie tried rocking her and singing to her during a meltdown. The calming impact was amazing, and Maddie began to request singing and rocking when upset. Callie was essentially training her two-year-old in self-soothing.

One day, at speech therapy, Maddie was stressed and beginning to fall apart. She looked at her mom with tear-filled eyes and said, "B-I-B-I." She knew exactly which special song she needed. The therapist got a little gospel concert as Callie gently sang "The B-I-B-L-E" into Maddie's ear, and then they worked hard together in the rest of her session.

Six-year-old Alex struggled with regular meltdowns, so his mom, Sheila, printed off cartoons from a book on kids' brain function.[2] She used its feelings chart to help him identify and communicate his emotions. She also explained the cartoons that illustrated basic strategies for the calm parts of his brain to help the angry parts, and she encouraged him whenever he used a strategy. When he was calm, she asked him questions about how he thought he could solve his problem. Alex felt respected by Sheila's effort to teach rather than criticize, and his responses to his emotions improved dramatically.

Some key skills for overcoming meltdowns are flexibility, problem-solving, and the ability to wait and delay gratification. So consider: How much effort have you put into proactively teaching these skills? Flexibility is a great starting place. Jen used a stick and a pipe cleaner to teach four-year-old Jonah this skill.

> "When people don't get what they want or expect and they're *rigid*," I said, pressing the stick, "they just keep trying to make things go their way, and then BOOM, they explode." The stick snapped in my hands.
>
> "Other people can bend and change when they need to, like sharing a toy when they didn't expect to, or being okay with a different kind of cereal one day. That's being *flexible* like this pipe cleaner—it can bend when it needs to and then it can straighten back out again like before."
>
> I built Jonah's sense of success with this concept by reminding him of how flexible he'd been on our recent vacation. He helped teach the rest of the family this cool idea at supper; over the next few weeks we all looked for times when we were flexible. The change has been amazing.

Another resource that has helped lots of kids learn to be flexible is a book about the cartoon hero Superflex.[3] (For more links to helpful resources for struggling kids, go to discipline thatconnects.org/links.)

A final, practical "you are capable" principle to help with meltdowns is to focus on and affirm whatever has gone well—for example, "I noticed you took a big breath, and that really seemed to help you calm down" or "You were *so* angry and you didn't hurt anyone. How did you do that?"

Ted's daughter Carlie had a prolonged, terrified meltdown on a steep, icy ski slope, repeatedly screaming, "I can't get down!" She finally inched her way down but stuck to the easiest slopes for the rest of their vacation. After some fresh insight, Ted told her how *brave* she'd been to calm herself and make her way down the slope. Carlie grinned in joy as she listened. The next time they went skiing, she challenged Ted to go down "the Wall" with her—the steepest double black diamond in the whole ski area! Ted said, "I was actually nervous too, but we both went for it!" By simply shifting his focus, Ted helped shift his daughter's identity from "fearful" to "overcomer."

What did all these parents have in common? They believed that their children were not out to get them but were uniquely created miracles of God. They knew their kids felt out of control inside, needed help, and had great potential to learn wiser ways of dealing with their stress. And they were determined to find out how to provide that "come alongside" help in order to unlock the treasure inside their kids.

"You are RESPONSIBLE": What consequence best teaches my child responsibility for his actions?

Do-over: In a difficult meltdown, usually both the parents and kids have actions they wish they had done differently. You can lead the way after everyone is calm by suggesting a do-over for both of you. Celebrate how much better that feels. This often paves the way for sincere apologies.

Make it right: Particularly as children get a little older and are able to remember and process what happened, they can be held accountable to make restitution for the impact of their meltdowns. This can be as simple as stating, "Yelling and screaming adds stress to the family. Before you enjoy special privileges, you can do something that adds encouragement and joy instead."

Planning a family game or helping to make a special meal, for instance—and then encouraging your child about it—helps him get out of the rut of misbehaving and can lift the tone in the family after the meltdown.

Lose the privilege: It's a logical consequence to put the object or privilege that sparked a meltdown on hold awhile, but focusing on punishment as the go-to tool for a child's outbursts almost always increases discouragement and resentment and makes matters worse. Effective consequences include encouragement and even a gentle smile: "It's really hard to turn off the iPad, so it will take a break. When you turn off the TV quickly at the end of your shows for a few days, I'll know you are ready to try again with the iPad." The message she gets is, "I want to give you your privilege back as soon as you show me you can handle it."

Defiance

To a certain extent this relates to a battle of which the apostle Paul said, "I find this law at work: Although I want to do good, evil is right there with me" (Romans 7:21). He's referring to selfishness, the desire to live for me and no one else. It's a sin problem every person has (every kid, every adult). Realizing this helps us to engage our children's defiance with grace-filled guidance, knowing that we are easily tempted by the same response.

Practical/biblical perspectives: Parents typically take a strong stand when dealing with defiance. They also tend to feel justified in their own anger and actions in the name of "setting kids straight." Given these dynamics, the question is, what are the children learning? Parents assume the answer is "their lesson" if the kids back down and comply, and "apparently, nothing yet" if they continue in defiance. But it's our thought that in both cases kids are learning far more about how to get power and control than they are about how to get through defiant conflict wisely and constructively.

For kids to overcome defiant attitudes, they need to feel *safe*, feel *understood*, and be given *healthy power*—power that functions within the guidance of an authority, with a goal of growing wise independence. When these three needs are met, we've seen defiance and attempts at unhealthy control of others greatly diminish. So we suggest a different strong stand on defiance: standing strong to communicate the four messages! (See chapter 2.)

Long-term vision for my children's lives: to grow in heartfelt trust in and respect for authorities (starting with parents), resulting in godly wisdom and sincere obedience. (See Luke 1:17.)

"You are SAFE with me": What's going on in me that affects how I engage with my child?

When kids defy us by doing the opposite of what we ask, in a certain way they hold up a mirror that shows whether we're walking in the "fruit of the Spirit"—particularly peace, patience, gentleness, and self-control—or in "the acts of the flesh"—particularly hatred, discord, angry outbursts, or selfish ambitions. (See Galatians 5:19–23.) The choice we habitually make when this mirror is up will be a strong example of walking in either faith or selfishness.

A parent's angry attempt at controlling a defiant child can create an unhealthy bond: "This is how we give each other *big* attention!" It also gives the child a sense of power over the parent's emotions. Both factors tend to fertilize and perpetuate the defiance—a payoff of sorts. Coming to the challenge peacefully, with a clear head, is of utmost importance.

It doesn't help to suppress frustration about a defiant child and pretend to be calm. Most kids read this in a heartbeat! It does help to examine our beliefs about the conflict and then bring God's grace and truth into the fray.

Some examples of helpful thoughts/beliefs regarding defiance:

- Anger and a need for control will only feed this cycle.
- My response can empower my child toward a wise decision.
- My child can learn to respond wisely with my help.
- This strong will has great potential for good purposes someday.

Steve and Kristi exemplified the impact of changing beliefs about defiance. They'd been very frustrated with their intense, defiant four-year-old, Sierra, who'd scream and refuse to take a time-out in her room after whacking her little brother. Further, she'd often refuse to do basic tasks, get herself ready for bed, or do anything else for which she wasn't in the mood.

Steve's unhelpful belief was, "If I don't win these power struggles, she's going to run the family." His anxiety about needing control had been fueling conflict. As he embraced Discipline that Connects, this belief became, "She's not my opponent, she's my teammate to solve these problems." Kristi's new beliefs included, "I mess up too. A lot. And Jesus teaches me patiently. I want to do the same for Sierra."

A defiant child believes, "You're against me, not for me. So I must be against you—it's the only way to protect myself." It was no surprise that when Sierra began to feel safe because she believed her parents were *for* her, her defiance decreased dramatically. She even learned to run to her room to calm herself down when she was unsafe and had hit her little brother.

Defiant kids are often anxious kids, and parents who see this can more easily have compassion, patience, and wisdom. A leading child psychiatrist stated, "Anxiety is one of those diagnoses that is a great masquerader. It can look like a lot of things. Particularly with kids who may not have words to express their feelings, or because no one is listening to them."[4]

Our son Daniel seemed a fearless, strong-willed kid. But in truth he had some high self-expectations and resisted any insinuation that he'd made a mistake or done the wrong thing. His bright, intense brain had an idling speed that ran high and revved up fairly easily into fight-or-flight. Because backing down left him feeling vulnerable or even ashamed, his default was "fight."

When we asked him recently to describe what was behind his childhood defiance, he said, "Easily given apologies or yielding would mean I was giving up my ability to assert myself and to hold strongly to my ideas of right and wrong, and of fairness. If I let people be unfair to me, it would be a slippery slope to being a pushover. I had anxiety about starting on that slope."

There's a reason your child is defiant, so consider (during a non-conflict time): Have you given her defiance power over your emotions? Is it possible underlying anxiety is playing a strong role in her behavior? Does she feel, for example, like a black sheep and believe she's not as loved as her easygoing sibling(s)? If so, she would tend to view parents as against her, not for her.

In the throes of conflict, kids need to feel safe or their defiance escalates. The more anxious the child, the more a quick, default *no* feels like his only safe response. One mom said, "Even if I announce we're going to do something fun, if it's a sudden request, Ava's immediate response is 'No!'"

The first imperative with intense confrontation is *buy time.* Immediate obedience needn't be the goal! Consider the parable about the two sons—one who pledged to obey but didn't, and one who was defiant but then changed his mind and did the task. (See Matthew 21:28–31.) Jesus gives grace for struggling people to have time to come to a place of repentance and obedience. In God's kingdom, delayed but heartfelt obedience trumps forced compliance any day. (See 2 Peter 3:9.)

So when your child answers you with "*no!*" you can ask, in a relaxed, inquisitive tone, "No? What's that about?" If he can't or won't reply, consider whether your request has any selfish intention. If so, confess it. If not, say, "I'm going to ask again in just a minute, to give you a chance to think about it." Other possibilities are, "You have big feelings about this. Let's take a few moments to calm down so we can figure out how we might solve it" or "You often make wise choices. You can think about this before you respond."

"You are LOVED": How can I connect or empathize with my child?

It's insightful to read how the FBI deals with hostage situations (talk about defiance!). If you search online you'll find they have a five-step protocol with practical steps and scripts to help agents de-escalate volatile situations:

1. Active listening
2. Empathy
3. Rapport
4. Influence
5. Behavior change

Think back to your last head-to-head defiant-child encounter. Did you spend any emotional energy on those first three steps? How concerned were you with your child's feelings and priorities? On a 0 to 10 scale (0 = not at all, 10 = extremely important), what was your number? What would your child say was your number? The more a child feels truly understood, the safer she will feel to let go of the defiance and listen to what's important to you as well.

See how it feels to sincerely say, "I know you hate emptying the trash. You have to leave something you love and go around the house to collect things others threw away. There might even be some yucky stuff in there. I remember when I was a kid, I really disliked loading the dishwasher and putting in everyone's sticky dishes." This communicates "I really do understand you" as the starting place from which to solve the conflict and use consequences if needed.

You can also try to help your child realize, "It's usually easier for parents to give in, but I wouldn't be a good parent if I gave you everything you want. I'm committed to being thoughtful about what's best." With that insight, you can still show that her needs matter by offering a yes with an explanation to offset the no: "Instead of a cookie you can have an apple with yogurt dip, to keep you healthy," or "Instead of another video game, we can get art supplies that develop the creativity God gave you." Even if she isn't thrilled with an option, offer it with a sincere smile and you'll convey "I'm for you, not against you."

"You are CALLED and CAPABLE": How might I acknowledge and redirect a gift gone awry?

Martin Luther, Harriet Tubman, George Washington, Rosa Parks, and Dietrich Bonhoeffer were all defiant. Maybe it's time we see defiance less as a problem to eliminate and more as a quality to reposition for good.

We spoke one day with a teacher at a Christian school about behavior problems with her students, but she actually seemed more upset about the obedient kids. She declared, "I can always tell the kids who have parents who demand first-time obedience. They do what you say but take no risks. They won't give answers unless they know they're right. But the kids who fight back—they're usually the bold ones, the creative ones, the energetic ones. Many of them are leaders. I love the chance to shape these kids!"

Can you embrace a vision to shape your potential leader?

When have you seen your child's tenacity and strong will show up in a helpful or honoring way? If she's old enough, have a "defiance conversation": "What's good about your intense determination? How is it helpful? What's hard about it sometimes? When does it cause problems? Let's see if we can both be determined to solve our problem about [whatever the issue is]."

How might I nurture capability in my child?

The knee-jerk *no!* reaction some kids have is like a super-highway in their brain. You can nurture capability by making it easier for your child's brain to turn onto a different road. For example, ask a question that prompts a yes: "Are you guys having some crazy fun down here?" "Is this the coolest picture you've drawn today?" This can build connection and gradually make it easier for your child's brain to respond well to your subsequent guidance or requests.

Your child may respond with defiance if he feels overwhelmed. Small requests, even "Could you please hand me that pencil," can create success momentum and provide a chance for gratitude and affirmation ("Thanks, buddy!") that will empower him for larger requests. What's important is not what you think he *should* be able to do, but what he *can* fairly consistently do.

What can you do to build on that level of success? It's important to ask yourself, "Is this request a just-right challenge for my child?" In a similar way, "What might I do to help you get started?" lets him know you expect follow-through but are for him and want to set him up for success.

As you identify key triggers for your defiant child—the issues that typically spark a power struggle—you can set aside time when all is calm to brainstorm those challenges. This meets his need for healthy power at the same time that you build teamwork and his capability for leadership and wise decision-making. Ask questions like "How do we all feel about this situation? How would we like to feel about it? When it goes better, what does each of us do to help make that happen?" Children as young as four have benefitted greatly from this approach. For a copy of the "From Power Struggles to Problem-solving" handout, with additional questions and a diagram you can print and show your child, go to disciplinethatconnects .org.

"You are RESPONSIBLE": What consequence best teaches my child responsibility for his actions?

Demands without choices are fertile soil for defiance. Again, kids need to feel *safe, understood,* and have *healthy power* to begin to grow beyond their defiance. Offering thoughtful options can meet this need and help them to take responsibility for those choices.

This is not wishy-washy parenting—it follows the biblical pattern in which God clearly lays out choices and their consequences, while conveying His desire to bless us:

> This day I call the heavens and the earth as witnesses against you that I have set before you life and death, blessings and curses. Now choose life, so that you and your children may live and that you may love the LORD your God, listen to his voice, and

hold fast to him. (Deuteronomy 30:19–20. For another example, see Nehemiah 1:8–9.)

As a young adult, our son Daniel actually helped us make this giving-choices concept highly practical for parents when he did some in-home work with challenging kids. He had profound insight (maybe from a little firsthand experience of his own) into the dynamics between a defiant child and a struggling parent as he watched interactions. For example, when a parent made a demand ("Put your toys away!"), the child often thwarted the parent by refusing. Daniel would watch parents get more demanding to attempt to force compliance. As the interaction escalated, the toys would no longer be on anyone's radar—the goal now was to win at expressing how unfair, rude, disobedient, or mean the other person was. From this place it was difficult for the parent to follow through on any constructive consequences.

The If/Then choices tool Daniel developed has helped many parents empower their kids for responsibility, not defiance.

- "*If* you put the toys away before dinner . . ." [*Describe the wise decision.*]
- "*Then* you can have them tomorrow . . ." [*Describe the wise decision's result.*]

   ". . . which would be really fun; that looks like a cool toy!" [*Encourage the wise decision in terms of your child's goals, which shows you're for her, not against her.*]

- "*Otherwise* we'll put them away for you, and you can have them again on Saturday." [*State the unwise decision's result gently so it doesn't feel like a threat.*]

   ". . . and I'm sure you can find other things to play with instead. . . ." [*Adding a little silver lining for the results of her choice reinforces that you're for her, not against her.*]

- "*You can choose* either way and that's okay; it's up to you." [*Then calmly disengage and walk away. Give her space to make her own decision. This minimizes her temptation to decide impulsively out of spite or resistance or gridlock. In essence, you get out of the way of her wise choice!*]

If your child chooses wisely, help her enjoy its blessing on everyone. "You decided to pick up your toys and worked hard at it. Now you get to play with them tomorrow, and you practiced being responsible. It was really helpful for me to be able to focus on dinner instead of cleaning up toys. I appreciated that."

If she makes an unwise choice, stay relaxed and predict a better future outcome. "Remember, you'll get these back on [day]. Maybe we can take out fewer toys so they're easier to pick up. We'll figure it out—you're learning."

Using If/Then choices helps us remember all the parts of engaging a defiant child in an encouraging and empowering way. This template:

- eliminates empty threats and communicates "You are safe."
- communicates "I am for you, not against you," which communicates "You are loved."
- encourages wise decision-making, communicating "You are capable."
- sets clear boundaries with reasonable consequences.
- increases likelihood of follow-through, which communicates "You are responsible." (In the above example, the child has a do-over chance in a few days, with loss of privilege until that time.)
- follows a biblical pattern; one such example is laid out in Deuteronomy 30:19–20.

See an If/Then choices practice worksheet at disciplinethat connects.org/links.

Lying

Most parents make it their goal to get kids to stop lying. At face value this seems reasonable; however, it tends to pit parents and children against each other as opponents from the start. Children are bound to lie as they grow up, and parents are bound to catch them. Over time this can become a contentious hide-and-seek match. Kids get better and better at hiding lies, and suspecting parents grow less trusting and work harder to catch and punish them. We've seen this dynamic snowball until kids and parents utterly despise each other.

This is why we advocate a different goal. We've consistently seen much better success when parents seek to validate and place high value on truth-telling instead of putting big energy into punishing lying. This is not to say we don't confront lies— rather, we de-emphasize the punitive approach.

This "truth-telling promotion" goal is validated by a study in which elementary-aged children were set up with the opportunity to tell a lie. Dr. Victoria Talwar, an expert on child lying, found that reading to kids *The Boy Who Cried Wolf*, which emphasizes the dangers of lying, did nothing to curb— and even slightly increased—their lying during the experiment. Most of them lied when given the chance. (The authors of the article also found that kids who are frequently punished for lying don't lie less; they just get sneakier and better at it.)

Conversely, reading to kids *George Washington and the Cherry Tree*, which promotes the benefits and good feelings involved with truth-telling, reduced lying by 43 percent! Most of these children told the truth when given the chance.[5]

We want to share an approach that highly values truth-telling and treats lying with grace, because we've seen it powerfully open children's hearts to the Holy Spirit's conviction about being deceptive versus telling it like it is.

Practical/biblical perspectives: The very nature of Jesus is truth: "I am the way and the truth and the life" (John 14:6). True intimacy with people and with God depends on honesty. Telling the truth builds trust. False statements that sound good or smooth over a situation are the "kisses of an enemy." (See Proverbs 27:6.) Habitual lying leads to hardness of heart and broken relationships. Knowing all this to be true, the paradox of teaching kids to tell the truth is to demonstrate grace when they lie while advocating strongly for the benefits of truth-telling. As we faithfully speak of and demonstrate the blessings of "speaking the truth in love," kids will listen and learn (Ephesians 4:15).

Long-term vision for my children's lives: to value intimacy, trust, and honesty; to build an identity of integrity that safeguards relationships with others and honors God.

"You are SAFE with me": What's going on in me that affects how I engage with my child?

Research suggests that a primary reason kids learn to lie is that their parents model lying. Are you aware of any little (or big) ways you are dishonest and say what you think people want to hear?

Beth was angry and punitive when her son stayed late at a party and then lied to her about the absence of parent chaperones. She failed to consider that before he left, she'd suggested a deceitful excuse to leave the party if there were no parents: "Just tell your friends you have a headache." The message was, lie to your friends to do what I want, but you'd better not lie to me to do what you want.

What do you feel when your child lies, and how do your feelings affect your response? If your own hurt or anger is the primary driver, your child may feel guilty not because lying is wrong but because it upset Mom or Dad. So she'll either get craftier about not getting caught or take the lying elsewhere.

Communicating "You are safe with me" when a child lies means that I learn to respond to her out of my compassion and not my hurt.

"You are LOVED": How can I connect or empathize with my child?

Imagine telling a bold-faced lie to someone you feel really safe and connected with on a heart level. Deception doesn't match the relationship's quality; it feels off. Children usually lie because they feel anxious and/or disconnected from us. They may even be working hard to counteract shame and fear of rejection. Working hard to connect more deeply with a dishonest child can give him the courage to tell the truth.

Patty and Carl were convinced that their ten-year-old son's frequent lies were another sign that he just didn't care about them or their values. But as they persevered at being more affectionate and encouraging with Devin despite his difficult behavior, they saw a variety of changes—he began to tell them he loved them, and sibling conflict began to subside.

Then one night a breakthrough happened. Devin locked his room so he could break the rules and play his DS at bedtime. His dad stopped by twice to connect; both times the door was locked, and both times Devin quickly hid his DS before opening. "The lock must be sticky," Devin lied, and then, "Boy, it's really sticky." Though suspicious, Carl chatted lovingly with him both times.

After this, Devin had a chance to think about what he'd done in a context of feeling secure and loved instead of being accused and defending himself. A bit later he slipped out of bed and put a note on Carl's computer. "Dad, I have something really bad to tell you."

When Carl came in, Devin began sobbing. "I lied when I told you the door locked itself. I was playing on my DS."

Carl listened gently and affirmed his honesty. Later, he sent his son this text: "Devin I am sad that u lied to me but I am proud that u made the right choice to admit your sin. It honors both God and me. It shows that you are maturing. I love you no matter what. You can always talk to me. Even if it is hard - Dad."

Devin still occasionally stretches the truth, but Carl has not known him to tell another bold-faced lie since that day. This is the safety and connection that empowers kids to be honest.

"You are CALLED and CAPABLE": How might I acknowledge and redirect a gift gone awry?

Kids who lie just might be using a few good "gifts gone awry" to do it . . . creativity, confidence, good memory, even a desire to keep everyone happy. Our son Noah went through a year or so of struggling with truth-telling. He was definitely a "get along with everyone, love to keep the peace" kid who didn't want to disappoint us.

Here's how a conversation about this might go with a child who's lied to you. "I really appreciate your _____ [name the good trait] in this. This is not the most helpful way I've seen you use it, though. It's important to me that we keep a close, trust-based relationship. What are your ideas about that?"

How might I nurture capability in my child?

Parents tend to set kids up to lie by asking them about something they know the child would not want to reveal. This can be very discouraging for the child, especially if the parent then punishes her. She feels trapped—either she admits a shameful truth or she lies to evade trouble at the risk of getting caught and punished. The result is she's even less trusting of the parent.

When you know your child might be tempted to lie, set him up to tell the truth. Instead of "Did you brush your teeth?" say, "Let's quick check your toothbrush before you leave. Think I'll find it wet or dry?" He'll almost certainly tell the truth since avoiding detection is so unlikely. When he says "dry," you can respond by affirming his true answer. For instance: "You could have lied about that, but you didn't. When you tell the truth like this it helps me trust you more. Thanks! I really appreciate it. What'll it take to get that toothbrush wet?" This shows him you're for him in the challenge of learning to tell more truth instead of against him in the battle to catch and punish lies.

Parents can also help children learn to value honesty by "catching" them telling the truth without prompting. Kids tell the truth far more often than they lie. Especially for younger kids: Listen to her tell a story about her day, or ask him his opinion on something. Any time you hear truth is a chance to affirm, "You're telling the truth, aren't you! Feels good, doesn't it?"

When there's natural opportunity, tell stories from your own life about times you told the truth even when tempted to lie. Get the kids talking about times they told the truth when it was hard.

Since kids often lie to keep the peace, a great opportunity to affirm truth-telling is when they're angry, spouting off, and *not* keeping the peace. We can affirm the gift of honest expression gone awry: "You're really ticked off about this! I think it'd be best to talk about it when you're calmer so I can understand clearly, but I really appreciate how honest you were just now. Even if it's hard to hear, that's really important to me." This sends him strong messages: "Your honesty matters more to me than your delivery" and "Heart connection is more important than outward behavior."

"You are RESPONSIBLE": What consequence best teaches my child responsibility for his actions?

Lying results in a valuable chance to help your kids learn to tune in to that subtle, unsettled feeling of God-given conviction, which truly is the ideal consequence to teach them responsibility for their words. At a relaxed time, talk together about the "knot in their stomach" they might experience when they lie or do something else hurtful. Help them view this as a good thing, a sign of maturity, even a gift—God's protection of their life and relationships. His Spirit guides us into truth, and truth, including the truth about our sin, sets us free. (See John 16:13; 8:32.) Share about a time you lied or were deceitful, how you felt God's conviction, how you made it right, and how you felt afterward.

We gently helped our son Noah learn to tune in to that Holy Spirit stomach knot. He began to come to us (sometimes in tears), "Mom, Dad . . . I lied again." This gave us a rich opportunity to affirm his tender conscience and honesty, and extend forgiveness. This was integral to his growth into the meticulously honest young man he is today.

Do-over: The first lies usually show up in two-year-olds. An interaction might go something like this: "Honey, did you mess your diaper?" Somehow kids already have a sense of this as a problem, either feeling ashamed about it (based on how adults respond to a smelly, messy diaper) or not wanting to stop what they're doing. So they lie. "No."

The way to encourage them to be truthful is to be sure there's a big, expressive reward for telling the truth. Stage a do-over with a light-hearted tone to set your child up for a truthful response: "Honey, I'm going to look in your diaper now. What's in there?" Now the child knows you're going to look, and he will likely say "Poopy." If not, you can prompt it: "Can you say *poopy*?" When he says it, give some big expressive energy and say, "That's right! You told me the truth!"

With older kids, you may realize you've trapped them in a lie. For example, you asked suspiciously, "Don't you have homework tonight?" and got "Uh . . . no." Rather than up the ante with "Don't lie to me," take a breath, add some warmth and humility, and take a do-over. "I realize my tone and question weren't helpful; maybe they made you defensive. I'm sorry. I want to give you a better chance to tell me the truth. If I were to check the school ParentLink website, what would I see? Do you know for sure, or should we check it together?"

Lose the privilege: As kids get older, lies get craftier. Certainly if the lie is about use of a privilege, like screen time or car use, then a consequence of losing that privilege may be appropriate. But with craftier lying comes a deeper layer of issues to address—of disconnection, discouragement, or shame, etc., which may have prompted your child to lie. Resorting to removing a privilege without addressing those issues is likely to make the lying worse.

Make it right: The most important "lying factor" is relationship. Trust is broken; confession and forgiveness are needed for restoration. So ideally, consequences relate to restoring relationship and reconnecting in some way.

Since children tend to lie less to someone with whom they feel closely connected, a possible consequence could be that she will plan an outing to reconnect with the parent she deceived. One dad's guideline for his daughter was that if he caught her in a lie, she was grounded until she reconnected with him by sharing something she hadn't ever told anyone. This unusual rule communicated that his priority was closeness and trust with her.

Disrespect/Sass

Few things push Mom or Dad's buttons like a kid mouthing off or getting aggressive. Usually we shift into "I'm in charge here" posture, and proclaim, "Don't you *dare* talk to me that way!" or "You will *not* treat your sister like that!" or "Go to your room *now*!" These anger-energized responses set an example children are likely to follow.

The principle taught: Anger equals power.

We're reinforcing the very behavior we're trying to curb . . . unless the child is anxious or easily intimidated. (If this type of child doesn't feel safe expressing anger, he may begin showing it passive-aggressively to get back at a parent. He may pick on a sibling, fail assignments, or act in other ways that are less overt or obvious but more destructive in the long run.)

When a kid gets angry and abusive, less-assertive parents may shrink away from the outbursts, which is no more constructive than being domineering. It teaches her she's in charge. The principle is the same: Anger equals power. But now the child has it all.

Neither passivity nor angry control by a parent holds a child accountable for her poor choices. Without true accountability, she's unlikely to develop the heart of compassion and kindness toward others that her parents desire for her. However, when parents have both the confidence and self-control to thoughtfully and spiritually address what's happening, their kids will feel more respected and likely will be more responsive to discipline.

This approach is not a quick, "Now say you're sorry!" Scripted, forced apologies teach a child to lie or merely speak memorized words to get out of trouble. They also learn to avoid the painful process of true reconciliation.

Reconciliation is tough work. Understanding the complexities of each unique situation requires thoughtfulness and vision. The thoughtful parent's goal is not immediate control but rather helping a child to:

1. identify and honestly communicate his difficult feelings.
2. comprehend the other person's point of view.

3. grow in skills for healthy and God-honoring conflict resolution . . . with God's love and grace permeating the whole process.

Why is this so difficult for kids?

When young children first enter the conflict resolution arena, they have very limited language and problem-solving skills but a whole lot of intense emotions. This overwhelming combination pushes them to fight-or-flight self-protection skills when angry or stressed. These are essential functions when there's true danger, yet they also kick in whenever we simply feel threatened. In fight-or-flight, the brain provides quick access to bold aggressive or defensive responses but efficiently blocks access to less-necessary cognitive skills like articulate language, awareness of feelings, or problem-solving. (When I'm attacked, I don't need to ask the attackers what they're feeling!)

So when your tyke is ticked, she has easy access to aggressive responses like punch/shove or "You dummyhead/I hate you," and truly very limited access to "I'm really frustrated that you want me to stop this fun and get to bed" or "I'm angry that Logan took my truck; I want it back."

The same basic principle is true of us adults—we're just a little more sophisticated at our disrespect. Remember: Kids read facial expression, tone of voice, and body language, and they react to the intent behind them more than they respond to our actual words. So when your child says to his sibling, "You *idiot*," if you respond with a pointed finger, clenched jaw, and furrowed brow, "That is *not* acceptable behavior, young man!" you might as well be saying, "Knock it off, you idiot!" because the emotional impact is nearly the same.

Attempting conflict resolution in a state of intense anger is like attempting surgery with a sword. The tools available are meant for a different job. So—calm first, communicate second. Kids need much practice—with supervision and affirmation—to learn the necessary skills and build easily accessible brain pathways to respectful conflict resolution.

Practical/biblical perspectives: John the Baptist's calling was to prepare the way for Christ (see Luke 1:17; John 1:23), and turning parents' hearts toward their children was crucial to doing this. Connected parent-child relationships aren't about silencing disrespect or saying the "right" things. The Lord can't stand inward contempt covered up with spiritual talk and outward obedience. "These people . . . honor me with their lips, but their hearts are far from me. Their worship of me is based on merely human rules they have been taught" (Isaiah 29:13).

The upshot of this is, God isn't concerned about what's coming out of your child's *mouth*, He's concerned about what's in your child's *heart*, and whether or not it's well-connected to yours. And probably, to whatever degree you can get past the hurt from your child's disrespect, so are you.

"You are SAFE with me": What's going on in me that affects how I engage with my child?

Start by considering your own beliefs and feelings about conflict:

- What were my family's rules about conflict and respect?
- Do I consider anger and conflict inherently bad?
- If my child lips off to me, do I instantly feel threatened or angry?

Most parents would say yes to that last question. (We certainly remember the feeling.) One vented, "Oh, the eye-rolling and sass—it's driving me crazy! How do I stop it?" Unfortunately, this desire is the very thing that feeds sass. In Jim's outreach, a frustrated teen once said that when she couldn't get life to go her way, "At least I can get my old lady to jump around and act crazy." Her mom's big reaction was just what she was looking for. So consider: Is my child stressed, discouraged, or anxious—and wanting my intense attention? Showing care and concern for those issues builds true respect and connection.

Parents who are satisfied with a zipped lip as an outward show of respect aren't usually looking below the surface at their child's heart. What is she mumbling about you as she heads off to her room? And what might she be texting friends when she gets there? Shutting down expression of boiling emotions is almost sure to erode whatever respect a child has for a parent.

True respect isn't demanded; it's earned with the kind of character your child *naturally* respects. And that's a good thing. Parents want their kids to look up to and emulate people with deep character. Humility will help us be among those people.

. . . .

Megan had been concerned about Evan's increasing disrespect with family members. As she sat down to address it with her son, she saw his defenses rise and felt God prompting her to start with a different approach. "I've noticed you've been struggling more with being respectful, and . . . [noticeable pause] I'm wondering if I've been disrespectful to you recently." Evan immediately responded, "Yes!" and poured out hurts from his mom's responses to him in recent weeks. This resulted in a deep connection, forgiveness, and a significantly increased tone of respect in their home. For Megan, this was humbling and difficult but richly rewarding.

. . . .

In our house we often earned every bit as much respect from our kids when we regrouped after we'd blown it as we did from wise responses in the heat of the moment. I (Lynne) remember trudging down the stairs to reconcile after Daniel and I had a disrespectful exchange. As I went, I thought, *It's my job to get this started. At least my kids will know what to do when they blow it.* When I entered his room, he was lying on his bed, leaning back with a grin. He greeted me with, "I knew you were coming." My first thought was, *You little stinker.* My second was, *He trusts me to reconcile. That's really important.*

Think of people you profoundly respect. How is it you feel that way about them? What might you do to draw that kind of respect from your kids?

And then, as you think more deeply about this, how can you prepare yourself for your child's disrespect so you can stay peaceful in the heat of the moment? Here are some thoughts to slow down and cool off the interaction:

- We don't have to stay stuck; I can do this differently.
- His disrespect doesn't mean he's a bad kid or I'm a bad parent.
- I guide him toward true respect when I stay respectful and lead with grace.

I (Jim) have faced the ultimate disrespect from troubled teens. Many times my first greeting from a new kid at our youth outreach was a scowl and scornful demand: "Who the f--- are you?" I learned to smile, unfazed, and say, "Hi. I'm Jim. That's quite a greeting. I look forward to getting to know you." As I developed connections with them, I also guided them toward responding in much better ways out of their own unique gifts of self-expression.

"You are LOVED": How can I connect or empathize with my child?

Think about times you're disrespectful to others. It's most often when you're stressed, anxious, discouraged, or ashamed. Your kids are no different. Caring about what's driving the disrespect and reaffirming your love anyway conveys a mighty message of unconditional love. Tara, who'd taken our online course, was learning to look below the surface into her sassy, intense four-year-old's heart and give voice to the stress and difficult feelings.

> Our family was traveling, and we were making our way through a crowded hotel. We were all tired and stressed. Cecelia was over-stimulated and began to melt down as I was carrying a big load of our luggage. She escalated till she loudly screamed, "I hate you! I hate you!" We suddenly had the attention of lots of people. I was deeply hurt—she'd never said this before. [Tara teared up sharing this painful memory.] I was tempted to give a quick, harsh response. But I remembered I wanted to do this differently, so I set down my load and prayed, *Jesus, I don't know what to say right now.* That cleared my spirit and I was able to consider, *What does she need right now?*
>
> I started by kneeling down to her level and giving voice to her experience: "It's really crowded and noisy here, isn't it? But no matter what you say to me, or whether or not you mean it, I love you and I'm never going to stop loving you." She jumped into my arms, and I held her until she calmed down. It must have met a deep need in her soul, because for several weeks after that she seemed so much more resilient and joyful.

"You are CALLED and CAPABLE": How might I acknowledge and redirect a gift gone awry?

Passion, expressiveness, and confidence are among the good gifts that can sinfully show up in disrespect. A child's quick responsiveness can become misguided aggression. A strong sense of justice may lock a child on to getting what he thinks is fair. Honesty can be harshly blunt, leadership domineering, and insight negatively critical. Wit often feeds sarcasm. The list goes on.

When dealing with disrespect, acknowledging a child's good gifts gone awry tends to temper our own black-and-white, judgmental responses and calm everyone. One day my (Jim's) harshness toward Bethany prompted Daniel's sarcastic retort, "Way to go, Ogre!"

It was quite a bit later when we were both calm enough to discuss this interaction. I acknowledged that he'd used his bold wit and compassion to defend his little sister. That set the stage for us to discuss how it might have gone better on both our parts.

If there's a way to incorporate the good gift in the solution, that's even more helpful. In our home, kids sometimes used powerful words to hurt others. We guided them to calm down, process the conflict, and, when ready, use powerful words to heal the damage they'd inflicted.

How might I nurture capability in my child?

Some parents think it's an effective consequence to remove a child's door from the hinges if she slams it. Clever, yes. Constructive, probably not. This is the message: "What I care about is stopping your outward display of disrespect so I feel back in control." To show you care about what's beneath the sarcastic barbs, rolling eyes, or slamming doors, don't suppress but empower!

I (Lynne) made numerous grand pronouncements to Daniel on occasions of disrespect, complete with eyes popping and veins bulging: "You can't talk to me that way!" But then I would step back and consider my statement: *Unhelpful. Untrue. And probably a bit amusing to my insightful son.*

I also clearly remember the first time I said this instead: "I'm feeling really upset right now, and I don't want to be disrespectful to you, so let's take a break and talk about this later."

It was a breakthrough for us, as Daniel soon began to imitate this with a slightly blunter version: "Mom, I'm really ticked off!

297

I need a break." Our discussions thereafter were much more productive and respectful.

If you're concerned about disrespect, how *do* you want your kids to deal wisely and respectfully with their upset feelings? And how can you help them learn it? Here's another example to help you create what would work for you:

> I'd like to understand the real message beneath the eye-rolling (or door-slamming). We are too upset to talk about it now, but before the end of the day I'd like you to put it in a few clear, respectful sentences so I can understand. I think that will help us both. (You could even ask your child to write this down so you can think carefully about how to respond.)

"You are RESPONSIBLE*": What consequence best teaches my child responsibility for his actions?*

The ideas above pave the way for a do-over to discuss the underlying issue in a helpful, respectful way. This holds kids responsible for their actions and builds skills to avoid disrespect in the future. Ideas in the "Peace Process" section (see under Sibling Conflict) may help as well to guide the discussion.

If kids are hesitant to have this discussion, they may be anticipating a lecture. You can help them feel more at ease about how it will go and then ask them to set a time. If necessary, put some distracting privileges on hold until this is accomplished. If you're careful to focus on understanding and solving (not criticizing), and then you affirm whatever either of you did well during the process, you just might find this kind of discussion happening more often.

When the disrespect flew in our house, we worked to make sure we took responsibility to reconnect well afterward. Sometimes it was doing something fun after discussing our conflict. Sometimes it was just making sure all hurts were resolved and we were in a good place with each other. One day Daniel criticized the dinner I (Lynne) had planned. I upped the ante with a sarcastic retort. He dropped a couple of explosive name-calling zingers. After sincerely apologizing for my sarcasm and crankiness, I asked him to write eight "kind and true" statements to offset and set straight the two "unkind and untrue" bombs. Finding that piece of paper years later was really entertaining: "You are not a nincompoop; You are not a sarcastic piece of feces; I love you; You rock the house; Thank you for the meal; You make good food; You are very tolerant; You da woman!" (And I'm sure we had a pleasant meal after that!)

Sibling Conflict and Aggression

- "If another believer *sins against you*, go privately and point out the offense" (Matthew 18:15 NLT, emphasis added).
- "If you . . . remember that someone *has something against you* . . . go and be reconciled to that person" (Matthew 5:23–24 NLT, emphasis added).

Jesus' words remind us that those who have the problem solve the problem—not everyone else in the family who has an opinion about it! A fun reminder from *The Message*: "You grab a mad dog by the ears when you butt into a quarrel that's none of your business" (Proverbs 26:17).

Long-term vision for my children's lives: to experience gospel grace in conflict and learn the values and skills that will equip them for authentic, connected, joy-filled relationships. (Think of the divorce and family pain that could be avoided, as well as the gossip, division, and bitterness in the body of Christ, if we all were clearly taught these values and skills as children.)

"You are SAFE with me": What's going on in me that affects how I engage with my child?

Consider:

- Am I fearful about what my child will be like as a spouse/parent?
- Am I worried I'm raising a child who will bully others?
- Am I worried my less-assertive child will be bullied, a perpetual victim in life?
- Do I have baggage about how sibling relationships went in my home?
- Do I engage sibling conflict with some variation of "Here we go again" and a ready-made judgment about who's at fault?

As I (Lynne) have shared (see chapter 10), I could have answered yes to all those questions. Dealing with my baggage was the starting point of real change. I determined what was true to counteract each of those hurtful thoughts, and then I hung on to those truths for dear life as I entered my kids' conflict with a new question: "Lord, what's the opportunity here?"

This determination was fueled by my passion for "my kids to have the kind of relationships in life that Jesus bought for them on the cross!" Jim and I both had faith that God's grace and love would trickle down over our messy conflicts and, over time, do amazing things. We were not disappointed.

In a similar way, Max, father of three feisty kids, heard the Discipline that Connects messages and got passionate about communicating them in family conflict. "Now instead of yelling and punishing, I go into my kids' fights proclaiming, 'We are going to have a safe and loving home!'" Max grinned as he added, "What kid doesn't want that?" His statement and conviction opened his children's hearts to what he'd say next:

"What you're doing right now is not safe and loving. You can take a break till you're ready to resolve it that way." His kids recognized the change in his heart and followed as he led with grace. And longstanding patterns began to change.

So what's your passion that will help you persevere?

"You are LOVED": How can I connect or empathize with my child?

Need for understanding and encouragement is common to all struggling kids. Start with simple statements that show you understand and care: "This is really hard, isn't it? I remember fighting with my brother" or "I know how important _____ is to you." Sitting between kids, an arm around each, also can convey acceptance and encouragement (and buffer the interaction).

In some of the families we worked with who made wonderful progress with sibling conflict, we had parents ask, "What does Mom or Dad do that is helpful and not helpful when you kids have a conflict?" Answers were very similar, focused on kids' need for understanding and encouragement. An intense, articulate eight-year-old said it best: "It really helps when my mom comes over and quietly talks to me and reminds me that I can do this and she believes in me. It does not help when my mom yells at us when we fight because it makes me feel broken down when I already need help."

"You are CALLED and CAPABLE": How might I acknowledge and redirect a gift gone awry?

When kids battle, there may be a variety of gifts or good qualities gone awry: They want to spend time together and feel important to each other, they have creative ideas about how things should go, they stand up for themselves, they have strong emotions, they have a strong sense of justice, or they have leadership potential. Call those out and suggest a more honoring use:

e.g., "What's fair is really important to you. That's something God built in you to bless people with. When you've calmed down, I bet you'll be able to use that to help come up with a solution that works both for you and your sister."

How might I nurture capability in my child?

When a child can't resolve a conflict without disrespect, the temptation is to tell her what to say, or dictate a solution to bring about an immediate end. What does she learn from this approach? That she's incapable and needs you to solve her problems. Not what you want her to learn, right? Just like learning to walk or to write one's name, learning conflict-resolution skills is gradual, with plenty of falls or messes along the way.

This process is a lot easier when kids understand why it's worth the effort. It's human nature to go halfheartedly at something if you think you're being forced into it with no idea why. If kids see the awesomeness of truly resolving conflicts well, they'll make far more progress than if they think they're doing the drill Mom or Dad mandates. (See "The Duct-Tape Approach to Reconciliation" activity near the end of chapter 17 for help explaining.)

"The Peace Process"

Here's a simple suggested process with specific ideas for facilitating and building conflict-resolving capability in your kids.

1. **Calm down.** This step is for reflecting and regrouping, *not* a timed punishment. (See Psalm 4:4.)
   - Model calming yourself, and guide kids to do the same. "Wow, you guys are pretty upset right now. Let's all take a little break to calm down and think about how to solve this." (Even if you aren't upset, this gives you a chance to pray for wisdom.) Encourage them to choose

a favorite way to calm—relaxing in a comfortable (non-distracting) place, drawing, riding their bike around the block once, taking deep breaths . . . whatever works for them. One four-year-old learned to take "dragon breaths" (long inhale through nose, slow "fiery" breath out through mouth), then encouraged others in his family to do the same.

- While kids are resting, give an assignment to think through, e.g., "What did you feel and want? What do you think your sibling felt and wanted?" Challenge them to see how closely they can anticipate each other's answers when they get back together.

- If they're open to it, you can remind them of God's love and mercy in the midst of our conflicts.

- When children comply with taking a calming break, affirm how helpful that is. This affirmation often changes the tone of the rest of the interaction.

- If emotions are extremely high, it may take quite some time for fight-or-flight brain chemistry to subside. Kids can either write or draw the main ideas they want to discuss so that later that day they can recall important details. Keep these sheets safe in a clip, file, or box, and use a timer or sticky note to make sure the issues don't get dropped. One mom stated, "Lots of times our kids fight in the mornings getting ready. It's helped a ton to keep notebooks in the car to jot down what they're upset about. It calms them down, and we remember to solve it after school."

2. **Understand each other.** Help your children learn to identify and express their own feelings/perspective and listen to and understand the other person's feelings/perspective. (See James 1:19 and Ephesians 4:15.)

- Establish rules as a family about how to address conflict. (For example, we had "Say what you feel and want, but speak the truth in love. Yelling, mean words, or name-calling means you're not ready.") During this process, gently restate these rules, and remind kids of previous successes in following them.
- Make sure kids address each other, not you.
- Vary the questions as needed for kids to be successful. To identify feelings, young children usually need simple choices, e.g., "Are you sad or mad right now?" Some might respond well to, "What was important to you? What do you think was important to your brother?" Older children can answer more open-ended questions: "You seem upset. What's that about?" Kids can restate what's said until all feel understood.
- Understanding other people's perspectives and feelings can be very difficult for a child who's more intense, active, or anxious than typical kids. *You Are a Social Detective!* and other helpful resources are available at socialthinking.com.

3. **Find a good solution.** Work together to bring about forgiveness or create possible solutions and/or compromises. (See Ephesians 4:32 and Philippians 2:3.)
   - For some children, this step may be as simple as asking, "What do you want to do to solve this?"
   - Children may understand each other but not necessarily want to apologize. It can feel shameful and difficult to choke out the words "I'm sorry." A question that helps is, "Now that you've listened to each other well . . . if you could do it all over, is there anything you'd do differently?" This can lead to, "That's good insight. What would you like to say to your sister/brother about

that?" or "Do you want a do-over?" One youngster who found it very difficult to apologize did much better if he started with, "I wish I hadn't_____." This often led to, "I wish I had_____ instead," and a heartfelt apology often followed.

- Remind kids that part of growing up is thinking about everyone involved, not just themselves. If they're open to it, you could read Philippians 2:3: "Do nothing out of selfish ambition or vain conceit. Rather, in humility value others above yourselves." Then ask, "What's the one thing that's most important to each of you? How could your solution include those things?" Remind them of any previous successes at finding solutions.

4. **Celebrate!** Celebrate their success. Review any positive effort or attitude you noticed, however slight. (See Philippians 4:8b.)

- Who wants to do the hard work of conflict resolution if you always end up feeling ashamed, hurt, or frustrated? When parents are faithful to do the final step of celebrating *anything* that went well, kids are much more eager to try it again next time. A sense of progress begets more progress. So it's vital to leave kids feeling like they've really accomplished something.

- Even if it was a time-consuming and messy process, help kids see whatever contribution each of them made to the solution. This is especially important if other kids are watching. As one mom put it, "Leave them feeling good about what they did well, instead of ashamed of what they did wrong." Based on how the brain grows new patterns (positive or negative), this is really good advice. We've found that parents who do the first (calming) and last (celebration) steps well can often come to let their kids muddle through the resolution process on their own to grow skills independently.

Once our kids learned the routine and rules for resolving, we'd structure a calming break if the conflict was intense, or simply ask if they needed help resolving. Whenever they were ready to solve the conflict on their own, we'd send them into our room to sit on opposite sides of the bed (a "demilitarized zone") until they'd resolved their issue well enough to meet in the middle for a hug. This automatically started "celebration," which we'd finish off when they returned by affirming their process or asking what they had done well.

The assistance children need fades over time as they learn these four steps, until maybe you'll only need to say something like, "Looks like you guys are having a hard time right now. You've worked through tough things before. What help do you need to resolve this peacefully and respectfully?"

One day I (Lynne) was chatting with an acquaintance when our kids came running up, blurting out their sides of a conflict. I structured them as usual, and when they emerged from our bedroom about five minutes later chattering happily, my friend's jaw dropped. "How'd you get them to do that?!" I assured her there was no trick, that it was the result of a lot of practice on everyone's part and perseverance through the many times we thought we were getting nowhere.

This can take a *long* time. But be patient—the effort is infinitely worth it!

"You are RESPONSIBLE": What consequence best teaches my child responsibility for his actions?

We've seen children from two-year-olds to teens solve their own conflicts and take responsibility for their actions with a little encouragement and some thoughtful questions.

Four-year-old Caleb would often hit his younger brother if Luke got in his way when they played. One day Luke came running, crying and accusing Caleb of hitting him. Instead of angrily punishing Caleb, this time Alicia chose thoughtful questions to engage his awareness and problem-solving. She gently asked him if he hit Luke, and he answered, "Yes."

"Was that a good thing to do or not such a good thing?"

"Not such a good thing."

"Hmm. Well, what do you think you should do about it? What good things could you do with your hands for Luke? What do you think you could do to help you remember that you shouldn't hit him?"

Feeling respected and empowered, Caleb's face lit up. "We could make a chart!" Alicia gave him some paper and a pen; he traced his hand and drew Luke as a stick figure near it. He asked her to help him write "No hitting." He was on a roll and made two more pictures of other things not to do to his brother: "No pushing" and "No taking toys away from Luke." Caleb and Alicia tacked up the picture where the boys often played, and he apologized to Luke.

The next day, they were drawing pictures when Luke decided it was fun to keep turning the lights on and off. Caleb got upset and walked over to Luke. Trouble seemed to be brewing, when suddenly Caleb ran down the hall. He came back with a smile on his face. "Mom! Mom! I was going to hit Luke and I didn't. I ran to look at my chart and saw 'No hitting,' and I didn't hit Luke!" Alicia told him that using his self-control was really a grown-up thing to do. He was *so* proud of himself, smiling ear to ear.

When kids start to be disrespectful, a simple, non-condemning "Oops, how about a do-over?" can be all they need to regroup and try a more respectful approach. Bethany was quick to back up little Noah in conflicts with their older brother. Of course, Daniel would feel ganged up on, and "Butt out,

Bethany!" was often his harsh response. Over time we helped him learn (through lots of repetition) to take a breath and say, "Bethany, this is not your issue." Do-overs help with changing patterns and developing skills, because kids end a conflict by practicing and feeling good about a wise, kind response.

There was lots of conflict in Kelly and Tim's blended family of teens, so they all decided to do do-overs when they blew it with each other. Modeling this was the key. The next day, Tim, feeling sick and crabby, told his kids their delay in shoveling the driveway was laziness. As they resentfully went out to shovel, one muttered, "*You* should do a do-over." When they came back inside, Tim humbled himself to apologize, adding, "I wish I'd said, 'Hey kids, I'm really feeling sick today. Would you please shovel the driveway?'"

Several days later his daughter ridiculed her brother for a low test score. He snapped back. She stormed off, slamming her door. Tim was tempted to come down on her but let her think about it. She soon messaged her brother to apologize and ask for a do-over. And reconciliation's value was growing.

Scripture strongly emphasizes the importance of true reconciliation. God's priority for us, even before worship or offerings, is first to go reconcile our conflicts. (See Matthew 5:23–24.) A way to reinforce this value is to convey, "Your relationships are your first priority. If you have a conflict with someone, all other distracting activities are on hold until that's resolved and you've reconciled well." Restricting privileges in this way encourages kids to reconcile but doesn't demand it immediately when they aren't ready.

- For older kids: When you've done the hard work of reconciling, you can resume contact with your friends, regain use of your computer or phone, go to the game/mall/party, etc.

- For younger kids: Once you've worked this out, you can play with your sister again, have the toys back (the ones that led to the conflict), and so on.

These consequences have an important goal—to restore the harmony that's ours in Christ! They will make good sense to children *if* we proactively talk about reconciliation as a wonderful gift rooted in the gospel's grace and peace. And *if* we model it and value it in our own relationships!

Once the consequences that move kids toward working it out are in place, kids can wait until they're ready—they get to make this call. Then parents can come alongside them to facilitate conflict resolution. This is not for the faint of heart. We have many times started well only to be drawn into unhelpful emotions and dynamics. But having a strategy and practicing again and again have strengthened us to dive in and stay the course. For more depth and practical ideas, you can sign up for our sibling conflict online course at disciplinethatconnects.org/links.

* * *

Sibling *aggression* brought about some of the most difficult situations for us to stay peaceful and purposeful. When there was strong aggression (verbal or physical) on the part of one child, two important principles emerged as we helped kids reconcile, including consequences as needed:

Focus first on strengthening the one who was wounded. The initial important lesson we learned along the way is to avoid our default response of focusing our initial or biggest energy on confronting the offender.

Jesus' timeless conflict resolution instructions are aimed at *empowering*:

If your brother or sister sins [against you], go and point out their fault, just between the two of you. If they listen to you, you have won them over. But *if they will not listen, take one or two others along*, so that "every matter may be established by the testimony of two or three witnesses" (Matthew 18:15–16, emphasis added).

The emphasis is not on punishing the one who sinned or sending another person to do the confronting—it's on supporting the one hurt to confront the offender with only as much assistance as needed. The goal: sincere repentance.

When our first response is to comfort and empower, we build empathy in the aggressor as she listens to the feelings of the child she hurt. It also empowers the one hurt to set a consequence or boundary, which the parent enforces. "Sounds like you want to take a break from playing with Maya right now. Okay, Maya, did you hear that? Where are you going to choose to play for a bit, other than the toy room?"

This priority of "comfort and empower" is a win/win/win. It tends to calm the parent; conveys safety, caring, and confidence to the hurt child; and gives the aggressive child a chance to think on what happened. It also avoids rewarding him with lots of intense attention. No more whacking sis just to get a big Mom/Dad reaction!

Impose only constructive consequences. In this challenge with aggressive conflict, we also learned that imposed consequences are constructive only to the degree that they move kids toward a heartfelt apology and forgiveness. So right along with the consequences we used, we put in place teaching about reconciliation: "If you used your hands to hurt, you can reconcile by using your hands to help" and "It takes several healing statements to repair the damage from one hurtful statement."

We taught our kids Scripture as part of their discipleship for conflicts. A favorite was Proverbs 12:18: "The words of the reckless pierce like swords, but the tongue of the wise brings healing." When children are reckless, give them an opportunity to be wise as part of their consequence.

Restitution consequences that were constructive and helpful for our family included:

- The consequence for physical aggression was putting all distracting privileges on hold until the child had resolved the problem by doing something kind for the one hurt or threatened. The aggressed-against child could give input also.

- For name-calling or strong verbal disrespect (something unkind and untrue), reconciliation was four both-kind-and-true statements, including setting the untruth straight e.g., "You're not a stupidbutt." (Based on Ephesians 4:15.) It was important that this did not become a rote formula, so at least two of the statements had to be fresh and creative. Sometimes the four statements included some pretty silly stuff ("Your eyes match"; "You aren't an alien"). Occasionally, if the offending sibling got stuck for new ideas, the "victim" offered a suggestion. This process often set the tone for fun and connection afterward.

Our kids came to increasingly value this process. We helped them notice the joy that came with restitution and reconciliation, contrasted with how the conflict felt before it was resolved: "Now you're living out the true heart God gave you for your sister/brother." We used these times to discuss God's forgiving and reconciling nature, seeking to disciple through our discipline.

What was the fruit of all this effort? We have been blessed to watch our children (now in their twenties) grow to be dear friends who love to hang out together and have healthy, compassionate relationships with others. In his late teen years, Daniel said, "I love apologizing, because I can take the wrong I've done, cast it off, and be free of it and have it be forgiven by both God and man. It's beautiful!"

Notes

Chapter 12: Building the Wisdom Kids Need

1. Merton P. Strommen and Richard A. Hardel, *Passing On the Faith* (Winona, MN: Saint Mary's Press, Christian Brothers Publications, 2000), 59, quoting Bradley J. Strahan, *Parents, Adolescents and Religion* (New South Wales: Avondale College, 1994), 25.

Chapter 16: Understanding *Why* My Child Is Misbehaving

1. Chip Heath and Dan Heath, *Switch: How to Change Things When Change Is Hard* (New York: Random House, 2010), 154.

Appendix Section A: Self-Motivated, Responsible Kids

1. Commission on Children at Risk, *Hardwired to Connect: The New Scientific Case for Authoritative Communities* (New York: Broadway, 2003), 31, 38–39.

Appendix Section B: Peaceful Daily Routines

1. Mary Sheedy Kurcinka, *Sleepless in America* (New York: Harper Perennial, 2006).

2. John Trent and Gary Smalley, *The Blessing* (Nashville: Thomas Nelson, 2001).

Appendix Section C: Growing True Respect and Reconciliation

1. Harvey Karp, *The Happiest Toddler on the Block*, dir. Nina Montee (Los Angeles: The Happiest Baby, Inc., 2004), DVD. Also see Ross W. Greene, PhD, *The Explosive Child: A New Approach for Understanding and Parenting Easily Frustrated, Chronically Inflexible Children*, 5th rev. ed., (New York: Harper, 2014).

2. Daniel J. Siegel, MD, and Tina Payne Bryson, PhD, *The Whole-Brain Child: 12 Revolutionary Strategies to Nurture Your Child's Developing Mind* (New York: Bantam, 2012).

3. Stephanie Madrigal and Michelle Garcia Winner, *Superflex Takes on Glassman and the Team of Unthinkables* (Santa Clara, CA: Think Social Publishing, 2009).

4. Dr. Laura Prager quoted in Caroline Miller, "How Anxiety Leads to Disruptive Behavior: Kids Who Seem Oppositional Are Often Severely Anxious," Child Mind Institute, childmind.org/article/how-anxiety-leads-to-disruptive-behavior/ (accessed 02/03/16).

5. Po Bronson, "Learning to Lie," *New York Magazine*, nymag.com/news/features/43893/, February 10, 2008.

Jim and Lynne Jackson have conducted over 1,300 workshops for parents and privately coached more than 1,000 parents since the early 1990s. They are media spokespeople for a variety of parenting issues, frequently speaking at churches and parenting conferences. The Jacksons have three children and live in Minnesota. For more information, visit www.connectedfamilies.org.